Blue Laws and Black Codes

D1127977

PETER WALLENSTEIN

Blue Laws

AND

Black Codes

Conflict, Courts,
and Change in
Twentieth-Century
Virginia

University of Virginia Press   Charlottesville and London

BOWLING GREEN STATE
UNIVERSITY LIBRARIES

University of Virginia Press
© 2004 by the Rector and Visitors of the University of Virginia
All rights reserved
Printed in the United States of America on acid-free paper

First published 2004

9 8 7 6 5 4 3 2 1

Library of Congress Cataloging-in-Publication Data
Wallenstein, Peter.
   Blue laws and Black codes : conflict, courts, and change in twentieth-century
Virginia / Peter Wallenstein.
      p.   cm.
Includes bibliographical references and index.
   ISBN 0-8139-2260-7 (cloth : alk. paper) — ISBN 0-8139-2261-5 (pbk. : alk. paper)
   1. Law—Virginia—History.   2. Civil rights—Virginia—History.
3. Social change—Virginia—History.   I. Title.
KFV2478 .W35 2004
340'.115'09755—dc22

                                                              2003015695

For My family

Contents

Maps and Tables

Preface

IN THE 1980S I RETURNED TO VIRGINIA AFTER MANY YEARS AWAY and began teaching at Virginia Tech, where I found an abundance of intriguing yet neglected topics in Virginia history. At that point I was finishing a long-term project on public policy in the Deep South in the nineteenth century, and I soon turned my attention to similar matters for the Upper South in the twentieth century. Much was very different, of course, but the focus of my work continued to be on public policy and legal history, as these themes relate to education, transportation, racial identity, the exercise of power, and everyday life.

The chapters of this book began life as stand-alone pieces, whether conference papers or even brief reference entries. Several chapters at one time or another struck me as opening up promising areas of inquiry for entire books by themselves: on the history of the Virginia Supreme Court; race and gender in the legal profession; litigation comprising "the case against Jim Crow" in Virginia; the 1960s southern sit-ins and the resulting court cases. My work on the law of interracial marriage has, in fact, led to an entire book, one that covers 300 years and every part of the nation: *Tell the Court I Love My Wife* (2002).

Regardless, these particular topics have long seemed to belong together. I have in mind, as I usually do in my books, two audiences: fellow academics and general readers. For members of the academy, I think I have fresh things to say on every subject, on particular issues and on broader questions. To my fellow citizens I offer a series of engaging stories, each designed to illuminate how the legal and political systems have operated regarding various issues in one American state over the past hundred years. To both groups, I have wanted to demonstrate how, often through citizens' day-to-day activities and the day-to-day workings of political institutions, a not-so-distant past became such a different present.

To students in courses in Virginia history, the Civil Rights movement, American politics, legal history, southern history, or the twentieth-century United States, I wish to tell you that I originally wrote a number of these essays for students in my classes, particularly my Virginia history classes. In fact, though, I did not do it all. I believe in undergraduate research at a research institution; and various undergraduates, as well as graduate students, did work that has contributed toward the making of this book. For my students as well as myself, the teaching and the research were related facets of one enterprise.

I have placed acknowledgments at the start of the notes to each chapter. Yet here is a good place to express my indebtedness to the Virginia Foundation for the Humanities and Public Policy, which twice—in summer 1989 and summer 1992—provided me with space and funds in Charlottesville, where I did much of the work on chapters 1 and 3. I wish to salute my colleagues at the Virginia Center for the Humanities, especially several fellows from 1989: Hoda Zaki, Rafia Zafar, Paul Gaston, and the elder statesman from China among the group, whom we affectionately called Professor Shi. I am grateful, too, to the Virginia Tech Department of History's Frank L. Curtis Fund, which supports research in Civil War or Virginia history. I began trying out my emergent ideas regarding Virginia history at annual meetings of the Virginia Social Science Association, and I subsequently published small portions of this book in the *Virginia Social Science Journal*. I wish to acknowledge my friends and associates in the VSSA during the years I was most active in the organization—especially Bernard "Bud" Levin of Blue Ridge Community College; Greg Weiss of Roanoke College, editor then of the *Journal*; and political scientist John Ramsey and geographer Don Zeigler, both of Old Dominion University. Here, too, I wish to express my appreciation for the encouragement that came from Kermit Hall and Paul Finkelman as I worked on this book, as well as the astute comments that J. William Harris and Charles W. McCurdy offered in the closing stages. Virginia Tech undergraduate Erin Mooney assisted with the index.

I wish also to thank several people who shared with me their own compelling stories. Without their voices, several chapters would have been less substantive and less accurate. In particular I have in mind Elsie Tucker Thomas, Oliver W. Hill, Roland D. Ealey, Ford T. Johnson Sr., and Ford T. Johnson Jr. for various dimensions of chapters 3 through 5, as well as Louise Proffitt Spencer for chapter 1 and Mildred D. Loving for chapter 6. I hope that I have recounted their stories in ways that they will recognize as authentic and that others will find accessible and illuminating.

As for dedications, this book is for the many members of my extended family. It is in memory of my grandparents, the Wallensteins and the Van Duynes, children of the nineteenth century; my father, Crandall R. Wallenstein; my uncle Raymond Van Duyne; and my cousin Frank Wallenstein. It is for my younger brothers and sisters—Ckris, Andy, Kathe, Nancy, Mark, Holly, and Faith—and my mother, R. Carol Wallenstein. It is for Colton Wallenstein, the family patriarch, and for the children and grandchildren of my brothers and sisters, the newest additions among them children of the twenty-first century. And it is for Sookhan, always.

Blue Laws and Black Codes

Introduction

Amending Virginia, Amending America

Lawyers are men. "Colored" people cannot marry "white" people. Public amusements must remain closed on Sundays. On these and other matters, popular beliefs and public policy underwent changes so dramatic in the past hundred years, Virginia in the 1990s was hardly the same place as Virginia in the 1890s. This book explores the transformation.

Blue Laws and Black Codes emphasizes the past century or so in the history of one state. Yet, in degree, Virginia can stand as a proxy for the entire South, even the entire nation (indeed for much of the world), as traditional ways of doing things and governing behavior have undergone change, have even disappeared, and new ways have come to the fore. Thus, while my book uses materials from the history of Virginia, it raises and addresses larger questions, first in the legal history of the U.S. South, second in American political culture. The first three chapters could perhaps have been largely crafted from materials on any American state. The next three, in particular, derive far more from the legal history of the South. The ways in which the later chapters differ from the earlier ones can help define what is southern about southern history.

Changing a Constitution through Judicial Interpretation

Exploring the history of Virginia in the years since the Civil War, *Blue Laws and Black Codes* emphasizes the period from the 1890s through the 1960s. Each of the chapters takes a fresh look at Virginia, the South, and the United States. The theme of conflict, law, and change captures the approach I offer toward linking conflict with change, explaining how Americans have made their way, on all manner of matters, from one set of social rules to another. My subtitle—*Conflict, Courts, and Change*—locates the venue where much of the policy conflict and legal change took place.

Some years ago a book appeared under the title *Amending America*. It focused on formal amendment to the U.S. Constitution.[1] My book has taken a related but substantially different approach. While tracing change in the statutory and constitutional law of Virginia, it emphasizes ways other than formal amendment to the U.S. Constitution or the Virginia constitution. Indeed, formal amendment appears in these chapters only briefly and on infrequent occasion, as when the Twenty-fourth Amendment to the U.S. Constitution (1964) banned payment of a poll tax as a requirement for voting in federal elections. Far more often, the language of the written constitution remained the same, but its meaning underwent significant reinterpretation.

My book takes the approach that in successfully amending the legal and constitutional framework of life in Virginia, a wide range of actors— citizens, lawyers, legislators, judges, delegates to constitutional conventions—brought change to the way people lived in the Old Dominion. *Blue Laws and Black Codes* emphasizes a single American state while frequently framing the inquiry in broader regional and national contexts.

Life at the end of the twentieth century was organized around rules that often contrasted sharply with the rules that governed life a hundred years earlier. Social, cultural, economic, and political change had pushed, or at least facilitated, changes in the legal system. At the same time, the legal system had fostered many kinds of change. In seeking to shape the world through changes in the law, people used various political tools, from electoral and legislative politics in the state and in the nation to civil or criminal cases in state or federal court. The law mediates conflict, and it mirrors change, causes change, legitimates change.

Blue Laws and Black Codes offers a series of case studies in how the law interacts with change in society, culture, the economy, and the political system. In different ways each chapter illustrates how Americans have routinely employed legal concepts and legal venues to work out their differences and either promote or retard some kind of change. A legal idiom— a discourse about what "the law" is or ought to be and whether a given statute is "constitutional"—has played a central part in American political culture; the comment "there ought to be a law" is applied to almost anything at all. Law and policy have been changed—or not—in legislatures and constitutional conventions, through access to the state and federal courts, through appeal to the state and federal constitutions, through formal amendment to constitutions, and through reinterpretation of existing language.

At the outset it should be stated that this book is both more and less than a history of Virginia in the past century or so. It is less, in that it is by no means a comprehensive history of twentieth-century Virginia; it is not even a comprehensive legal, constitutional, or political history. That is not its intent. Rather, highlighting selected issues, it does not seek to include others, and it is often centered on activities in state and federal courts, not the state legislature. At the same time it is more than a full history of Virginia in that it situates Virginia in a regional context, even a national context. The emphasis is on Virginia. Yet as frequent references to other states reveal, developments in Virginia in many ways have resembled those in other states across the South, and the region has often participated in broader national patterns.

Regardless, each chapter unfolds against a backdrop of the structure of power and the system of state politics in Virginia. An overview of that system and that structure will provide a framework in which to place the seven chapters.

Virginia Politics: The Nineteenth Century and the Twentieth

Virginia politics in the first half of the twentieth century resembled in many ways Virginia politics in the first half of the nineteenth century. In both periods the same white men who dominated the economy also dominated the political system. Between the American Revolution and the Civil War, the great issue of the day was slavery. The Civil War brought an end to slavery, but disputes over race persisted. In the generations that followed, the great issues centered on the maintenance of white power and privilege in a world without slavery.

Other issues were important as well, and they, too, were constantly caught up in matters of race as well as power. Acting at about the same time that other states did, the Virginia General Assembly established a Literary Fund in 1811 to promote educational opportunity and a Board of Public Works in 1816 to promote transportation improvements. Again, the first three decades of the twentieth century in Virginia, as in many other states, brought a resurgent commitment to public schools and public roads.[2] Virginians, like Americans elsewhere, had to answer questions like: What activities should the state and local governments carry out? Who should pay for them, and who should benefit? The political system was centrally implicated in the well-being and prosperity of all Virginians. Who controlled politics mattered to everyone, for the answer to that question largely determined the answers to the other questions.

The political history of Virginia across the nineteenth century can be understood in broad terms as a three-way struggle among western whites, eastern blacks, and eastern whites. Black Virginians had no vote before

1867, but their presence and their actions forced issues that white Virginians had to face.[3] White Virginians, for their part, were at no time in full agreement about the great issues of their day. The struggle among the three groups materialized at every point and in every venue: in debates in the state legislature and in constitutional conventions; in decisions about slavery, secession, and war; in confrontations over political power, state taxes, public schools, and public roads.

In the generation before the Civil War, middling and landless white farmers between the Blue Ridge and the Ohio River sought a greater say in state politics and policy making. In a constitutional convention in 1829–30, meeting to renovate the Constitution of 1776, they demanded—but failed to obtain—universal white manhood suffrage and a legislative apportionment that would give them a louder voice. In 1832, in the wake of Nat Turner's rebellion, they led a charge in the House of Delegates against slavery but, given the system of apportionment, were narrowly turned back in their effort to put slavery on a gradual path to termination. In a subsequent constitutional convention, in 1850–51, they obtained a wider suffrage and a reapportionment. But the new constitution also restricted their power to tax planters' slaves and thus obtain enhanced revenues with which to fund education and transportation for their part of the state. And the new constitution expressly denied the legislature authority to do anything to restrict slavery; eastern whites wanted to eliminate any chance of a renewal of the debate that had taken place two decades earlier.[4]

In 1861 Virginia's leaders took the state out of the United States of America and into the new Confederate States of America, but over the next four years the Union fought, in the end successfully, to bring the seceded states back into the Union. The Civil War transformed Virginia. Conflict did not end when the war did, but slavery came to an end. Reconstruction brought the enfranchisement of black men, and former slaves served in the state legislature until late in the century. But the western region proved far weaker in postwar state politics than it would have been had West Virginia not gone its separate way during the war.[5]

In 1865–66 the Virginia legislature adopted a new black code, a collection of laws that distinguished the legal status of black residents. Not only did the new code replace the old slave laws, it also replaced many of the provision that had long denied even free black Virginians a broad range of rights that white Virginians enjoyed. The new provisions permitted black Virginians to testify in some court proceedings, for example, and legalized their marriages. But the postwar Virginia black code also increased the penalties for a number of crimes popularly associated with blacks; introduced a new vagrancy act under which freedmen could be put to work without pay on plantations; prevented blacks from testifying in court proceedings that involved only whites; and perpetuated the ancient bans on black voting and officeholding.[6]

The Virginia black code was far less restrictive than its counterparts in some Deep South states—unlike Mississippi, Virginia did not prevent black landownership—and it elevated the legal status of black residents in many ways. But it also represented just another chapter in Virginia laws that denied equal rights, a base line from which black Virginians would push for greater freedom during Reconstruction and on for the next hundred years.

Congress soon changed the rules that governed Virginia and its sister states of the former Confederacy. First it passed the Civil Rights Act of 1866 to neutralize many of the restrictions in the postwar black codes, and then it took over Reconstruction in 1867. At the outset of Congressional Reconstruction, the Virginia electorate—redefined to include black voters as well as whites—went to the polls in 1867 to elect delegates to a new constitutional convention, one that would make sure the state had a public school system and a biracial electorate. Republicans controlled the state constitutional convention of 1867–68 (often called the Underwood convention, after its presiding officer, John C. Underwood). The Constitution of 1869 provided for public schools and black suffrage. The Republicans also took the governorship in 1869, but they did not control the legislature, and a struggle ensued over control of the state. Meanwhile, the new rules propelled Virginia toward reshaping education in the state.

Before 1865 schools for black Virginians were illegal. During and after the early postwar years, by contrast, a new system of public schools, established in 1870, made space for black children and white children alike, though in separate schools. Higher education followed a similar path. Implementing the new federal land-grant system of higher education, the legislature divided Virginia's Morrill Act funds, allotting two-thirds to a new white school, present-day Virginia Polytechnic Institute and State University (founded in 1872), and one-third to a black school, present-day Hampton University (founded in 1868).[7]

Through the 1870s the Democratic Party insisted on full payment of a huge public debt for transportation improvements left over from the prewar period, even at the cost of seeing the public schools wither for lack of funding. Challenging the ruling Democrats' power and policies, a biracial coalition—Republicans and disaffected Democrats; the majority black, a large minority white—took power, winning both houses of the legislature in 1879 and the governorship in 1881. The Readjuster movement challenges conventional assumptions about late nineteenth-century southern politics, as class trumped race, and black political power flourished in a biracial coalition in Virginia. And it challenges the conventional periodization of southern history, for Reconstruction can be said to have continued in—or even come to—Virginia later than the 1877 cutoff customarily taken by historians to mark its end.[8]

The new regime "readjusted" the public debt, slashing payments on it, and expenditures for public schools surged. The legislature also eliminated the connection between a poll tax and voting rights, and it established a public college for black Virginians, the Virginia Normal and Collegiate Institute—present-day Virginia State University. The Readjuster legislature sent William Mahone to the U.S. Senate for the 1881–87 term, and Mahone took his seat as a Republican. The Readjusters' policy initiatives persisted long after their loss at the polls in 1883 (when Democrats exploited a racial incident in Danville to stampede white voters). In 1888 the Petersburg area elected a black congressional candidate, John Mercer Langston, a former president of Virginia Normal and Collegiate. By the late 1890s, however, black Virginians no longer held any political office, and for the next half century no black officeholders could be found anywhere in the state.[9]

Yet significant portions of the Readjusters' legacy persisted. Their successors accepted the Readjusters' settlement of the debt question. Although the new regime reduced the Virginia Normal and Collegiate Institute's funds and terminated its collegiate curriculum, they let the school survive (as Virginia Normal and Industrial Institute) and continued to fund it. Those successors did far more toward educating white Virginians. In particular, they inaugurated higher education for white women in institutions created to train public school teachers. First, they established a school in Farmville (present-day Longwood University). By World War I each of the four great divisions of the state had such a school for white women: two east of the Blue Ridge (today's Mary Washington College, north of the James River, as well Longwood, in the Southside) and two west of it (today's James Madison University, in the northwest quadrant of the state, and Radford University, in the southwest).[10]

Between the 1880s and the mid-twentieth century, society and politics in Virginia underwent a whitening that transformed both. Long before the "Great Migration" from the Deep South that took place between the 1910s and the 1960s, large numbers of black Virginians moved north to Washington, Baltimore, Philadelphia, and New York. That migration was well under way in the 1880s; between 1880 and 1900 the white proportion of Virginia's population surged from 58 to 64 percent. The 1900 census counted 1,192,855 whites in Virginia and 661,329 blacks. Between 1900 and World War II, the black population figure stagnated while the white figure doubled, and the white proportion climbed past 75 percent.[11]

Yet large numbers of black Virginians remained in the Old Dominion, as did memories among white Virginians of a time when white dominance could not be assumed. A counterrevolution in the early twentieth century targeted black Virginians for political neutralization. In the constitutional convention in 1901–2, by means of a poll tax and other measures, Virginia's traditional elite circumscribed the political activities of its rivals and thereby resumed, or solidified, its control over state politics.[12] Slavery did not return under the new regime, but segregation, sharecropping, and disfranchisement left black Virginians with only a down payment toward social, economic, or political freedom.

Into the 1960s a white oligarchy dominated Virginia politics through an organization long controlled by Senator Thomas S. Martin and, after him, Harry F. Byrd Sr. In a representative statement Byrd, newly nominated by the Democratic Party as its candidate for the governorship in 1925, declared his policy commitments in anticipation of his inevitable victory in Virginia's one-party political system. "The supremacy of the Democratic party in the South," he insisted, must be perpetuated. Any "evils in the continued and unchallenged government by a single political party" could not hold a candle to "the much greater evils in a political condition . . . where the negro vote either controlled or held the balance of power."[13]

Something else had been going on as well. When the Constitution of 1902 placed new restrictions on voting rights, it required even previous voters to re-register. At about the same time that Byrd was gearing up to win the governorship, William C. Pendleton, a white Republican from western Virginia, a former Readjuster, was finishing up a book he called *Political History of Appalachian Virginia*. In it, he wrote, "It was painful and pitiful to see the horror and dread visible on the faces of the illiterate poor white men" as they waited "to take their turn before the inquisition" that would determine whether they were permitted to register and retain their status as voters. "Still more horrible" was it, he said, "to see the marks of humiliation and despair that were stamped on the faces of honest but poor white men who had been refused registration and who had been robbed of their citizenship without cause."[14]

The author had reason to exaggerate, and he may have taken poetic license. Then again, he was describing something that must have happened time and again as the 1902 constitution's disfranchising provisions did their work to trim the Virginia electorate. Given the language of the Fifteenth Amendment, blacks voters could not be targeted by race. A device like the poll tax did not necessarily distinguish between black and white. Black men and white men, too, were forced from electoral politics, had their voices silenced, were "robbed of their citizenship without cause."

But of course there was cause, ample cause. The interlude of Readjuster power revealed the potential for all to see, and in the eyes of some, that potential had to be curbed. As a consequence of the deliberate efforts of the disfranchising convention at the dawn of the century, the political world of Virginia in the twentieth century took on contours not radically different from those dating back before the Civil War. The presence of any black voters at all, to be sure, demonstrated that change had taken place. Change was real, but it could move in more than one direction, and by very early in the twentieth century, much of the revolution, the dual revolution, of the nineteenth century—the democratization of politics on the white side of the great racial divide, and then the democratization across that divide—had been undone.

If some white voters were eliminated along the way, either of two attitudes could be adopted. One was that some costs would necessarily be incurred, and the whites who fell by the wayside would have to be sacrificed for the greater good—although their interests might still be looked after, in a world of white solidarity, by their politically active white neighbors. The other attitude at the time was that those who were eliminated may well have been renegades who, back in the 1880s, had betrayed white Virginia by lending their support to black Virginians in the Readjuster coalition.

From that latter perspective, a reduced electorate had a double advantage. The new regime clipped both wings of the old Readjuster coalition, black and white. From the perspective of people inclined to support a movement like the Readjusters, the reduction of western white voters compounded the hit that the region's political power took when much of western Virginia became a separate state. Race, class, and region were all at work in the struggle for political power, although the dominant rhetoric focused on white racial solidarity and white racial supremacy. Though a system of public schools had taken root after the Civil War, far greater state and local funding went into schools for eastern whites than for any other group.[15] Into the 1960s eastern blacks and western whites would continue to have little say in state programs and to see little benefit from them.

In sum, the electorate of the early twentieth century looked remarkably similar to that of the late eighteenth, and was certainly a far cry from the "Underwood electorate" of the Constitution of 1869.[16] The 1910s looked more like the 1840s, 1810s, or even 1780s than like the 1880s. Yet those people and groups who had been pressed out of politics did what they could to keep a foot in the doorway. Resistance never went away. The dominant groups had to be vigilant, because the nondominant groups kept nipping at their heels. Republicans challenged Democrats. Blacks challenged whites. Western Virginia challenged the east.

The relative lack of change from the first half of the nineteenth century to the first half of the twentieth carried no guarantees of permanence. For one thing, great struggles during that hundred years had generated enormous turbulence. For another, in 1920 women—or, at least, many white women—gained the right to vote as a consequence of the Nineteenth Amendment, which removed gender as the basis for denying political rights.[17] Moreover, each of the other obstacles to a wider political participation also came under attack. In the 1920s, the 1940s, the 1960s, the struggle continued, as each side resisted the efforts of the other.[18]

The Virginia Supreme Court

The Virginia Supreme Court of Appeals was always involved in the struggles among various groups of Virginians. Through most of Virginia's history, vacancies on the state's highest court have been filled by the legislature, so its personnel have reflected the dominant tendencies of public life in the Commonwealth. Under the Constitution of 1851, though, the court was briefly elective. The revamped electorate under that constitution—reflecting virtually universal white manhood suffrage—chose the court's members. It did so subject to the requirement that each of five great geographical divisions of the state be represented by someone chosen by the voters of that district.[19]

After the Civil War the state constitution put judicial selection back into the hands of the legislature. In practice, the legislature continued to apportion judgeships among the state's major regions, though of course the western part of Virginia was far smaller than in the 1850s, since much of it had been split off when West Virginia was organized during the Civil War. New divisions fractured Virginia politics in the postwar world, as Republicans contested Democrats and as black Virginians sought to obtain and hold some power in state affairs. During the Readjuster period an entirely new slate of judges took their seats on the Virginia Supreme Court of Appeals, and in 1895, at the end of their twelve-year terms, another entirely new roster replaced those men.[20]

From the 1890s to the 1960s, the same dominant group that elected state governors and controlled the state legislature also controlled the state judiciary. Dissenters had little say on any issue in any branch of state government. Some institutional changes are nonetheless worth noting. In

1928, for example, the members of Virginia's highest court, formerly carrying the title of judge, became known as justices, and the president of the court also received a new title, chief justice. Moreover, the Virginia Supreme Court, formerly known as the Supreme Court of Appeals, took on its shorter formal name (which I often use here for convenience' sake) under the Constitution of 1971.[21] Into the 1980s, the court remained all white and all male, but then that, too, began to change. *Blue Laws and Black Codes* explores a range of issues that came to the attention of the court before the white male makeup of the court itself changed.

Eight Windows: The South and the Nation in the Twentieth Century

Each of the essays in this book revisits a past that, though largely vanished at the dawn of the twenty-first century, was central to the texture of life and the role of law a hundred years before. Some among these pasts are so forgotten now that the mere allegation that they once existed might elicit incredulity among some readers: a labor tax to work the roads, a law against Sunday sports or shopping. Much the same might be said regarding other messages from the past: a ban against women practicing law; a host of Jim Crow laws and customs including a ban on black students in law schools; laws that made it a serious crime to marry across racial lines; and various measures that restricted voting.

The greater a reader's surprise at these vanished restrictions, the more do we have a measure of how much changed in the course of the twentieth century. And none vanished without a struggle. In each case the struggle took many years and a host of actors to accomplish. Each struggle can tell us much about how the legal culture in Virginia has operated and, by extension, the political culture in the U.S. South and even across America. And each can illustrate the ways in which citizens have worked to change the laws—or to keep those laws from being changed.

Americans may often voice a wish that judges would just apply the law and not make law. In practice, nonetheless, every American retains the right to seek—in the courts—validation of his or her own preference concerning what the law is or ought to be. Despite the rhetoric, Americans wants judges to make law, the right law, even if there is, of course, no agreement on what that is. Similarly, we could say that all Americans are committed to a narrow view of what their constitutions, state and federal, permit lawmakers to do, unless, of course, it is something that we want to see done.

Each of the chapters explores some facet of this feature of American political culture, the vital role that constitutions play in shaping the field of routine politics and the vital roles played by judges' interpretations of those constitutions, at citizens' request, at citizens' insistence. Each exemplifies Americans' active participation in a political culture in which it is assumed that one can go to court and perhaps obtain a favorable ruling on what the law is and how it applies to a given case.

Chapter 1 is about the emergence of horseless carriages and hard-surfaced roads. It details the context in which a young Virginian declined to go out and—as local authorities assumed he would, in accordance with the law—work, without pay, for two days on the local roads. "The Case of the Laborer from Louisa" led to an 1890s decision by the Virginia Supreme Court that ended Virginia's reliance on the old corvée system of a tax paid in labor: unpaid labor to construct and maintain public roads. Most states found other ways to move away from a system that had been virtually universal, but Virginia's way came via a split decision by the state supreme court as to what the state constitution permitted and what it did not.

Chapter 2 explores the Sunday closing laws, the so-called blue laws that restricted on Sundays a broad range of activities that were perfectly legal on other days. The rise of challenges to such laws can illustrate the operations of American political culture. Moreover, business behavior and consumer customs alike have helped shape, and have been shaped by, the changing application of Sunday closing laws. Virginia supplies a case study. This essay, "Necessity, Charity, and a Sabbath," traces the history of Virginians' efforts in state courts to get the blue laws interpreted they way they wanted. Whatever the outcome in one particular case or another, efforts in the courts to curtail or even eliminate those laws ultimately met with success.

Chapters 3 and 4, which take us to law school as well as to court, discuss diversity in the legal profession—diversity in terms of race and gender. "These New and Strange Beings" emphasizes the emergence of women lawyers in modern America, with Virginia offering a case study from the 1890s to the 1970s. "The Siege against Segregation" examines the impact of another significant new group in shaping the rules that govern a whole society. Emphasizing the decade of the 1940s, it explores the impact that black lawyers had in propelling one southern state beyond segregation and into a new era of civil rights. The first of these two chapters, on gender, conveys the lengthy conflict over whether women, white or black, should be permitted to enter the legal profession. The second, on race, emphasizes the significance that diversity in the legal profession could have on the course of legal development.

Chapters 5 and 6, which continue the story—begun in chapter 4—of the Civil Rights movement, relate the law to dining establishments, courtroom seating arrangements, and even the racial identities of prospective marriage partners. "To Sit or Not to Sit" traces the background as well as the significance of two cases brought by Virginians to the U.S. Supreme Court in the 1960s. It highlights the story of one young Virginian who challenged segregated lunch counters in one case and segregated courtrooms in another. "Racial Identity and the Crime of Marriage" tracks the development and application, between the 1870s and the 1960s, of one American state's laws against interracial marriage. It also tracks the challenges to those laws in state and federal courts, and it concludes with a case that a Virginia couple took to the nation's highest court. Each of these three important cases from the 1960s—one on lunch counters, one on courtrooms, and one on marriage—ended with a ruling favorable to the forces of change. Each was a very long time in coming, and each contributed to the dismantling of the old rules of race that had permeated law as well as custom across the state and the region.

Chapter 7, "Power and Policy in an American State," explores the twin phenomena of voting rights and legislative apportionment. Like other southern states between the 1920s and the 1960s, authorities in Virginia had to address challenges to restrictions on the right to participate in the process of selecting public officials. Like other American states in the 1960s, Virginia also had to redraw the maps that outlined legislative districts and thereby structured the distribution of power among various social groups, defined by region and class more than by race or gender. Thus was altered the relative ability of one group or another to gain a favorable hearing for its policy agenda, to get some things done and prevent other things from happening.

The new rules of the 1960s continued beyond the 1990s to frame power and policy in Virginia, a fairly representative American state in these matters, though even more representative of the South. Changes in the makeup of the Virginia Supreme Court, as chapter 8 shows, offer a measure of the changes in race and gender that are revealed by a history of twentieth-century Virginia in particular and of America in general.

Symbol, Substance, Process

These chapters demonstrate the American system of law at work, and they demonstrate American politics at work to retain or change various laws. The process of lawmaking—in courts, in legislatures, even in shops, homes, and streets—is on display as much as is the substance of the law, and we see the process at work as citizens contend over the substance. In chapter 7 we see more a struggle over the process itself as citizens contended indirectly over substance. Repeatedly, too, we see Virginians engaged in symbolic politics, as they deal with policy issues that have symbolic importance to them.

These three concepts underlie the content of this book, give each chapter a significance beyond itself, help connect them. When Virginians contested with each other over voting rights and legislative apportionment, they were contesting directly over matters of process, and only indirectly over matters of substance. The procedural questions had to do with voting and representation, while the substantive issues had to do with taxation, education, and transportation. The issues of process were contested not only because of their close connection to substance but also because of their symbolic importance—because of what they said about who had a right to rule society and politics in Virginia.

Groups of Virginians had long struggled against each other over voting rights. Long ago—in the pre–Civil War years—western white men insisted they were citizens, too, and should have the right to vote no matter how little property they owned. Symbolism, substance, and process were all tied together. Eastern whites had resisted such a move toward political democracy as an extension of the franchise, and they resisted a reapportionment of the legislature even more, seeing powerful implications for such substantive matters as the security of slavery, the level and class distribution of the tax burden, and the level and regional distribution of public spending on schools and roads.

On other issues, too, this tripartite conceptual approach helps us understand what seemed at stake. For most people, for example, interracial marriage was a matter of symbolism; in fact, perhaps no matter of substance was more freighted with symbolism. Many whites insisted that the ban on black-white marriages be retained to safeguard their own images of themselves as a people apart. Many blacks just as fervently wanted the ban to go—and with it the symbolism that no black Virginian was good enough to marry any white Virginian—though, like whites, African Americans might generally frown on the idea of interracial sexual or marital relations. For some individuals, white and black, the matter seemed a question of life itself; for them, the opportunity to marry the person they loved, even if that meant crossing the color line, was very much an issue of substance. Regardless of perspective and regardless of whether the matter was more one of substance or of symbolism, process came into play when people jousted over whether state or federal courts should decide a case and whether state or federal laws should govern the outcome.

Virginia as the South, Virginia as America

Virginia in the 1980s and 1990s proved dramatically different from what it had been in the 1880s and 1890s. The entire South did. In fact, all of America did. The changes did not just happen. Each of this book's chapters helps explain how some of the twentieth century's changes came about. Although no state is identical to any other, the story in Virginia can suggest much of what was going on in other states, and in fact I have often been explicit in drawing comparisons between Virginia and other states.

At some times and on some issues, Virginia was distinctly a state of the South, while on other matters such was less the case. In the century after the Civil War, black codes were mostly—and increasingly—a regional phenomenon. Blue laws were national. By the mid-1960s the statutory ban on interracial marriage was very much a regional phenomenon. A century earlier, though, there was far less contrast on that issue between the South and the rest of the nation. In the 1960s the poll tax was also a regional phenomenon, yet rural privilege in the scheme of legislative apportionment still had perhaps as much force in Colorado or New York as in Tennessee or Virginia. The labor tax, the Sunday closing laws, the male monopoly on the legal profession—if such regulations as these lasted longer in the South than elsewhere, it was not by much. Rather, each was embedded in the life of the nation for much of America's history.

By placing Virginia in the twin larger contexts of region and nation, one can see with enhanced clarity what features were primarily southern and which were national in scope. The core difference between the South and the rest of the nation during most of the period of this study lay in the strength and persistence of legal distinctions based on race. Far greater in the South than elsewhere was the salience of issues of law and policy related to matters of power, privilege, and racial identity. That remained true into the second half of the twentieth century, just as it had been true in the nineteenth, both before and after the Civil War, before and after the end of slavery.

The individual chapters can each stand alone, but they tell us more when brought together. After these several journeys through the American past, the epilogue offers some concluding thoughts regarding their connections and ramifications, as Virginians and indeed Americans everywhere made their way through the twentieth century and toward a new millennium.

1

The Case of the
Laborer from Louisa

Conscripts, Convicts, and
Public Roads, 1890s–1920s

R EVEREND LITTLEBERRY JAMES HALEY (1832–1917) WROTE IN
mid-January 1882 that he had stayed at home in Louisa County on
both Wednesday and Thursday that week: "The roads are too awfully
muddy to travel."[1] He is one of three central Virginians whose stories illustrate how people traveled before the twentieth century and how the
coming of the horseless carriage and hard-surface roads transformed the
traditional patterns of life and work in the region. These three men involved themselves in three major developments in the law between the
1890s and the 1910s that led to Virginia's highway system: a court case in
the 1890s; state legislation in 1906 following a formal amendment to the
state constitution; and federal legislation in 1916.

Pastor Haley's Muddy Sundays

L. J. Haley spent fifty years, beginning in the late 1850s, as a Baptist
preacher in various churches, mostly in central Virginia's Louisa area,
where his eight children grew up. To fulfill his obligations at South Anna,
Trinity, Hopeful, and elsewhere, he knew that he could not count on good
weather or good roads, and he could not always wait for the weather, or the
roads, to get better. In addition to preaching Sunday sermons, he had to
visit the faithful and officiate at baptisms, weddings, and funerals. Moreover, as county superintendent of education for a while, he had to go to
Louisa Court House from time to time to take care of school business.

Writing of one of his churches in February 1888, he noted, "I go to
Hopeful. What a ride thro the mud!" Two weeks later he found the "roads
utterly desperate" and "traveling almost impossible except on horseback
and that bad enough." The next February proved no better. He went to
Hopeful on a "very rainy day"; his riding horse, Old Fred, got him home

again that night, but the reverend found it "a very disagreeable ride," with "mud and slush everywhere."

When it came to longer trips, trains sometimes proved Pastor Haley's salvation. One time he reported contentedly: "I go to Richmond with my little boys, Littleberry and Bunny, and they see the *city. A Big Thing* with the little boys. Go down on an excursion train, one dollar round trip. Boys half price. Spend the day in Richmond." On a spring day in 1882, he performed a marriage in the morning—"$5.00"—and then took a train from Fredericks Hall to Warrenton for a meeting that evening of the Baptist General Association.

The years passed, and Haley's reports about travel by horsepower during the winter months remained as bleak as the weather. In 1908 a January thaw came to Louisa. On the twenty-fourth, he reported that he had found a "good congregation" when he got to Little River, but "the roads are very bad, as muddy as I ever saw them."

During the first third of the twentieth century, nevertheless, transportation—in Louisa and Albemarle Counties and across the nation—embarked on as great a change as the railroad had brought in the middle third of the nineteenth century. In the year 1893, two brothers, bicycle mechanics in Springfield, Massachusetts, developed the first successful American automobile powered by gasoline, and by 1896 they were producing and marketing cars at the rate of one a month. Also in 1893, Congress established the Office of Public Road Inquiry in the Department of Agriculture.[2] Thus began both the age of automobiles in America and the era of the Good Roads movement. Both would find their way to central Virginia and begin their transformation of life there before the 1920s.

Like Pastor Haley, two more people, one each from Louisa and Albemarle, exhibited Virginia's system of transportation in their daily lives. And each took actions that worked directly to facilitate the changes.

Judge Duke's Sunny Everydays

Richard Thomas Walker Duke Jr. (1853–1926) lived on Park Street in Charlottesville, where he and his wife Edith raised five children. A lawyer, he served for a time beginning in 1888 as judge on the city's court. Judge Duke, like Pastor Haley, kept a diary, commented on the weather, and traveled a lot.[3]

Duke had a sunnier disposition than did Haley. His diary for the year 1892, for example, is sprinkled with entries like that for February 13, "beautiful aurora at night," or that for October 5, "an exquisitely beautiful moonlight night." Yet his capacity for enjoyment does not fully explain his failure, as a rule, to connect his descriptions of the weather with his accounts of his travels. Rather, much of Duke's travel, including his trips to New York City and West Virginia, was by train, so the weather had little influence on his plans or his outlook. Perhaps it was, as he wrote in January, "raining all day," but he "left for Richmond . . . on first train." A week or so later, on a day that was "warmer and clear," he "went to Orange at 11 o'clock, on C & O," and returned by train at 1:30. Duke often specified that he had traveled on the "F.F.V.," the Chesapeake and Ohio Railroad's name for the plush Pullman cars on the "Famous" or "Fast Flying Virginian," which began its runs in 1889 and ran north directly to Washington, Philadelphia, and New York.[4] Passenger trains facilitated Duke's constant travels and helped sustain his sunny disposition. He concluded each trip away from his home and family with a sigh of relief and gratitude, "All well thank God."

One might summarize Judge Duke's experience with transportation by observing that like Pastor Haley, he found travel by train preferable, even essential, when going much beyond the county boundaries. Duke happened to make such trips more often than Haley, and he tended to make much longer trips. As for local travel, one gathers from the two men's diaries that local roads in the Charlottesville area were superior to those in Louisa County. The larger towns in Virginia, as elsewhere in America, could take advantage of a bigger tax base and a denser population to build and maintain better roads than could small-town and rural America. Charlottesville did so.[5]

Judge Duke's diaries for 1892 supply many glimpses of his life in his hometown and its immediate surroundings. There, he was almost always moving with the power of a single horse. Again and again on Sunday afternoons, he wrote about local trips with his wife, Edith, or their children: Mary, who turned seven that year, Walker, who turned five, and Jack, four. At the end of January, he noted, "Edith & I drove to Sunny Side," the home of his aging father just to the west of town. Judge Duke had what he called "a sweet day" in October when he "rode to Sunny Side on Queen, Walker accompanying on his donkey. Edith & children coming on later." At Sunny Side the donkey "started off with Walker & I shouted 'Where are you going.'" Said Walker: "'I ain't going anywhere. It's the donkey.'"

Some travel on horse or in carriage, of course, was to other places, for other purposes, or without Edith or the children. One Sunday in January he went "after dinner to Sunny Side on horseback. A cold ride, but I rather enjoyed it." In May: "drove at night to the Univ[ersity]" regarding his Scottsville friend "Tom Martin's candidacy for the U S Senate." In June: "Edith & I drove to Edge Hill & took tea in the afternoon. Lovely afternoon." In July: "drove" to Rio Station, where he spoke to a group of Sunday school children. And in October: "Edith and I drove" to a church near Whitehall, "where I spoke to quite a large crowd of men women & children" and enjoyed a picnic. "Then by Pace's Old Mill to Ivy Depot. . . . A delightful day."

Everyman's Working the Roads

As late as the 1890s, in Virginia as in perhaps every state in the Union, an American adaptation of the *corvée*—a French term for a universal system—supplied the labor that constructed and maintained many, even most, of the public roads in rural areas. The system called for a tax, not of cash but of labor, a few days of work without compensation each year. Variously known as "statute labor" or "road duty," it provided a means whereby local governments might avoid the levy of cash taxes by securing labor without cash payments. It had been under attack for many years.[6]

By the years around 1900, states began to take legislative action against the labor tax. Vermont, for example, outlawed the labor tax in 1892, and the last of the states—in the South as well as the North—had done so by the early 1930s. But in some states, legislatures proved too slow for one citizen or another, who called on the courts to rule whether public authorities had the right to demand that free men work the roads. Until either legislative repeal or judicial invalidation, Americans had to appear when ordered to put in their quota of labor, or at least of time. Alternatively, as a rule, they might send a substitute or pay a cash tax.

As Pastor Haley could surely have testified, in Louisa County, Virginia, as elsewhere, authorities had little success in their struggle with the perennial problem of bad roads. In June 1890 the board of supervisors noted "the heavy complaints made of the bad condition of the public roads and the many difficulties in the way of securing effective Road work with the proper economy." A year later the board, writing that it was "fully aware of [the] present bad condition of the public roads," promised to continue its efforts "to do the best that the County finances will allow," but it pointed out that the county had more than 500 miles of roads to look after and warned that "our only hope of good roads is in a much larger outlay of money."[7]

Although authorities continued to make use of the labor tax, they recognized that a better way must be found. One such way might be convict labor, which had been tried in other southern states and other Virginia counties. In a split decision in 1889, the board rejected a resolution to adopt "the convict system," but it arranged the next year for the use of thirty-seven convicts for two months' work if the costs could be kept under $1,000. Some leading Louisans, like their counterparts elsewhere, favored hired labor over either the labor tax or convict workers. Regardless of which system might be adopted, the board called for putting the roads "under State Control, with hired labor or convicts and the Superintendance of a practical road engineer." Louisa County's supervisors, when they resorted to the labor tax, did not view it as a particularly good system, only as the best available.

That was the situation in Virginia in June 1892, when William F. "Pete" Proffitt received his orders to work the roads of Cuckoo District in Louisa County. Under an act of the state legislature, Louisa authorities could call him and all other able-bodied men between the ages of sixteen and sixty out to work the roads for two days each year.[8] Proffitt, however, declined to appear for work. As his daughter put it many years later, "Young men had to go out and work on the road," and "he just contested it."[9]

The law provided for such a contingency. The road overseer for Cuckoo District, J. C. Thacker, assessed him $1.00 for his failure to work, an amount to be paid in cash or to be obtained by seizing property of that value from him. Proffitt declined to pay the fine, and he owned nothing worth a dollar. It was time to force him to work the fine off, as well as costs, at $.75 for each day's work. The costs were set at $2.40.[10]

The Louisa County Court ruled that the fine was legal and ordered Proffitt to pay it or work it off as the law provided. Again, he balked. After Deputy Sheriff Frank H. Anderson arrested him, in the first week of November, Proffitt applied to the Virginia Supreme Court of Appeals for a writ of habeas corpus for false imprisonment. In view of Proffitt's claim that the Louisa road law violated the Virginia constitution, the state's high court agreed to hear the case.

Willis W. Proffitt, William F. Proffitt's father, was one of the leading farmers in the Pendleton area of Louisa County. Proffitt and his wife, Bettie, owned their own farm, free of mortgage. On it they raised their six children, with William the next youngest. Various kin (including Bettie's twin sister, Nancy) lived on the family homestead, which had been in Bettie's family since well before the Civil War. W. W. Proffitt and the road overseer, J. C. Thacker, were both proprietors of small gold mines. As for Pete Proffitt, he was twenty-two years old and either working the local mines or living at home as a farm laborer at the time he refused to work the roads in Cuckoo District.[11]

Pete Proffitt's Test Case

Proffitt's case was in fact designed as a test case. His leading attorney, William E. Bibb, was a principal in organizing the effort to test the road laws in the courts. Letters to him offer tantalizing glimpses of the origins of the test case. In May 1892 W. W. Proffitt wrote Bibb from nearby Pendleton: "I submitted the proposition of ours [of two days ago] to Mr. Thacker & my son. They would not agree to it. Thacker says he will make no move whatever until he is indemnified, now if [Louisa County Court] Judge [Frederick W.] Sims wants a case according to his so called law," and if he met their conditions, "we are ready." [12]

As the test unfolded, some participants grew more anxious about their roles in thwarting the law. At the same time, some of them voiced their opinions of Virginia's laws governing labor on the roads. In June, L. B. Glass wrote Bibb from nearby Mineral City, "I take the [occasion] to write you I could not get thare to see you personally in Regard to Working the Road." He and "Mr William C Harper," who worked "at the copper mines together," "want to know [what] they . . . intend to do. I see there are new orders issued to the . . . overseers of Road[.] I understand them to say that all parties that refuse to Work & of no property over the limits of Homestead shal be reported & shal be arrested by the sherif & be made to Work damages out & cost before released[.] . . . can the[y] do so[?] What Steps Shal Wee Take to defend our selfs[?] let us know me & Harper all about it." Then, reflecting the community's hostility toward the labor tax, he commented, "The people are more down on it than the[y] ever have been."

A month later, in July, W. A. Towsey, having grown even more anxious than Glass, wrote Bibb from Pendleton on stationery of the Chesapeake and Ohio Railway: "How is it that some of the road overseers are warning their hands in since they were at the Court House Monday? Did they get new instructions which stirred them up? I could not get to Court & can't find out why they have made a move. Ben Smith & Geo Spicer have been out after their hands. Please let me know at once if I had better wait longer or proceed as the others are doing. I did not think Mr Sims would urge them to do any thing until the test case has been tried." Towsey went on about what he clearly understood as a test case: "I thought it was understood between you and him to let every thing stand until after the trial. I heard that Ben Smith said he had tried to get out of it but could not keep from going to work any longer [for] if he did he would have to pay a fine of $30.00. Please let me hear from you at once. The money I promised is ready when called for and I know a good many more who are prepared to do the same."

Proffitt's petition for release argued that the Louisa road law violated the Virginia Constitution of 1869. According to this line of argument, the levy that had led to Proffitt's arrest was "nothing but" a poll tax. Yet the state constitution stipulated a maximum $1.00 poll tax, to be collected by the state and used exclusively for the schools, and a further $.50 poll tax, to be levied by the local authorities (the county or the town or city) to support the local government. The state had levied the $1.00 poll tax every year under the Constitution of 1869, and Louisa County had levied the additional $.50 every year as well. Again in 1892, as in every year, these taxes were being charged Louisa's citizens, and yet here the county was seeking to levy still more poll tax, a tax that clearly exceeded what the constitution permitted. Or at least so young William Proffitt argued.

The state supreme court granted the writ, and Proffitt gained his release, pending the outcome of a decision on the future of Virginia's road laws. Thus Virginia's highest court confronted a constitutional challenge to the traditional means of securing a labor force to construct and maintain rural roads.

The Virginia Supreme Court's Decision

Proffitt's lawyers—three of them—took his case to Virginia's highest court, where the state attorney general attempted to persuade the five judges to uphold the labor tax. Argument took place on March 17, 1893, but the court did not render its decision in Richmond until almost a year later. "The question is," said the court on February 1, 1894, "does the [road act] impose a capitation tax in the form of road service?" The court ruled that it did. Whether collected in cash or labor, road duty was a tax, and a commutation of a dollar went beyond the limit that the state constitution had established for local poll taxes. The tax was unconstitutional, so the arrest had been unlawful.[13]

The court had spoken, albeit with a divided voice. A majority of three judges decided for Proffitt. Two dissented. By the narrowest of margins, the laborer from Louisa had kept his freedom, and Virginia's laws requiring road duty had been struck down. In an exuberant note, one of Proffitt's attorneys, R. Randolph Fauntleroy, wrote Bibb: "I see the Supreme Court has, at last, decided the Proffit case. So—we *won!*"[14]

The next day, the *Richmond Dispatch* printed a story, under the headline "The Road Law Unconstitutional," about "one of the most important opinions handed down yesterday." The decision of the court "practically annuls the present road law of the State of Virginia" requiring men to work the roads each year or employ a substitute or pay a fine.[15] One of the more important decisions handed down that entire term of court, it would force either an amendment to Virginia's state constitution or a change in the way labor was secured to work the roads.

Beyond Virginia: Other Decisions on Challenges to Road Duty

Examining how other states dealt with road duty in the late nineteenth and early twentieth centuries points up three important features of the Virginia story. It suggests the near universality of the labor tax in the 1890s. It demonstrates that challenges to the constitutionality of such schemes were arising in various states, again not just in Virginia. Yet looking at how other jurisdictions dealt with questions of the sort that Pete Proffitt took to the Virginia Supreme Court also sets the Virginia conclusion apart.

Challenges to the constitutionality of the labor tax arose in various states, north and south, east and west, in the late nineteenth century and the early twentieth. Details varied, but the laws were fairly similar, as were the usual grounds for challenging them. Challenges could be brought on the basis of an interpretation of either the state or federal constitution. Recurrent themes in the challenges were that the laws imposed "involuntary servitude" and that they denied "due process." The rulings in turn pointed toward the system's long history and characterized it as demanding just another "public duty," like jury duty or militia service, legitimately demanded under the state's "police power." Courts typically deferred to the legislature as the place to go in quest of changes in the law of labor on the public roads. Two cases from other southern states, together with three from outside the South, illustrate the larger story and provide a context for developments in Virginia.

In Leavenworth, Kansas, C. F. W. Dassler refused in 1884 to perform two days of labor, refused to pay $3 cash instead, and refused to pay a $5 fine, so he languished in jail. The Kansas Supreme Court rejected Dassler's argument that his confinement violated the state constitution's ban on imprisonment for debt, and it rejected, too, his argument that it violated the ban in both the state constitution and the Thirteenth Amendment against involuntary servitude: "The power to impose labor for the repair of public highways and streets has been exercised from time immemorial, and comes within the police regulation of the state or city." Dassler was not a

"slave to the state"; no claim he had made could relieve him of his obligation to work the roads.[16]

In Ohio, William H. Dennis fared no better. The Ohio Supreme
Court ruled in March 1894—the month after Proffitt had won his case in
Virginia—that the law requiring Dennis to perform two days of labor on
the roads or pay $4 did not violate the state constitution. It did not impose
involuntary servitude on him, nor, in the court's judgment, did it impose
a "poll tax for county or state purposes" as forbidden in the Ohio constitution. In other states, too—including Indiana and Oklahoma—supreme
courts insisted that the labor levy was not a poll tax.[17]

The North Carolina Supreme Court was yet another that declared the
labor tax not a poll tax and directed any complaints to the legislative department. In 1906—the year Virginia, having already abandoned the labor tax, enacted a major new road law—that court ruled that T. J. Wheeler
must indeed contribute four days of labor in Wake County or pay $2.50 in
cash. The option to convert the labor tax to a cash payment was itself a recent innovation, as was Wake County's combination of a labor levy, a
property tax, and the work of "county convicts." For nearly two and half
centuries, the court said, "the roads of this State were worked solely by the
conscription of labor." North Carolina courts had held the labor tax valid
in "countless trials for failure to work the roads." Though the court was
prepared to humor Wheeler and give the question "full deliberation," it
could offer no relief. The labor levy was a matter of law for the legislature
to reconsider, not one of constitutionality for the courts to intervene in,
and "not a poll or capitation tax." The tax was a matter of the state's police
power, and "working the roads by labor" was "a police regulation or a public duty" that had nothing to do with the Fourteenth Amendment.[18]

The North Carolina Supreme Court had other things to say, too,
about the labor levy and its history. A duty, it said in one decision, "so long
recognized as such, which was universally exacted at the time of the adoption of the present Constitution, and which has been recognized ever
since, can not now be deemed and held a tax, and, therefore, unconstitutional." As a 1905 decision acknowledged, however, "The change to working the roads by taxation has been complete in most civilized countries,
but has been slower in this State than in most."[19]

Another court challenge to the labor tax emerged in Florida, where
Jake Butler refused to put in six days of work on the roads in Columbia
County. He also refused to hire a substitute, pay a cash commutation of
$3, or accept a jail term of thirty days, the maximum the law allowed. Un-
like people in other states, Butler not only took his case to the state su-

preme court but, failing there in 1914, carried it to the U.S. Supreme Court. There he pinned his hopes on his interpretation of the Thirteenth Amendment's ban on "involuntary servitude" and the Fourteenth Amendment's requirement of "due process."[20] Arguments based on state constitutions had no play here, but perhaps federal judges, unlike their state counterparts, would be convinced by his reading of one Reconstruction amendment or another.

The U.S. Supreme Court proved no more receptive to Butler's arguments than had the Florida Supreme Court. Neither the Thirteenth Amendment nor the Fourteenth could serve Butler's purpose, a unanimous Court ruled in 1916. The Thirteenth had borrowed its language from the Northwest Ordinance, yet almost as soon as the Northwest Territory was organized, its legislature enacted a labor tax on the roads. "From Colonial days to the present time[,] conscripted labor has been much relied on for the construction and maintenance of roads," said the Court. The Thirteenth Amendment "certainly was not intended to interdict enforcement of those duties which individuals owe to the State": jury duty, military service, and the like. "The great purpose in view was liberty under the protection of effective government, not the destruction of the latter by depriving it of essential powers." As for the Fourteenth Amendment, "to require work on the public roads has never been regarded as a deprivation of either liberty or property."[21]

The Supreme Court continued its history lesson in rejecting Butler's plea: "In view of ancient usage and the unanimity of judicial opinion, it must be taken as settled that"—unless some provision of the state constitution could save the day in state court—"a State has inherent power to require every able-bodied man within its jurisdiction to labor for a reasonable time on public roads near his residence without direct compensation." Like jury duty or militia service, such labor was "part of the duty which he owes to the public." In Butler's particular case, the Court could see "no failure to observe due process of law in the exercise of the State's undoubted power."[22]

The U.S. Supreme Court pointed Jake Butler back to his state's lawmaking authority, much as the North Carolina Supreme Court had pointed T. J. Wheeler to the state legislature for redress. After the 1916 federal decision, indeed, there was little point in looking anywhere but each state's legislature for a change in the laws and procedures for financing transportation improvements and recruiting a labor force for work on rural roads, city streets, bridges, and highways. Even more than before, Virginia continued to stand out in that its judiciary had interpreted the state constitution as the basis for invalidating the labor tax.

The only other state where a court decision threw out the labor tax is instructive in its similarity to the Virginia story. William Hassett challenged Nevada's Road Act of 1873, which levied a $4 annual tax for road purposes, also payable through two days' work on the roads. Nevada's 1864 constitution authorized a poll tax of at least $2 but no more than $4, the proceeds to be divided between the state and the taxpayer's county. With Nevada's Revenue Act calling for a poll tax of $4 and the Road Act another $4, Hassett claimed he was being taxed at twice the rate the constitution permitted.

The Nevada Supreme Court agreed with Hassett. "Taxation may be levied in money, service, or in kind; it is no less a tax," the court ruled in 1874. Regardless of whether levied in labor or cash, the Road Act mandated a capitation tax—a poll tax—and therefore exceeded the legislature's authority under the Nevada constitution.[23] Thus the Virginia court was not the sole exception to the usual pattern of deference to the legislature, reliance on a narrow concept of taxation, and upholding of the labor tax.

Virginia's Constitution and Its Supreme Court Decision

The Virginia court could have cited the Nevada decision, though it did not. Just as the Nevada constitution supported that state's court decision in opposition to the labor levy—and just as other states' courts cited the history of their state constitutions in upholding the labor tax—the history of the Virginia state constitution could support the Virginia court's opinion.

A look at the convention of 1867–68 that framed the Virginia Constitution of 1869 clarifies two things about Proffitt's case. Convention proceedings displayed strong disaffection toward the labor tax. And various delegates' understanding of their handiwork appears entirely consistent with the 1894 majority decision. The Virginia Reconstruction constitution—the one that, according to Proffitt, banned Louisa County's call for his involuntary labor—had occasioned a lengthy discussion of the labor tax. Delegates to the convention found it fairly easy to settle on a poll tax of $1.00 to support a new system of public elementary schools. How to pay for all the other operations of local government, however—and especially how to provide for maintaining the public roads—occasioned vigorous debate. In the end, by authorizing local governments to levy a $.50 poll tax "for all purposes," delegates had reason to think they had folded the traditional labor tax on the roads into the new cash tax.[24]

When the judges of the Virginia Supreme Court found themselves called upon to rule on Proffitt's case, it was the Virginia constitution, not some other state's, that they had to construe. And that constitution had emerged after a full discussion of the very questions they had to address. The supreme courts of Ohio and North Carolina might rule that under their states' constitutions, the labor tax was not a poll tax. The Virginia Supreme Court, in view of the split vote on the Proffitt case, could easily have ruled that way too, but three judges could draw upon a different history, and they came to a different conclusion.

Aftermath of the Court's Decision

Messages to the General Assembly from two Virginia governors—one delivered before the court's decision, the other after—reflect the importance of the decision and forecast the future of transportation in the Old Dominion.

Just weeks before the court's decision, Governor Philip W. McKinney called for action by the legislature. In an extended commentary on the need for roads and the powers of government, McKinney declared that the national government had no authority to supply county roads and that in any case the costs were too great. The state, for its part, was expressly denied authority, under its own constitution, to supply internal improvements. The counties would have to act, and he hoped that they would. Any combination of local bonds, the labor levy, a local property tax, and tolls might serve the purpose. Regardless of details, he asserted, "The necessity for better roads is conceded, and it is equally true that the people cannot expect help from the Federal Government, nor from the State Government, and, therefore, they must build the roads for themselves."[25] As it turned out, the big change in Virginia's roads would come when neither of Governor McKinney's statements about the state and federal governments was any longer true.

Governor Charles T. O'Ferrall, who took office on New Year's Day, 1894, one month before the court handed down its decision, picked up the theme at the legislature's next biennial session, in December 1895. The Supreme Court of Appeals, he reported, "has held that road service cannot be required of the citizen, and I am glad of it, for long experience had fully demonstrated that the compulsory system was 'penny-wise and pound-foolish.' Our roads, then, must be worked entirely by taxation. This is settled." He urged legislators to "evolve some measure which will redound to the advantage of every section of our State, by securing better ways for getting from point to point and conveying our products to the railroads and markets."[26]

One possible response to the court's decision was to amend the state constitution, overturn the decision, and re-create the recent past. Once again, men would be subject to demands for uncompensated labor on the roads each year. Within days of the court's decision, such an amendment was proposed. One version, approved in the House of Delegates, would have doubled the maximum annual poll tax that local governments might levy to $1.00 and would also have doubled the maximum labor tax to four days. The Senate reduced both figures to their previous levels of $.50 and two days, and the House accepted the changes. To go into effect, the proposed constitutional amendment had still to gain the approval of the next legislature and then the approval of the electorate in a referendum. Instead, the 1895–96 session declined to approve the amendment, and thus the effort to override the state supreme court failed.[27]

Later in the same year that the court handed down its decision, in October 1894, a convention of "good roads" proponents met in Richmond. Various participants spoke their minds, and they organized the Virginia Good Roads Association. Participants in the Richmond meeting approved the court's decision to outlaw the old system, an action they saw as prodding public policy in the direction that they hoped it would go anyway. One, a lawyer from Richmond named George L. Christian, observed that "by the late decision of our Court of Appeals, we have no general road law at all now, and I don't think the amendment proposed to the Constitution will meet the needs of the case." Another agreed: "For years past I have been a strong advocate for the abolition of statutory labor; the Supreme Court of the State now sustains this opinion, and such labor will not hereafter be available." The convention spent much of its time debating questions of how to finance the roads and how to secure a labor force, hired or convict.[28]

Meantime, Louisa County authorities had taken a new direction. In 1892, soon after William Proffitt refused to perform his uncompensated labor, Louisa County began to levy a separate tax on property for road improvements. The cash was spent for the construction and repair of bridges, for land taken for roads, for buying timber and hiring teams, and, increasingly, for hiring free labor to work on the roads.

From Conscripts to Convicts: Virginia's Road Law of 1906

In the first decade of the new century, the state legislature brought a new dispensation in Virginia travel. First, as Governor McKinney had noted back in 1893 while Proffitt's case was still in the courts, the Virginia constitution had to be amended before the state could invest in roads. The

Convention of 1901–2 replaced the 1869 constitution's flat prohibition against state investment with the phrase "except public roads." Even though delegates could not anticipate the developments of the 1910s and 1920s, they wanted to leave it up to the legislature whether to invest public money in public roads. Moreover, they displayed some concern that without the change in language, a court might determine that the state had no authority to put convicts to work on the roads.[29]

Given the new language, the state was free to act. Though efforts began immediately, big changes in state policy did not come until 1906. As it happened, L. J. Haley was elected to the House of Delegates from Louisa County for that session and thus had an opportunity to participate in the establishment of the state's new policy. Urged on by Governor Andrew Jackson Montague and then, in particular, by his successor, Governor Claude A. Swanson, the legislature enacted a new framework for the promotion of road improvements in Virginia. One law created a state highway commission to include one civil engineering professor each from the Virginia Military Institute, the University of Virginia, and Virginia Agricultural and Mechanical College and Polytechnic Institute. Another law provided for working large numbers of penitentiary inmates on convict road gangs. Delegate Haley voted in favor of establishing both the State Highway Commission and the state convict road force. Two years later, in 1908, the legislature appropriated $250,000 for allocation to the counties, on a matching-funds basis, for road improvements. The state had provided a basis for a system of highways.[30]

Though black residents of Louisa County far outnumbered whites, all the chief actors in the case of the laborer from Louisa had been white. Beneath the political maneuvering of turn-of-the-century Virginia was a bedrock reality: black workers could be pressed into service under a new regime that replaced conscripts, regardless of race, with convicts, most of them black. The Virginia chain gang, comprised largely of black workers—receiving no more compensation than had their conscript predecessors—labored in the years ahead to build better roads and bring Virginia into the automobile age. Meanwhile, roads in black areas of towns or counties were far less likely to be improved than were roads in white neighborhoods.[31]

Throughout central Virginia, the age of automobiles was coming into full view. In Culpeper County, for example, the first resident to buy a car did so in 1905. It is true that the second did not do so until 1910, that for the next few years each one to follow was written up in the local newspaper, and that some early owners put their new vehicles up on blocks in October and back on the roads only in June. But more and more town residents owned cars and drove them on new and improved roads. Culpeper County's historian notes that among the Fords and Buicks, the Maxwells and Marathons, one favorite was the E-M-F, "named for manufacturer E. M. Flanders, but in Culpeper popularly called 'Early Morning Fix.'" In a move designed to answer the prayers of the next generation of Reverend Haleys in the region, in 1917 "the four Baptist churches in the Jefferson-ton circuit gave Rev. Charles B. Clement a Ford touring car."[32]

Livery stables and blacksmith shops took on new tasks. By the 1920s full-service gasoline stations had arrived. In Crozet, Ernest L. Sandridge opened the first one in 1923.[33]

From 1906 to 1917

As late as Judge Duke's diary for the year 1906, in many ways little had changed. He still took the train for longer distances and drove his carriage or walked around home, as when he went "to U of Va Library in the af-ternoon" from his home on Park Street. Again and again, he "drove to Sunny Side." On an afternoon in June: "Drove with Edith to Monticello & back by Ficklin's hill—An exquisite view—lovely drive."

In June that year, he came back from a trip to Washington, D.C., with a photograph of a friend, at the wheel of an automobile, with whom he had just gone on a different kind of short excursion. Back home, however, when he wrote in his diary about going for a drive, he was still being pro-pelled by a single horse, as when he "drove the new mare to Monticello." One local trip in the spring is particularly remarkable. He left home for a little less than twenty-four hours: "Left at 1:55 p.m. & drove to Scottsville by 5:45 p.m." That evening he "delivered the address at the closing exer-cises of the Scottsville Graded School on 'Some fallacies of the present theories of education.'" After spending the night at the home of Major J. C. Hill, "Maj of father's old Regiment—the 46th," he "left Scottsville at 8:55 [a].m. Pleasant drive—arriving at 12:30 p.m. To U of Va in after-noon." He had made the twenty-mile trip each way in less than four hours, and he finished each leg of the journey full of energy and ready for more.

Let another ten years or so slip away. The year is 1917, and we find all kinds of change. Judge Duke pays a $10.00 phone bill, $12.32 for "Elec-tric Lights," and $64 for a "Majestic range." In Washington he goes to the theater and sees a "film." And in New York, where in August it was "ex-ceedingly hot," he wrote that "an electric fan would have been the summit of earthly bliss."

Given all these kinds of changes, we should not expect that trans-portation had stayed the same. For one thing, the Virginia road legislation of 1906 had had a decade to show results. Some of the changes were in the landmarks that Judge Duke passed. He and Edith drove by the "new Extract Factory." He took a "new road," he wrote, or had to specify that he went by way of "the old road from Ivy Creek to Sunny Side." On the first day of summer, Duke reported: "In the afternoon—with Edith—drove to the new 'Lee Bridge' across the Rivanna at Hydraulic, going over the new road from the top of the hill beyond the coloured church. . . . The old Hydraulic mill is gone—to this mill in the summer of 1864 [during the Civil War, at the age of eleven] I rode with my first sack of corn to be ground into meal."

Given the world he recorded in 1892 and 1906, some of the changes by 1917 are startling. In October, Duke went by auto "to Scottsville in 1 hour," a tremendous compression of time. Duke's son Eskridge, who turned twenty-four and completed his law studies at the University in 1917 and whose automobile, "Eck's auto," appears as a central character in his father's diary entries that year, went off in May with three friends "to Staunton," forty miles away and across the Blue Ridge.

The old verbs, to drive or ride, still referred to travel by carriage or on horseback, but new verbs appeared. In February, a friend "autoed me out to Country Club, then to St. Paul's. Walked home." In March: "In the afternoon motored to Bradford."

The train remained the vehicle of choice for longer travel, but the automobile was replacing the horse on shorter trips, as the 1917 diary reveals. In February, Duke went by train to Roanoke for the afternoon, and when he returned that evening, "Eskridge met me with his car." After a trip by train to Washington and Richmond, "Home at 10 p.m. Eskridge met me. All well, thank God." On another occasion Duke wrote, "To U of Va in Lile's auto. Met Edith at church & back with her in Sally Rucker's auto." A Sunday jaunt, too, was likely to be by car. In one entry in the dead of winter, when in the old days the travel conditions that Reverend Haley customarily reported might have been expected, Judge Duke wrote contentedly: "In the afternoon in Eck's auto—we went to the Owensville Road & beyond in the Ivy road, as far as the McAdam had been finished." Whatever the merits of the new roads, though, the new machine could have its own problems. In April, Duke was part of an excursion "in Eck's car beyond Owensville. View exquisite. Puncture coming back. . . . I walked about a mile & broke down myself." But there was no going back to the old days.

Even Pastor Haley, in his eighties, enjoyed the benefits of the automobile. In August 1914 one of his sons came with his family for a visit: "Willy Haley, wife and daughters from Clifton Forge came down in their automobile today." Two months later Haley made it clear that the old means of transportation still had its place: "At Louisa C.H. . . . Went up in buggy with neighbor Mr. Sergeant." But the next May, Willy drove down for another visit, this time staying the night before going on to Richmond for a day or so, and Mrs. Haley went along on the excursion. A few weeks after that, Haley himself took a ride in the new contraption, and he marveled at the ease and the speed: "Attend a meeting of Bank Directors at Louisa. Went up with H. R. Terrell from Buckner in his automobile. We went from Mineral to Louisa, about 5 miles in ½ hour."

In the 1990s William F. Proffitt's daughter still remembered her first car ride, back in 1906. As for William F. Proffitt, he never owned an automobile. Into the 1920s, when the first of his children got a car, the family traveled about by horse and buggy. In the meantime, in 1921, authorities sought to improve what is now State Road 605. Proffitt, just as he had protested the labor tax almost thirty years earlier, contested the coming of a road that threatened to pass through the middle of the family farm. This time, he lost.[34]

Promoting a New Generation of Transportation Change

During 1916, soon after the U.S. Supreme Court's ruling in the *Butler* case from Florida, Congress passed a Federal Highways Act as well as a bill establishing the National Guard, both of them in the interests of national security as the United States continued to seek to stay out of World War I. Federal power had a role to play, a role supported even by members of Congress from Virginia—a state that had denied such powers, to the state and federal governments alike, back in the 1890s. (And military service would soon prove once again a major obligation by a citizen, "part of the duty which he owes to the public," as the Supreme Court phrased it in *Butler*.)

Following the Virginia Supreme Court decision in 1894 in the *Proffitt* case and the Virginia General Assembly's legislation in 1906, the 1916 Federal Highways Act was the last in the series of three great initiatives that shaped ground transportation in Virginia in the twentieth century. Congress passed, and Virginia-born president Woodrow Wilson signed, a bill that launched the federal government on what, though it started out small, turned out to be a massive role in the promotion of good roads.

The bill reflected in large part initiatives taken by Virginia congressmen and senators, including Judge Duke's friend Thomas S. Martin as well as the other U.S. senator from Virginia, former governor Claude A. Swanson. Federal funds would supply half the construction costs of some new highways throughout the nation. The act required each state, before it could receive its share of matching funds, to establish a state highway commission, obtain approval of the main highways on which it wished to expend the funds for construction, and commit itself to maintaining such roads once they were built.[35]

Thus it is that in 1917 we meet Judge Duke in another guise, not traveling about as a lawyer or family man but working to promote the new world of auto transportation and good roads. The automobile carried him about in quest of good roads. In May he left "at 10:30 a.m. in Bailey's auto" for "Red Hill & inspected the land to be taken from Dr. Sheppe for the new road. Back by 1:30 p.m." In July: "At 10:30 a.m. in Auto . . . to Crozet where quite a large crowd assembled & discussed before the Board of Supervisors the propriety of bringing the National Highway thro' Crozet. Back at 5 p.m."

In January 1917 Duke's work as promoter took him to Norfolk. The board of supervisors urged Duke, nominally in his capacity as commonwealth's attorney (district attorney) in Albemarle County, to attend a big meeting in Norfolk, as he put it, to "look after the Good Roads & Federal Appropriation."

Perhaps the new funds would help rescue Virginia from its status, as one citizen of Charlottesville described it, as the home of "bad roads and high tolls." Roads, it was agreed, should serve at least two main purposes. One, without doubt, was to cut the costs of farm-to-market transport. Another—people in Thomas Jefferson's home county have long believed this—was to bring in tourists. Farm-to-market roads would have to be supplied, in the main, through local efforts. Property taxes and new machinery, perhaps as in Albemarle's case supplemented with convict labor, might improve the local secondary roads. But only federal authority and substantial funding, state and federal, could orchestrate and pay for the complex, costly effort of bringing in all-weather trunk-line roads that cut across county lines, even across state lines.[36]

Citizens of Charlottesville viewed the future as promising and threatening, in similar portions. From the history of railroads in previous generations, they knew the fate of towns that found themselves bypassed by transportation improvements. Would development come, or would progress pass them by? Talk at the time made it clear that Virginia would be crossed by several major highways, some north-south and others east-west. If possible, Charlottesville's leaders wanted to see that at least one of those routes passed through their town.[37]

That was why the board of supervisors sent Judge Duke to Norfolk. In his diary Duke recorded the outlines of the meetings there. On January 16 he presided over a meeting about the east-west routes. Two days later, he wrote, "I spoke for a route thro' Charlottesville. . . . Every little Hamlet & Cross Road put in vigorous claims for 'recognition.' Neither Roads nor Rome can be built in a day. Some one has to wait."

Charlottesville's leaders did not wish for their town to be one of those that had to wait. They recognized that one of the north-south routes must connect Washington and Richmond, and another would stretch the length of the Shenandoah Valley—and beyond—and pass through Winchester, Staunton, and Roanoke. Arguing against a route that would track from Culpeper through Orange, Gordonsville, Palmyra, and Farmville, they trumpeted the merits of a route that instead would head south through Charlottesville, Lynchburg, and Danville. The town newspaper called for continuing efforts at "securing this great and permanent benefit" for the Charlottesville area.[38]

Central Virginia's road maps traced the changes through the years. Charlottesville's efforts proved successful. Since the 1930s it has been at the meeting point of two roads in the federal highway system: Route 29, moving south from Washington to Lynchburg and beyond, and Route 250, connecting Richmond and Staunton. Nor did the changes end there. Under federal legislation in 1956, a new system of limited access, high-speed, four-lane, divided highways began to crisscross America. Among the newer highways is I-64. Passing by Charlottesville and more or less paralleling Route 250, which in turn follows the old Three Chopt Road dating from the eighteenth century, I-64 replaces the Chesapeake and Ohio Railroad as the main artery for passenger traffic east and west through central Virginia.[39]

State Constitution, State Statute, and Federal Law

Everywhere except in Virginia and Nevada, court challenges to the ancient corvée system were turned aside. Therefore legislation, often slow in coming, was necessary to put an end to the labor tax in most states. By the 1930s the ancient system had been virtually abandoned in both the North and the South. For approximately a generation, however, regional patterns diverged sharply. The North replaced conscripts with paid labor. As a rule, the South replaced conscripts with convicts, though by the 1930s it, too, was turning to paid labor.[40]

The Virginia Supreme Court interpreted the labor tax as inconsistent with the Constitution of 1869. But that constitution clearly banned state investment of tax money in public roads, a prohibition that the Constitution of 1902 removed. In the years that followed, state legislation in 1906 and an act of Congress in 1916 led to a new dispensation. In combination, the federal, state, and local governments pumped huge amounts of money into hard-surfaced roads in Virginia.

Not only money and engineering expertise but also planning and new regulations went into the making of the American highway system. Starting in 1925, Americans in general and Virginians in particular saw standard markers on their main highways. Those markers identified the roads in terms of highway numbers, even-numbered if east-west, odd if north-south, and supplied other information, too: curves ahead, narrow bridge, school zone. In Virginia, as elsewhere, some highways retained other names, recently bestowed by the General Assembly or the highway commission, the Jefferson Davis Highway, the Pocahontas Trail, and the Lee Highway. Passing through central Virginia were the Madison Highway, connecting Warrenton, Culpeper, Orange, and Gordonsville on its way from Maryland to North Carolina, and the Jefferson Highway, connecting Richmond with Staunton by way of Louisa and Charlottesville.

It took a number of years to bring all the components together in a new system for supplying a network of public roads. By the 1920s governors, legislators, and voters in Virginia, and congressmen and U.S. senators from that state and from others as well, together created the new road system. Federal funds, convict labor, a state highway commission: changes such as these began to work their wonders on the roads of Louisa County's Cuckoo District and across the nation.

A new source of revenue—a tax on gasoline—made possible the rapid expansion of America's system of all-weather roads. The gas tax worked as a user fee and did not require an increase in property taxes. Each state had to come up with matching funds to benefit from the new federal highway legislation, and during a ten-year period beginning in 1919, every state in the Union enacted a gasoline tax. Virginia levied a tax of three cents per gallon in 1923. Political struggles in the various states had less to do with whether to institute the tax—that proved easy—than with spending the proceeds. Efforts to divert the funds to uses other than road improvements began in the 1920s and spread widely during the depression years of the 1930s.[41]

Virginia never diverted the funds, but it could not escape the fight over the formula for their use on highways. How much of the money should be spent on city streets, how much on farm-to-market roads, and how much on primary highways? And how much should be spent in one section of the state rather than another? Those questions persist today.

Motor Vehicles and Year-round Roads

In the mid-1920s the *Charlottesville Daily Progress* carried an advertisement from the Portland Cement Company. "Road Building Far Behind the Automobile," the ad declared; "permanent roads are a good investment—not an expense." Making the customary comparison with the railroad era, the ad declared that "the great majority of our highways are as out of date as the single-track, narrow gauge railway of fifty years ago." Citizens should direct their legislators "to invest in more and wider Concrete highways now."[42]

Legislators acted, and roads improved, though in fact in the early years people who went out to buy an automobile had to ask themselves what road were they going to run it on. For regardless of which came first—chickens or eggs, fingers or forks—the incontestable fact is that cars got here sooner than did roads suitable for driving them on. But as the years passed, highways caught up with cars, and together they changed American life.

By the 1940s the State Highway Commission had set as a goal, and then celebrated as an accomplishment, "not one school bus day . . . lost because of mud on the roads!" By midcentury it had stated that "there is no comfortable living in rural Virginia without a motor vehicle and a passable year-round road."[43]

Judge Duke would have been pleased at the prospect. Had he and Edith "autoed" out of town in the 1990s and crested the Blue Ridge on Interstate 64, he might have written "simply magnificent—lovely afternoon." Pastor Haley, presented with a vision of such highways, might have seconded it with a hearty "Amen"; but had you stated the proposition as prophecy, you would have found him a devout nonbeliever. Haley's disbelief offers some measure of the transformation of travel in particular, and thus of life in general, in central Virginia in the century after young William Proffitt declined, back in 1892, to show up for work on the Louisa County roads.[44]

2

Necessity, Charity, and a Sabbath

Citizens, Courts, and Sunday Closing Laws, 1920s–1980s

THE ALLEGED CRIME—PLAYING PROFESSIONAL BASEBALL ON A SUN-
day—took place on the playing field of the Portsmouth Truckers,
who were playing the Richmond Colts. Frank D. Lawrence, half owner
and president of the Truckers, had offered free admission that day—
May 17, 1925—in hopes of generating greater interest in baseball and
attracting more paying customers during regular games. He was also seeking to test a Virginia statute that restricted Sunday baseball. After one in-
ning the Norfolk County deputy sheriff arrested the starting nine on each
side, as well as the two umpires. Called on account of arrests, the game
ended in a tie at one-all. The case went to the Virginia Supreme Court.[1]

The state of Virginia was in no way unique in having on the books, and
applying in the courts, a statute that banned a wide range of activities—
entirely legal on other days—from taking place on Sundays. Such laws
were sometimes observed and sometimes not, sometimes enforced and
sometimes not, and often contested. Newspapers told of skirmishes in
town after town and state after state over whether city parks, baseball dia-
monds, swimming pools, golf links, and movie theaters would be open or
closed on Sundays.

On Sundays in the early twentieth century, no baseball fan could attend a home game played by the Boston Braves, the New York Giants, or
the Philadelphia Athletics. By the end of the century—long after those
teams had each changed cities at least once—the restrictions had long
since vanished, but the change was neither automatic nor easily accomplished. Among states with major league baseball teams, the final holdout
was Pennsylvania, which repealed the ban in 1934.[2]

So in Virginia and in many other states in the South and the North
alike, residents in the 1920s did not have the option of taking in a silent
movie or a professional baseball game on the Christian Sabbath. Nor was

the 1925 challenge to such laws unusual in Virginia or elsewhere in America. To the contrary, Frank D. Lawrence joined a host of citizens who, finding the law in their way, challenged the law's interpretation, even its constitutionality.

Lawrence had as much reason to feel confident of a favorable outcome in the courts as in the legislature. Though he, like other Americans, might rail against judges who made law, he, like them, in a wide range of cases, often insisted that judges make law. Americans went to court to keep restrictions in place. Courts and legislatures were simply alternative venues to go to in search of any particular policy outcome.

In Baltimore, Maryland, for example, the city council passed an ordinance in 1918 to allow residents to play baseball, tennis, and various other games in public parks on Sundays, under certain conditions: they could so only between 2 P.M. and 7 P.M., so as not to interfere with church attendance, and they could charge no admission fees. A group calling itself the Lord's Day Alliance challenged the city's authority to pass such an ordinance, and the next year, in *Levering* v. *Park Commissioners*, the Maryland Court of Appeals agreed that a state law prohibited such play on Sundays. The case pointed up one state's application of the Sunday closing laws, one city's attempt to relax the ban, and one citizen group's successful attack in the courts against any such relaxation.[3]

The career of Sunday closing legislation, and in particular the history of challenges to it, exemplifies American political culture at work. At the same time, that history offers a window through which to watch changes in business law and consumer behavior in twentieth-century America.

Works of Necessity and Charity

The statute under which the ballplayers were arrested in Richmond in 1925 declared it a misdemeanor for any person to be found working on a Sunday "at any trade or calling . . . except in household or other work of necessity or charity." The exception, like the Sunday closing laws themselves, dated back hundreds of years. In 1656 the British Parliament had restricted work on Sundays, provided those restrictions did not "hinder" any "works of piety, necessity or mercy."[4]

In 1676 Parliament offered a parenthetical exception to the Sunday closing laws—"(works of necessity and charity only excepted)"—that echoed through the British North American colonies and their successor states. The same parenthetical phrase appeared in statutes enacted in Rhode Island (1679), Delaware (1795), and Massachusetts (1797). Other states used similar language. Thus, Virginia participated in a very broad pattern both in the colonial period, when it specified "(cases of necessity and charity excepted)," and after, as in a 1786 law that provided "except it be in the ordinary household offices of daily necessity, or other work of necessity or charity."[5]

Sunday closing was an issue, often a major issue, at many times and places in nineteenth-century America, even at the federal level. Early in the century, particularly in the late 1820s, Congress dealt with the contentious matter of whether there should continue to be mail delivery on Sundays (and the Sunday delivery of mail finally came to an end in 1912).[6] Late in the century, when Congress appropriated money to assist the 1893 World's Fair in Chicago, it stipulated that the fair remain closed each Sunday. The fair's directors subsequently returned the federal appropriation so they could keep the fair open every day, and wrangling in the courts ensued. The U.S. attorney general decided against appealing an adverse decision to the Supreme Court only because the case could not be heard until fall, and the fair would be closing then anyway.[7]

If Sunday closing could become an issue in federal policy and federal courts, it should be no surprise that similar scenes played out again and again at the local level. Should horse-drawn cars be permitted to run on Sundays in Philadelphia? Should theater productions be staged on Sundays in Oregon? Should shops be open on the Sabbath in Texas? What should be done about stagecoaches that ran, or markets that opened for business, on Sundays in Virginia? These kinds of questions came up time and again in nineteenth-century America. And in the twentieth century, similar questions came up in Virginia and in much of the rest of the nation.[8]

The twentieth-century cases in Virginia focused on questions of entertainment or shopping on Sundays. People running various types of businesses appealed to the state supreme court for relief from local efforts to close everything from swimming pools to movie theaters and to prevent the sale of everything from beer to motor oil. What types of economic behavior qualified under the exceptions of work of either "necessity or charity"? The judges themselves differed over definition and application, but the questions were consistent, and so were some rules for their application.

Perhaps nobody in the stands or on the field in Portsmouth, Virginia, on that Sunday in 1925 knew much about the long history of Sunday closing laws and practices. Regardless, the question arose: Could what the Truckers and the Colts were doing that day be characterized as work of either "necessity" or "charity"?

The remainder of this chapter traces two overlapping tracks through the years between the 1920s and the 1980s. One is a series of episodes in or near the city of Roanoke. The other is a series of cases that were appealed to the Virginia Supreme Court. In addition, there's a second story about Sunday baseball.

Law and Fact: Two Court Cases from 1922

The modern history of the Virginia court's rulings on Sunday closing dates from the 1920s. Judge Martin Parks Burks spoke for the Virginia Supreme Court of Appeals in 1922 in a case stemming from the arrest of the owners of Weyer's Cave, also known as the Grottoes of the Shenandoah, in Augusta County. The owners had installed electric lights, supplied guides, advertised widely, and charged admission. On Sundays they generally attracted their largest crowds, and some local churches objected. Following their arrest, the owners were convicted and fined $250. Attorneys for both sides agreed to seek a judgment from the state supreme court as to "whether the keeping open of these caverns and admission to them of visitors on Sunday, constitute a violation of . . . the 'Sunday observance law.'"[9]

According to Judge Burks, "The constitutional validity of the statute has not been called into question, and we do not doubt that it is a valid exercise of the police power of the State." He went on to note that the word *necessity* could surely be understood in a manner different in 1922 from that in the early years of independence. The precise meaning in any given case, however, would be up to the jury in that case.[10]

Judge Burks quoted a statement by the U.S. Supreme Court that "laws setting aside Sunday as a day of rest are upheld, not from any right of the government to legislate for the promotion of religious observances, but from its right to protect all persons from the physical and moral debasement which comes from uninterrupted labor." But he noted ruefully that while statements such as that one "clearly condemn labor on Sunday, and advocate the observance of the day as a day of rest," they "convey but little idea of how that rest is to be taken."[11]

Juries, he said, would have to decide how to apply the Sunday closing laws in such matters. "Issues of fact arising under the statute will have to be decided by juries who have been selected for their fitness for the service from the whole body of the people, and who, in this service, reflect the community opinion of moral fitness and propriety."[12]

Judges should decide the law; juries, the facts. "Where the act done is plainly a violation of the statute, as where a contractor, without emergency, is running a steam shovel on Sunday, or the act is plainly one of necessity, as where the owner lifts his ox out of the ditch; in either case, the question is one of law for the court. But if the act be one about which fair-

minded men might reasonably differ as to whether or not it is a work of necessity, then it is a question of fact for the jury."[13]

The statute did not supply complete guidance on what the Sunday
closing laws permitted or prohibited. What one community—by means
of a jury in a trial of this sort—judged acceptable, another might not.
Properly instructed by the judge and then left to its own devices, this particular jury in this particular case had decided to convict. The appeals
court did not see itself as "warranted in interfering with" that verdict.[14]
The Pirkey brothers would pay the fine. Weyer's Cave would be closed on
Sundays.

Another case, decided the same day, related to a swimming pool near
Roanoke that was kept open on Sunday afternoons. The Lakeside Inn
Corporation had opened a grand swimming pool at its amusement park
in Salem in 1920. In July 1921 a delegation appointed by the Ministers
Conference of Roanoke went there on a Sunday, bought tickets, looked
around, and then complained that they had been permitted to do so.[15]

At trial in the Roanoke County Circuit Court, Lakeside sought to introduce testimony from people including the county sheriff that, up until
the opening of the pool, there had been numerous complaints of "disorderly crowds" along the banks of Mason's Creek and the Roanoke River.
As that testimony was later summarized, "The persons living along the
banks of streams in Roanoke county in the vicinity of Roanoke city, and
persons passing along the public roads and streets near these streams, had
been shocked and embarrassed by the great number of nude men and boys
and partially nude women who could be seen on Sundays bathing or dress-
ing and undressing along these streams."[16]

The circuit court judge, however, excluded all such testimony. After
such testimony as the judge would admit was heard, he instructed the jury
that "the evidence in this case presents no element of necessity, either
physical or moral, within the contemplation of the Virginia statute for the
protection of Sunday."[17]

Lakeside had asked for very different instructions to the jury, each related to the question of the "necessity" of the work being judged, and each
in turn denied by the judge. For example, Lakeside wanted the jury to be
told "that the question of whether the act of keeping open the Lakeside
swimming pool on Sunday afternoons was a work of necessity within the
meaning of the statute is a question of fact for the jury, and that in determining this fact the jury may consider the manner in which the pool and
the premises and the business in connection with it were run, the effect
that the opening of this place has on the good order and moral welfare of

the community[,] and whether . . . the opening of this place is for the orderly and moral recreation of the public."[18]

Given the judge's restrictions on the testimony admitted and his instructions to the jury, Lakeside was found guilty of violating the Sunday
laws. On appeal, however, the Virginia Supreme Court observed that "under the testimony actually admitted, and the instructions given, the jury
could not well have found any other verdict than the one found." The appeals court reversed the trial court, overturned the conviction, and ordered a new trial. Should the corporation be again put on trial, members
of the jury "as the representative of the morality of the community" must
be permitted to hear the relevant evidence and come to their own judgment as to whether the law had been broken.[19]

The jury must be permitted to make determinations of fact, and in the
Lakeside case, in contrast to the case from Weyer's Cave, the judge had denied jurors that determination. Although it could scarcely bring an end to
contention over Sunday closing laws or to difficulties in enforcing them,
the court was laying down a broad rule that left it up to juries, as proxies
for local public opinion, to determine how the laws should be applied in
their own communities. In that way how the state's Sunday closing law was
applied to local affairs might vary a good deal.

What was a dead letter in one community might be very much alive
somewhere else. Indeed, by changing the law's application in this fashion,
a community could even revert to an earlier norm. Regardless, not everyone would accept the outcome in a local courthouse, so some cases would
continue to be appealed to the Virginia Supreme Court.

Sunday Baseball

When the state's highest court turned its attention in 1927 to the baseball case brought by the Portsmouth Truckers, Judge Jesse Felix West
spoke for a divided court. Upholding the twenty convictions, he wrote:
"The object of the statute being to make Sunday a day of rest, a person
who performs the same labor on Sunday which he performs in his regular
trade or calling on the other days of the week, cannot escape the penalty
of the statute by working without compensation, and claiming that he was
in fact playing and not working."[20]

Judge West took judicial notice of the fact that, the previous year, a
state senator from Norfolk County had introduced a bill that would have
exempted "athletic fields or outdoor sports open to the general public"
after 2:00 P.M. on Sundays. That the bill had failed, he wrote, gave "an

indication of the legislative policy in Virginia." Quite properly, the trial judge had instructed jurors that they might consider the connections between the baseball game and "the orderly and moral recreation of the public." And, as in the Weyer's Cave case, the jurors had elected to convict. That was that.[21]

Two of the five judges of the state supreme court remained unconvinced. Judge Richard Henry Lee Chichester joined Judge Burks in rejecting the majority's position that these men had, in fact, been playing professional baseball. In this they did not mean to deprecate the quality of play that Sunday afternoon in May 1925. Rather, although they agreed that "the playing of professional baseball on Sunday in Virginia" was a misdemeanor, they contended that "no one will deny the fact that a professional baseball player can play baseball for sport on Sunday as well as any other person, without violating the statute."[22]

Judges Chichester and Burks, although recognizing that the trial had followed the rules and that jurors had elected to convict, were unconvinced that the convictions were proper. They argued that "the question of Sunday sports and diversions should be left to the legislature." Seeing "reasonable doubt" that the legislature had intended that the statute apply to baseball players who received no compensation—though professionals, these men had received no extra pay for that day's game—the dissenters declared that the court should have overturned the convictions.[23]

Either way, Frank Lawrence could see—whether no professional teams could play, or players could not be paid, or tickets sold, if they did—no regular commercial games would be legally played in Virginia on Sundays anytime soon.

The *Richmond News Leader*, though it had called for a more relaxed application of the blue laws, editorialized that the decision, "by drawing a distinction between an amateur and a professional," would likely meet with citizens' approval "as a reasonable compromise of a vexing issue." The paper then pushed its own limited agenda: "If the court of appeals holds that an amateur may seek recreation on Sunday, why should the city continue to deny him the facilities for it? It might be well to make a test of this point." The editorial went on to note that the newspaper "has long believed that amateur sports on Sunday not only did no harm, but also offered an outlet for energies that might otherwise be misdirected. But the *News Leader* has never believed that professional ball or open theatres were necessary or desirable on Sunday in Richmond."[24]

In the Legislature and on the Playing Fields

Gradually across the twentieth century, more and more economic activities on Sunday gained legitimacy. In 1916 the Virginia legislature decided that delivery of ice cream on Sunday—provided that it had been made on any other day—should henceforth "be construed as a work of necessity." In 1932, no doubt determining that the growth of tourism and automobile travel made for a more generous definition of "necessity," the legislature acted to exclude the sale of gasoline and motor oil from the universe of restricted activities.[25]

By contrast, when the 1934 Virginia legislature faced bills designed to permit the operation of movie theaters as well as the playing of professional baseball on Sundays, both measures lost. Like the *News Leader* on the question of Sunday sports, legislators came to distinguish various activities. They were prepared to amend the law so as to legitimate some additional Sunday activities but not others.[26]

Efforts to change the operation of the law continued in the courts as well as in the legislature. Thus a new test case arose in 1934 at Bain Field in Norfolk. On April 29, with the Wilmington Pirates visiting from North Carolina, the Norfolk Tars took to the field. As in the 1925 test case, police moved in to make arrests. The eighteen starting players, together with three umpires, had to post bail of $11 each, but then, unlike in the 1925 game, play continued. A crowd of 4,500 watched the home team win, 3–2, in ten innings.[27]

Eddie Mooers, owner of the Richmond Colts, pondered these proceedings. He indicated that if the Norfolk test went well, he, too, would schedule Sunday home games. He did not wait. For the next Sunday, May 6, he took a page from the plans of the operators of local movie theaters and announced he was scheduling a charity game to benefit the Sheltering Arms Hospital. Then he announced that the game would directly challenge the blue laws. City officials notified him that they would enforce the law, though they would not shut down the game.[28]

On Sunday, May 6, owner Eddie Mooers and Manager Ed Hendee found themselves facing more than a legal challenge, as the visiting team dampened their parade by winning, 9–4. According to a newspaper writer, the Colts were suffering not only from a "dearth of hits" but also from a shortage of fielders "who can catch pop flies and who don't throw uselessly to first base to beat runners already there—and, in throwing, toss the ball wide or too high."[29]

Not only did the Richmond team lose the game at Tate Field. That Sunday, thirty participants were arrested—fifteen members of the Colts, twelve from Greensboro Patriots, and three umpires. Rather than collar the starting nine from each side, the police brought charges only when the game was over, and they included everyone who had played that day. Bobby Rice, the victorious Patriots' manager, had seen all this before. "Well," he sighed, "this makes the sixth time I've been arrested for this 'crime.'"[30]

Sunday Movies

Court cases could lead to relaxed enforcement of Sunday closing laws in two ways. If the state supreme court overruled a conviction on procedural grounds, local authorities might choose not to prosecute the case again; Lakeside may well be an example. And local courts sometimes made their own determination that certain activities should be brought under the "necessity" exception. In the city of Roanoke, for example, theater operator S. G. Richardson persisted in showing Sunday movies in 1935, and when he was brought to trial for violating the Sunday closing laws, the jury acquitted him. That local court decision brought a new dispensation in Roanoke, but it had no authority elsewhere.[31]

The issue arose in 1941 in Farmville, in the heart of the Virginia Southside, where the names of two movie theaters—the State and the Lee—reflected the dominant political culture. That culture required orthodoxy on matters of race, power, and the Lost Cause. What about Sunday movies?

Russell L. Williams, manager of those two theaters, was arrested on Sunday, September 14, 1941, for operating a theater in violation of Virginia's Sunday closing laws. In view of those laws, Farmville's residents could not as a rule attend movies on Sundays, but this was a special situation. With many area people urging that movies be screened on Sundays, the Junior Woman's Club of Farmville arranged with the owners to open the theaters as a charitable rather than a business venture. Any income in excess of operating expenses would go to the club for charity work, up to $1,000, an amount that it was anticipated would take from four to six months to accumulate.[32]

In the city of Roanoke, a local jury had decided back in 1935 that Sunday movies were acceptable, but that fact did not help Russell Williams some years later in Farmville. There, the jury found him guilty, and he appealed his conviction to the Virginia Supreme Court.

Speaking for that court, Justice Herbert Bailey Gregory viewed the case as involving work not of "necessity" but of "charity," a type of case the court was facing for the first time. Justice Gregory viewed the fact that the net proceeds would go to charity as "the principal element to be considered," and yet the trial judge had instructed the jurors that they could not consider that fact. Justice Gregory pointed to Virginia tax statutes that clearly recognized that movies could be shown for charitable, educational, or religious purposes. The court reversed the lower court and dismissed the case.[33]

But Justice Gregory did not speak for a unanimous court. In fact, in this illuminating transitional case, only Justice Edward Wren Hudgins agreed with both his conclusion and his reasoning. Chief Justice Preston White Campbell, dissenting, would have upheld the conviction. The three other participating justices—John William Eggleston, Henry Winston Holt, and Claude Vernon Spratley—concurred in the result but held that dismissal should have been on the grounds that Williams was engaged in a "work of necessity."[34]

Justice Eggleston explained: "Due to the complexity of our present day civilization and the strain under which we now live and work, relaxation and recreation are just as much necessities as food and drink." Back in 1779 "recreation was free and readily accessible to all. This is no longer the case. Nowadays recreation must be largely purchased from those who are engaged in the business of furnishing it." Eggleston concluded, "To deny to many people the opportunity of attending moving pictures on Sundays is to exclude them from their chosen form of recreation altogether, for that is the only day on which they are free from their work. Moreover, that is the day set aside both by law and custom for rest and recreation."[35]

Neither the judges' collective minds nor the law of Sunday closing had reached a new consensus. Some judges, however, were clearly willing to interpret the word *necessity* more broadly than had been typical in the past.

The Courts, the Legislature, and the Question of "Necessity"

In 1942 the Virginia Supreme Court heard a case that asked whether the sale of beer on a Sunday was "necessary." M. G. Francisco operated a general store in Hanover County. On the day he found himself charged with selling beer on a Sunday, he sold—as he customarily did on Sundays—gasoline and motor oil, tobacco and cigarettes, soft drinks, ice cream, and beer. At Francisco's trial, circuit court judge Leon M. Bazile— relying on two Virginia Supreme Court decisions, one from 1908 about Coca Cola and one from 1917 about the sale of tobacco—took it as a matter of law that the sale of beer on a Sunday could not be a work of "necessity" and left it for the jury to determine only whether in fact Francisco had made the sale.[36]

John William Eggleston, now the chief justice, spoke for the 4–1 majority in reversing the conviction and ordering a new trial. Relying on the 1922 decisions in the Weyer's Cave and Lakeside cases, he held the trial judge to have been in error in refusing the instructions requested by the defendant's attorneys that would have left it to the jury to determine the question of necessity.

Going further, Chief Justice Eggleston offered a "more practical definition" of *necessity:* "The work of necessity covered by the exception in the statute is not merely one of absolute or physical necessity, not merely something required to furnish physical existence or safety of person or property, but embraces as well all work reasonably essential to the economic, social or moral welfare of the people, viewed in the light of the habits and customs of the age in which they live and of the community in which they reside."[37]

The court went on to speak of cultural change as the basis for a change in how the law should be understood. Virginia's judges could not, Eggleston said, "shut our eyes to the known fact that the habits, customs, demands and necessities of the people, in some if not all the communities throughout the State, have undergone a change in the past twenty-five years," since those early cases on the Sunday sale of soft drinks and tobacco.[38]

"Many acts which were condemned in the past are now universally recognized as being works of necessity," the chief justice noted. "Were it not for the recorded cases"—he did not specify these—"one might be surprised to know that in the past persons have been convicted under the Sunday law for feeding livestock on a farm, for riding to a funeral, for traveling to visit sick friends, for riding to divine worship, as well as for operating trains and telegraph lines, carrying the mail, and printing newspapers."[39]

And the court took judicial notice of a 1938 state law that authorized local governments to adopt ordinances banning the Sunday sale of beer and wine. If on the face of it the Sunday closing statute prohibited the sale of beer on Sundays, surely no such ordinance would be required.

The appeals court remanded the case for a new trial. Francisco might or might not be found guilty by a jury that was permitted to rule on the facts. That remained to be seen, but Judge Bazile would have to let the jurors decide. He could not decide that the law was so clear that the outcome was predetermined.

In a concurring opinion Justice Gregory noted that in effect the legislature had accepted the court's interpretation of the law in *Pirkey* and *Lakeside,* in that despite all the legislative sessions since those decisions were handed down, the General Assembly had not chosen to undo the court's work. The appeals court's strong statement in 1942 of broader grounds for dismissing the case constituted as much a major new departure in Virginia in the law of Sunday closing as had the decisions twenty years earlier. The dissenter, Justice George Landon Browning, took a hard line and would have affirmed the conviction, but he was alone.

Adopting as a practical matter those broader grounds, the General Assembly eventually acted in 1954 to exempt the operation of movie theaters from the Sunday closing laws.[40] After that, all jurisdictions in Virginia would share the kind of law on Sunday movies that the city of Roanoke had settled on back in 1935. Roanoke had not, however, accepted that year the idea that all manner of businesses had become exempt from prosecution under the Sunday closing laws.

More than Peanuts

In the 1940s the American Peanut Corporation operated a retail store in downtown Roanoke, at 12 Campbell Avenue Southwest. Two years after the attack at Pearl Harbor, as American forces worked their way island by island toward the enemy Japan, the peanut store found itself under local assault by the Roanoke police and the Sunday closing laws. Joann L. Higgins, the store manager, was arrested in December 1943 for working on a Sunday. In hustings court a jury convicted her of the offense, and she paid a $5 fine. Soon afterwards she ended her employment as store manager, and Lionel R. Petitt took her place.[41] Little else changed.

The store operated on Sundays, much as any other day of the week, and on May 21, 1944, and again a week later, Petitt was arrested on the same charge as Higgins had been earlier. He too "did unlawfully conduct his usual business and employ and work his servants in the conduct" of that business, "not being a work of necessity or charity," in violation of the Roanoke city code.[42]

In J. Lindsay Almond Jr.'s hustings court T. Warren "Squeak" Messick represented Lionel Petitt, just as he had represented theater operator S. G. Richardson nine years earlier. Messick and his cocounsel, English Showalter, took the position that Petitt was indeed engaged in a "work of necessity" under the statute. What, they wanted jurors to determine, was "the attitude of the community in regard to other forms of business"? What was "the manner in which the defendant's place of business and the premises in connection with it were run"? And what effect did that business have "on the economic, social and moral welfare of the community"? Was it "conducive to the orderly and modern recreation of the public"?[43]

The community depended on access to such businesses as that managed by Petitt, though the judge refused to let the jury hear his testimony to that effect. Barely a block away, on Jefferson Street, Petitt wanted the record to show, one could buy nuts or popcorn any Sunday at the American Theatre, which had been showing Sunday movies now for nine years. In between the Peanut Store and the American Theatre, at the corner of Campbell and Jefferson, the United Cigar Store and Rosenberg Brothers sold nuts, soft drinks, chewing gum, candy, and tobacco every Sunday, just like any other day of the week. Right next door to the Peanut Store was the Roanoke Theatre, which also sold peanuts and popcorn.[44]

Convicted, Petitt appealed the case to the Virginia Supreme Court of Appeals. There the city's attorneys argued that the question of necessity had been presented to the jury in the case against Higgins, and the jury had convicted her. Why might anyone think that some six months later anything had changed? What could have happened in Roanoke "in so short a space of time" that such a "radical change" had taken place to "make something that was not a necessity on one Sunday become a necessity the next"? Quite aside from that, they insisted, "No reasonable person could, under any pretense, contend that the operation of a peanut store is a matter of necessity."[45]

Justice Hudgins, speaking for a unanimous court, insisted that Judge Almond should have permitted Petitt to introduce evidence that his selling peanuts on a Sunday was in fact a "work of necessity."[46] It was the jury's job to determine whether the defendant's action should be considered necessary. Instead, the judge had adopted the premise that a previous conviction of another employee at the same store for working on Sunday proved in itself that the work in question was not necessary.

Petitt's widow, Bernice Petitt, later reported that the store remained open on Sundays through the entire appeals process. He routinely worked there on Sundays during that time and afterwards.[47]

Continuing Prosecutions

And yet prosecutions for other violations continued in the years that followed. James E. Rich Jr. was convicted of operating a retail grocery store in Warwick on Sunday, June 12, 1955. He appealed his case to the Virginia Supreme Court, which pondered the nature of the evidence and the verdict of the jury. Had Rich's two stores, when they sold bread, milk, and cereal, been engaged in "work of necessity"? It was evident that they had not been involved "a work of charity."[48]

It was clear that many stores were open on Sundays in Warwick. Rich testified that he owned two supermarkets. One had been open since 1949, the other since 1953, and both had been open "seven days a week" ever since he "began business." John T. Christian, another grocery store operator, said he had opened his store on Sundays for many years, and he explained, "People need bread and milk and things like that on Sunday." R. L. Seaboldt, who worked as pharmacist and the manager of People's Drug Store in Warwick, told the court that his own store "was regularly open on Sundays for the sale of bread and various other items, such as were sold in grocery and hardware stores." Best of all, A. C. Smith testified that he "kept his grocery store, located across the street from the Court House of the City of Warwick, open on Sundays."[49]

G. W. Vaughan, a local resident, was the person who fingered Rich in the first place. He told the trial court that "because of religious convictions" he was "opposed to grocery stores being open on Sunday." Yet it became clear that, though he "did not make any purchases on that date," he had "made purchases from the same store on previous Sundays." He had to agree that his religious "convictions had not been strong enough" to prevent his making Sunday purchases whenever he "desired to do so."[50]

Speaking for the appeals court, Justice Spratley had no interest in considering whether the law under which Rich had been convicted was unconstitutional. Rich's lawyers had brought an argument, "raised for the first time in this Court," said Spratley, that the phrase "other work of necessity or charity" was so vague, or so "dependent upon the religious philosophy of the particular judge or jury trying the case," that it violated the Fifth and Fourteenth Amendments to the U.S. Constitution. That constitutional argument would not fly: "The enactment of Sunday regulations" was a valid "exercise of the police power," by no means on its face unconstitutional.[51] On the facts, however, there was ample reason to reconsider the outcome of the trial.

Justice Spratley observed that many of the grocery stores in Warwick were routinely open for business on Sundays. The prosecution had argued that this fact "showed that the needs of the community could have been filled on weekdays and on Sundays by grocery stores other than those of the defendant, while the defendant contends the operation of the other stores warranted the assumption of a necessity affecting the economic and social welfare of the people of Warwick, viewed in the light of their present habits and customs," such that "there can be no justification for excluding the defendant from an equal opportunity to relieve the necessity."[52]

The court took an agnostic stance: "In the absence of material relevant evidence, the correct conclusion is merely speculative." And that proved critical to the case's outcome. The justices reversed the conviction and dismissed the case. "We are not unmindful of the respect justly due to the verdict of a jury; but their verdict cannot be sustained unless it is supported by some evidence." Though the jury had elected to convict Rich, its verdict "was without evidence," for the state had "signally failed to carry the burden of proving" that the work he had been doing that Sunday in June 1955 was "not a necessity within the meaning of the statute."[53]

Continuing Challenges to the Statute's Constitutionality

In a 1961 case five operators of retail grocery stores in Richmond— Robert L. Mandell, Myron A. Fine, Gerald H. Fine, C. T. Covington Jr., and W. V. Harvey—filed suit for a declaratory judgment against the commonwealth's attorney of the city, T. Gray Haddon, seeking an injunction against his enforcement of Virginia's Sunday closing laws. They took two grounds, one technical in nature, the other constitutional. On appeal, Justice Lawrence Warren I'Anson spoke for a unanimous court in dismissing the technical objection and addressing the constitutional arguments.[54]

Did the Sunday closing laws, in violation of the state constitution, comprise "special legislation"? That is, did the law unfairly discriminate in favor of some businesses and against others? "This contention is without merit." Justice I'Anson observed that the current law remained sufficiently comprehensive "to close a great majority of stores" in Virginia "while leaving open restaurants, drug stores, recreation centers and filling stations."[55] He concluded that the statutory scheme was reasonably related to the attainment of the legislative goal: providing the people of Virginia a common day of rest.

But there remained the question of the federal Constitution. Did those laws deny retailers "equal protection of the laws" under the Fourteenth Amendment to the U.S. Constitution? Again, "This contention is without merit." On this federal question the Virginia court relied on a recent major decision in the U.S. Supreme Court, *McGowan* v. *Maryland* (1961), that neither the First nor the Fourteenth Amendment prevented states from enforcing their blue laws. In that decision only Justice William O. Douglas thought the First Amendment, with its clauses regarding an "establishment of religion" and the "free exercise" of religion, a bar to the criminal prosecution of businesses for operating on Sundays. By a margin of 8–1, the nation's high court upheld the constitutionality of Maryland's Sunday closing laws, and Maryland's blue laws differed in no essential way from Virginia's.[56]

Statutory Renovation and Local Option

Though clearly being attacked on constitutional grounds, both state and federal, Virginia's Sunday closing laws remained in force. In 1974, however, the legislature enacted a local-option feature. Each city and county gained authority to enact an ordinance stipulating that the Sunday closing laws were "not necessary." Yet before local authorities could act, voters had to approve a referendum on the question. And such elections could be held no more often than every other year, in even years.[57]

The same act renovated the schedule of economic activities that would escape the Sunday closing laws even in jurisdictions that had not approved such a referendum. The list of such exempt activities indicated how much had changed in the previous half century: "sale of food"; "sale of tobacco and related products"; "operation of motion picture theatres"; "athletic events and the operation of historic, entertainment and recreational facilities"; and various other categories to a total of nineteen, including "servicing, fueling and emergency repair of motor vehicles."[58]

One aspect of the new schedule would prove far-reaching. The 1974 measure shifted the emphasis from regulating the sale of certain items to regulating which industries or businesses might operate on Sundays. Soon afterwards, Bonnie BeLo Enterprises, operators of Farm Fresh Supermarkets, came to the Virginia Supreme Court, convicted in the city of Portsmouth of selling nonfood items—paper cups, paper plates, and a paperback book, *The Day of the Jackal*—on Sunday, November 10, 1974. Justice Alex M. Harman Jr. spoke for a unanimous court in 1976 that reversed the conviction and dismissed the case. Under the state's revised Sunday closing laws, all those engaged in the business of retailing food might open for business on Sundays. Now the court declared that a food retailer "is permitted, incidental to the operation of his business on Sunday, to sell such non-food items as are sold in the ordinary and normal course of his business."[59]

But the next year, 1977, the Virginia Supreme Court unanimously affirmed the conviction of Malibu Auto Parts for selling a quart of motor oil at its Virginia Beach store on Sunday, July 4, 1976. The *Farm Fresh* case, it seemed, offered no value as a precedent in the *Malibu* case. "Malibu's principal business [selling automotive parts and supplies] is not permitted as an exception to the Sunday Closing Laws." Moreover, the fact that motor oil could be purchased in Virginia Beach "in a drugstore, a supermarket, and a service station" on Sundays offered no basis for the contention that Malibu was being denied equal protection of the laws.[60]

Thus in the late 1970s the Sunday closing laws in Virginia—despite statutory amendments and local option—remained potent in some areas. But local option swept through much of the state in the 1970s and 1980s. And in many jurisdictions, when voters failed to approve a change, some retailers grew restive. Challenges continued.

The Best Little Warehouse in Virginia

One such challenge took place in Roanoke. In February 1986 Doug Carr opened a store there, Valley Liquidators of Roanoke. In it he sold everything from auto parts to answering machines and from ceiling fans to talking animals. From the beginning, Valley Liquidators—which Carr advertised as "the best little warehouse in Virginia"—was open for business seven days a week. In a referendum in November that year, a majority of voters in both Roanoke and Roanoke County determined to retain the Sunday closing laws, but Doug Carr stayed open each Sunday. Commonwealth's Attorney Donald Caldwell had lobbied the previous year against the law, but it had been kept, and his job was to enforce it.

On Sunday, May 31, 1987, Carr was charged with violating the law, the first person in the city to be so cited since the referendum. When a police detective gave him a summons, Carr said "thank you" and continued to work. When the officer told him he would have to close, Carr asked, "What are you going to do if I don't?" Told he would be arrested and taken to jail, Carr responded, "That's fine." Told, however, that all his employees would be arrested too, Carr relented. The store was closed the rest of that Sunday.[61]

Doug Carr knew an unjust law when he saw one. "It is unconstitutional," he remonstrated. "It is unfair." His comments focused on the inequity of it all. He was hardly the only person selling merchandise in Roanoke on Sundays. By that he meant both to protest his arrest and to explain it. "It's got to be a competitor" who brought the complaint, he observed, and most likely a flea market operator unhappy with Carr's low prices. Almost anything that he sold could be bought on Sundays at drugstores or flea markets, he growled. "Either shut 'em down or leave me alone."

Carr had to consider his options. With sales averaging $5,000 on Sundays, Valley Liquidators did about a quarter of its weekly business that day. And he ruminated on the importance of Sunday sales to the community. According to Carr, 80 percent of his Sunday sales went to people from out of town. After his arrest he declared, "They keep on, Roanoke is gonna be a ghost town." People would go away from Roanoke to spend their money, not come to the city. Merchants would lose business, and the city would lose sales tax revenues.

Carr got off on a technicality, but he warned: "I'm a little guy. I can't afford to take this thing to the Supreme Court." He went on, "If they charge me again, I'll have to close, period. I can't afford to pay the rent on this building and lose 25 percent of my business." But if he closed, he would move. "One more time and I'll leave the city. I'll move to one of the localities that will welcome a million-dollar-a-year business." [62]

Carr was, in fact, arrested again. This time, however, he won. Circuit court judge Roy Willett ruled on October 8, 1987, that Virginia's blue laws violated the state constitution. Although he had been inclined at first to uphold the statute, Willett determined that the blue law failed to fit "the present circumstances of modern life" and that, in view of its many exemptions, it was "virtually unenforceable." [63]

All of Roanoke city could open on Sundays. Doug Carr called Judge Willett's decision "the greatest thing that ever happened to the city of Roanoke," and Commonwealth's Attorney Caldwell, who had prosecuted Carr, announced that the city would not appeal the ruling. He explained, "Kroger can stay open and sell everything under the sun." Caldwell anticipated that surrounding jurisdictions might follow Roanoke, since Roanoke County and the city of Salem lay in the same judicial circuit as the city of Roanoke, and in fact the commonwealth's attorney for neighboring Roanoke County, Tom Blaylock, expressed an inclination to accept the ruling for the county.

Not everyone was happy. Charles M. Robertson Jr., executive vice president of Magic City Ford in Roanoke, had campaigned to keep the blue laws in the city, and now he was angry that, after the referendum had been won, a judge threw out the results. The decision "just burns me up," he declared. He foresaw a "mushrooming" effect, as more and more stores would open on Sundays. Magic City Ford would not be among them, he promised. "We feel like it's a day people like to be with their families." Rolen Bailey, director of the Roanoke Valley Baptist Association, spoke for another group that had hoped to keep what was left of Sunday closing. But he noted that, with all the exemptions that had been approved over the years, "they have taken the heart out of it, in my opinion," and its usefulness had been greatly diminished regardless of Judge Willett's ruling.

Retailers at Valley View Mall, leaders in the local effort to end the operation of the blue laws, moved quickly. By Sunday, November 1, the *Roanoke Times and World-News* contained advertisements like that of department store Miller and Rhoads, which urged consumers to shop "today." The Crossroads Mall announced, "Now Open Sundays," but Leggett, refusing to follow the crowd, had to specify in its advertising that it was closed Sundays.[64]

To the Plaintiffs' Great Competitive Disadvantage

Another challenge emerged in Virginia Beach. In 1985 several corporations initiated legal action against the enforcement of the Sunday closing laws there. These included two real estate development companies that operated shopping centers: Benderson Development Company and S. L. Nusbaum and Company, Inc. It also included six giant retailers: Best, Circuit City, Hechinger, K Mart, Rose's, and Zayre. Three efforts to get a local-option referendum passed in Virginia Beach had failed. It was time to resort again to the courts.

Attorney Mike Greenberger complained that Virginia's Sunday closing laws were the strictest in the nation, but that they were nonetheless ineffective. The legislature had exempted any number of types of retailers from the operation of the laws, and a local-option provision permitted individual counties and cities to opt out. Circuit court judge Edward W. Hanson Jr. rebutted such arguments by noting that the Virginia General Assembly had enacted the laws, the Virginia Supreme Court had approved them as recently as 1977 (in the *Malibu* case), and the voters of Virginia Beach had rejected local option in three successive referenda. Thus the current law in the city faithfully reflected "the expressed will of the Legislature, the courts and the people."[65]

The case went to the state supreme court. Judge Willett, together with the other people in Roanoke who commented on the ruling in the Carr case regarding "the best little warehouse in Virginia," knew that the Roanoke ruling might well prove temporary, overturned in effect if the Virginia Supreme Court upheld the blue laws and the Virginia Beach convictions. Which way would that court go?

In presenting their case to the state's highest court, the plaintiffs in *Benderson* insisted not only that "the current Sunday closing law is ineffectual, irrational, and discriminatory" but that "the Sunday closing law's constitutional defects are especially great under the Virginia constitution."[66] The state, with Mary Sue Terry as the attorney general, argued that the U.S. Supreme Court had consistently upheld Sunday closing statutes, and the state court should too, but lawyers for the retailers rejected the relevance of that statement.

They concluded their argument for overturning the Virginia statute: "Finally, our view that state constitutions frequently mandate greater scrutiny of state legislation and hence that *McGowan* and its companion cases

were [by no means the last] word on the constitutionality of Sunday closing laws is confirmed by the fact that, since *McGowan* was decided, almost
two dozen state courts have invalidated their states' Sunday closing laws in
whole or in part on state constitutional grounds." Such decisions had recognized that where, as was true in Virginia, "the presence of numerous exemptions has transformed the statute's effect from assuring rest to discriminating among businesses, the statute cannot stand as a matter of state
constitutional law." Under the 1974 law "any retail store which can successfully contend that it fits into one of the exempt categories may sell on
Sunday any merchandise it wishes, including the same items the plaintiffs
are forbidden to sell on Sunday." [67]

The Virginia Supreme Court proved receptive to this line of argument. Observing that "this appeal challenges Virginia's Sunday-closing
laws," it handed down its ruling in *Benderson* on September 23, 1988.
Speaking for the 6–1 majority, Justice Charles Stephens Russell cited the
retailers' contention that, while they had to close on Sundays, "a number
of their competitors selling identical products are exempt from the operation of those laws and therefore do business in Virginia Beach on Sundays, to the plaintiffs' great competitive disadvantage." [68]

The corporations had challenged the constitutionality of the 1974
measure both on federal ("equal protection") and state ("special laws")
grounds. The court chose to distinguish the one from the other. As the
U.S. Supreme Court had held in the 1961 *McGowan* decision, a state's Sunday closing laws would violate the Fourteenth Amendment's equal protection clause only if the distinction between goods that could and could not
be sold rested on "grounds wholly irrelevant to the achievement of the
State's objective." Under the Virginia constitution a statute could not get
off so easily but must, rather, bear "a reasonable and substantial relation"
to the legislative purpose. Did the 1974 law, Justice Russell asked, violate
the state constitution's ban against "special laws"? [69] The court majority
judged that it did.

Local option had transformed the legal environment. Rather than
"close a great majority of stores" in Virginia, as the court could say the law
did in 1961, the law's scope in 1988 was "sufficient to close only a small minority of stores." Moreover, "merchandise of every kind can be purchased
in every county and city on Sunday." In short, as plaintiffs had argued, "a
statutory scheme" that "began its life as a general law" had, "by attrition,"
become "a special law." [70] Having been reduced in their operation by statute and then by referendum, Virginia's blue laws could no longer pass constitutional muster.

The ban on special legislation had as its target "economic favoritism," and Justice Russell took notice of plaintiffs' arguments that "the many exemptions in the law make it impossible to enforce fairly. The defendant commonwealth's attorney admits . . . that he enforces the Sunday-closing laws only when called upon to do so by 'private complaint.' Plaintiffs contend that this state of affairs results in the law being used as a weapon by those who are privileged to do business on Sunday, to prevent would-be competitors from opening on Sunday."[71] They would have such a weapon no more.

In earlier decisions, the court observed, "we have held unconstitutional laws which were general when first enacted, but were rendered special by subsequent amendment." General laws could be rendered special through other means than legislative amendment, but if they became special, by whatever combination of means, they could no longer pass the test of general application. The Virginia Supreme Court did not expressly state that the state's Sunday closing laws were unconstitutional. Rather, it said they were unconstitutional "as applied to the plaintiffs in this case."[72]

Court as Forum, Court as Mirror

By the 1990s Virginia had, it seemed, resolved the question of whether businesses could operate on Sundays. Surely it seemed unlikely that the legislature would act to reverse the extension of exemptions that had led to the court's ruling that, if so very many businesses no longer faced restrictions from the blue laws, no business had to. In some places elsewhere in the nation, however, and in other countries, too, the issue persisted and clearly would do so for some time. Should the voters in Bergen County, New Jersey, put an end to the blue laws there? People with businesses at giant malls hoped they would; their smaller competitors hoped not. A similar issue divided people in France, where many store owners wanted the restrictions ended, but many workers hoped to retain their entitlement to work-free Sundays.[73]

The U.S. Supreme Court decided a case in 1985 about the right of a worker to refuse to work on Sundays in Connecticut, where the courts and the legislature continued to wrestle over the Sunday closing laws.[74] But the nation's highest court had nothing new it wished to say about whether a state chose to retain or end its blue laws in general. The U.S. Supreme Court had not moved beyond its approval of Sunday closing legislation in the 1961 *McGowan* case.

The Virginia Supreme Court, by contrast, declining to address questions arising from the First and Fourteenth Amendments, based its decision in 1988 squarely on the Virginia state constitution. Doing so, the Virginia court went far beyond what most members of the U.S. Supreme Court felt they could or should do. In the 1970s and 1980s, the courts in Virginia faced questions that they chose to handle on the basis of their readings of their own state constitution. So did those in various other states, some of which also axed their blue laws.[75]

In an expression reminiscent of the rhetoric of the Age of Jackson 150 years before, the Virginia Supreme Court insisted in late 1988 that the legislature not provide unfair and unequal economic opportunity for retailers. Other things were surely also at work to produce the decision in *Benderson*. As early as 1932, when the legislature approved the Sunday sale of gasoline, lawmakers had recognized that tourism constituted a major industry in Virginia; and tourism, by its nature, invalidated any assumption of an immutable sum of sales. If Sunday sales from customers in transit added a bonus to local sales—as Doug Carr contended regarding his store in Roanoke—then Sunday sales did not simply spread a fixed sum of sales across an additional day. Pointing in a different direction were the three judges who, back in 1942, had agreed with the court in overturning Russell Williams's conviction but wanted to acquit him on grounds that he was engaged in "work of necessity" rather than "work of charity."[76]

From One Paradigm to Another

The paradigm had changed in the years since the 1920s and 1930s. Back in 1935, in prosecuting the case against Sunday movies, the Roanoke commonwealth's attorney had argued that if Sunday movies could be construed as "necessary," then there could be nothing wrong, either, with "opening a shoe store, a barber shop, a beauty parlor."[77] That logic led in 1988 to a conclusion opposite to the one the Roanoke prosecutor had sought, and the court decided that all such businesses could be open.

As the Virginia Supreme Court made its way from one paradigm to another, it prodded at some points, and impeded at others, a process in which, across the twentieth century, more and more retailers could operate on Sundays, and convictions became harder to obtain and harder to sustain. The premise in the 1988 decision was possible only because many Virginians had eased the way. Various retailers, charged with and convicted for Sunday sales, forced judges and legislators to rethink the Sunday closing laws. In staying open, contesting the law—taking their challenge to the courts—they had promoted incremental, even wholesale change. By 1988 most retail establishments were open on Sundays, or at least could choose, without regard to legal considerations, whether to open. Restrictions against the minority that remained constituted invidious discrimination.

The Sunday closing laws changed because of what happened in shops and on playing fields as well as in legislatures and courts. Citizens acted, and thus they forced judges and juries to question the meaning of the law. Again and again, the questions led to new answers. Both sides resorted to the courts to make law, and the cases that they brought often led to new law. Changing attitudes thus crystallized into a new environment—social, economic, and legal. No longer does any baseball player, movie operator, or retail salesperson in Virginia face arrest, conviction, and a fine for working on Sunday.

Some things changed outside the course of lawsuits and legislation, and some things did not change at all. The Virginia Supreme Court spoke in 1922 about the kinds of behavior that would constitute a clear violation of the Sunday closing laws, for example, "where a contractor, without emergency, is running a steam shovel on Sunday." Evidence at construction sites suggested that, as the twentieth century turned into the twenty-first, contractors no longer had to concern themselves with that kind of restriction on their activities. Yet deer hunting—evidently quite another matter—was not yet a legal option on a Sunday.[78]

Mrs. Petitt can bring us back to what changed during her lifetime as a consequence of laws and lawsuits. She grew up in the Roanoke area in the 1920s and 1930s, and in the 1990s she remembered going with her family, years before, to Lakeside Pool for picnics on Sunday afternoons. She remembered that as early as the mid-1930s, the movie theaters were open on Sunday afternoons, and she was sure that she went to a Sunday movie at one time or another. In later years she went to Roanoke-area malls on an occasional Sunday. Yet late in her life she remained unsure that shops ought to be open on Sundays. Remembering her husband, she noted that if you have to work on Sundays to keep your job, that job can keep you away from your family. Still, if the shops were open, she was not against giving them business, and she would sometimes get to Valley View, or Crossroads Mall, or Tanglewood, even on Sundays.[79]

In Roanoke the last of the Sunday closing restrictions fell in October 1987. In Virginia Beach and other cities and counties in Virginia that had not yet put an end to the blue laws, the end came in September 1988 with the *Benderson* decision. And what was happening in Virginia was not so different from developments elsewhere in America. Lionel Petitt's behavior, like Doug Carr's and, before him, S. G. Richardson's—in staying open, contesting the law, taking on a challenge in the courts—had promoted change in Roanoke, and their counterparts elsewhere in Virginia and across America had taken similar actions. Across the twentieth century, consumer customs had changed. So had business behavior. So had public policy, whether announced in local courts, appellate courts, or legislatures.

3

These New and Strange Beings

*Race, Sex, and the Legal
Profession, 1870s–1970s*

IN 1848 EVERY ATTORNEY IN VIRGINIA WAS A WHITE MAN. IN THAT regard Virginia was representative of the South, indeed of virtually the entire nation. Over the next century and a half, much would change, and albeit in very different ways, Virginia would once again typify regional and indeed national patterns.[1] This chapter explores some of those changes in Virginia, the South, and the nation. While the emphasis here is on gender, race offers a comparative means of gauging change; and of course change had to take place in both race and gender for there to be black female attorneys. Such change relates to the variable participation by men and women and by Caucasians and African Americans in public life, their leverage in public policy, their power to use the law to shape relationships and opportunities.

In 1848 an early wave of American feminism produced the Seneca Falls Declaration of Sentiments. A small band of feminists meeting in upstate New York indicted the American scene, made demands for change, and voiced commitment to secure those changes. Speaking of "a history of repeated injuries and usurpations on the part of man toward woman," the declaration charged that "he" had blocked "her" from exercising "her inalienable right to the elective franchise," "denied her the facilities for obtaining a thorough education," and "monopolized nearly all the profitable employments."[2]

In short, the group at Seneca Falls, New York, called for three things nowhere available to women in the United States in 1848: the right to become a lawyer, the right to secure access to the training to become a lawyer, and the right to vote. Having adopted the Declaration of Sentiments, the same group produced a set of resolutions that called on "woman" to reject the legitimacy of these and other restrictions. She should, they insisted, have some say in formulating the laws that governed her, and she should take action to overcome the restrictions. The resolutions declared "that the speedy success of our cause depends upon the zealous and untiring efforts of both men and women, . . . for the securing to women an equal participation with men in the . . . professions."[3]

In pre–Civil War America, African Americans encountered tremendous obstacles of all kinds, which often proved far greater than those faced by white women. Yet by the time the Seneca Falls Convention issued its resolutions, three black men in the North had recently become lawyers, although no woman of any racial identity would manage the feat until after the Civil War. Macon Bolling Allen was admitted to the practice of law in Maine in 1844 and in Massachusetts the next year, and Robert Morris Sr. was admitted to the bar in Massachusetts in 1847. George Boyer Vashon, though turned away in Pennsylvania in 1847 on the basis of his racial identity, was admitted to the practice of law in New York in January 1848.[4]

In Virginia, race and gender would have both remained insuperable obstacles for many years after 1848 had it not been for the Civil War, the emancipation it brought, and the Reconstruction that followed it. Emancipation and Reconstruction, in combination, fast-forwarded change on the racial front throughout the states that had formed the Confederacy. By the mid-1870s black lawyers were as likely to be found in the South as in the North. By that time, an occasional female attorney could be found as well—outside the South.

To Be Black and a Lawyer in Virginia

Before the end of slavery in the 1860s, one of Virginia's statutes declared it a crime for anyone to conduct a school attended by African Americans; and a white woman, Margaret Douglass, went to jail in Norfolk for a month in 1854 for teaching black children—free black children—in violation of that law.[5] The law against black schools ended when slavery did, and before long—from 1867 into the 1890s—black Virginians were shaping the law themselves by voting in large numbers and even holding political office.

Some became lawyers. In the two decades after Confederate general Robert E. Lee surrendered his army to Union general U. S. Grant at Appomattox Courthouse, a number of black men joined the ranks of practicing attorneys in Virginia. Some first studied law at the fledgling Howard University Law School in Washington, D.C., organized in 1869 by John Mercer Langston, a mixed-race native of Virginia who had grown up in Ohio, where he had graduated from Oberlin College in 1849 and had been admitted to the practice of law in 1854. Later, after his time at Howard University, Langston presided for a time over a black college in Southside Virginia, an area that he represented in Congress in 1890–91.[6]

In fact, every state of the former Confederacy had admitted its first black lawyer to the bar by 1873, as the world in which Margaret Douglass could be jailed rapidly receded. Not only could black children go to elementary school, but black adults could study law and become lawyers.[7] Walthal G. Wynn, who graduated from the Howard University Law School in 1871, became Virginia's first black lawyer when he was admitted to the Virginia bar that same year.[8]

Another early law graduate at Howard from Virginia was Robert D. Ruffin. Born a slave in King and Queen County in 1837, he fought in the Union army during the war, earned his law degree in 1874, and subsequently served as sheriff and, in 1875–76, as a member of the state legislature. Howard law graduates William C. Roane and Robert Peel Brooks both became lawyers in Richmond in 1876. On at least one occasion in 1879, black lawyers both prosecuted and defended a black defendant when Roane, who was serving as commonwealth's attorney (the Virginia equivalent of district attorney) in Richmond, prosecuted a black man whom Brooks was representing. Among the black attorneys who began to practice in Virginia in the 1880s were James H. Hayes, Thomas Calhoun Walker, Giles Beecher Jackson, and William Micaijah Reid.[9]

During the early 1880s black legislators found themselves part of a Readjuster majority. One of them was Alfred W. Harris, who was born to a free black family in Fairfax County in 1854 and graduated from the Howard University Law School in 1881. Harris practiced law in Petersburg and, beginning in 1881, represented Dinwiddie County for four successive two-year terms in the House of Delegates. Early in his time in the legislature, he pushed successfully for the establishment of Virginia Normal and Collegiate Institute, the black public institution of higher education that John Mercer Langston soon served briefly as president (and that by 1979 became Virginia State University).[10]

Black men continued to gain election to the Virginia legislature as late as the 1889–90 session, when James A. Fields served in the House of Delegates. Born a slave in Hanover County in 1844, Fields graduated in the first class at Hampton Institute, in 1871, then taught school before earning his law degree from Howard University in 1881, the same year as Alfred W. Harris.[11] By the 1890s, however, black Virginians found themselves squeezed out of the political sphere, and no black Virginian gained election to any political office after the 1890s until the 1940s (see chapters 4 and 7).

A second generation of black lawyers in Virginia joined the profession between the 1890s and the 1920s. These included Thomas H. Hewin, Joseph R. Pollard, and J. Thomas Newsome. In fact, some families produced two generations of black lawyers. Andrew William Ernest Bassette Sr. became a lawyer in the 1880s, and A. W. E. Bassette Jr. graduated from Howard University Law School in 1906. Alfred W. Harris's son, B. F. Harris, practiced law, like his father, in Petersburg. William Micaijah Reid's son Thomas Harris Reid joined his father's firm in Portsmouth after graduating from Howard in 1915.[12]

Until the 1920s no law school in Virginia accepted black applicants, which is why black lawyers in Virginia had earned their law degrees outside the state. From 1922 to 1931, however, Virginia Union University in Richmond offered a law program. For the first time black students—men and women—had access to a formal course of legal studies in Virginia. The program remained small, however, and did not last long; only six of its graduates were admitted to the Virginia bar.[13]

To Be a Woman and a Lawyer in Virginia

By the 1920s black women were practicing law in Virginia. George Washington Fields, a graduate of Cornell University Law School, began practicing law in Virginia in 1890. His daughter, Inez C. Fields, graduated from Boston University Law School in 1922 and, after practicing law in New England for a few years, returned to Virginia and joined her father's practice in Hampton.[14] Her presence epitomized a new kind of change in the legal profession. That she was black and female offered two reasons she had had to go out of state to obtain a law degree. But by the late 1920s she was back in Virginia, practicing her craft. By that point other black women and a number of white women were lawyers in Virginia.

Occasionally a woman, white or black, had sought to practice law in Virginia in the half century before the 1920s. As early as 1880 Providence Crute, a black woman in Richmond, told the census taker that she, like her husband Nelson Crute, was a lawyer.[15] The Crutes may indeed have been doing legal work, but the Richmond city directories do not list them as lawyers, and neither appears ever to have been admitted to practice in any court.

The first evidence that a woman sought admission to the legal profession in Virginia came in the late 1880s, when Annie Smith, a white woman in Danville, forced the issue. Her lawyer-husband, Presley A. L. Smith, had studied law at the University of Virginia; she had studied law with him, and they planned to become law partners. In June 1889 Annie Smith went to a local judge, sought to be licensed as a lawyer, but found herself rejected on grounds of gender. She petitioned the legislature for redress, but to no avail. The state Senate considered but rejected bills, in the 1889–90 session and again in 1891–92, that would have permitted the licensing of women as lawyers. Before completing action on the question, legislators found it the subject of thigh-thumping humor, as one harped on whether, if a woman might become a lawyer and might choose a law partner, she might choose some man other than her husband: "The idea of my partner for life becoming the legal partner and associate of some other man! [Laughter.]"[16]

Annie Smith may be the anomalous female lawyer reported in the 1890 federal population census (table 1). Born in Ohio in September 1865, she was twenty-three, a year younger than her husband, when she launched her effort to join the profession. Their first child was born the next January, about the same time that the legislature denied her petition.[17]

Thus into the 1890s no woman, white or black, had managed to obtain a license to practice law and represent clients in the courts of the Old Dominion. There, as elsewhere, gender proved an even greater obstacle to entry to the legal profession than race did. A small number of black men had been practicing law in Virginia since the 1870s. Elsewhere, beginning in 1869 with Arabella Babb Mansfield in Iowa, women had begun to gain admission to the bar of one state, then another, sometimes with relative ease, more often after battles in the courts and legislatures.[18]

Meanwhile, however, various court decisions had made it clear that the matter was, by and large, one for states—in particular, state legislatures—to decide. The Illinois Supreme Court ruled that if Myra Bradwell was to become a lawyer in that state, the legislature would first have to change the statutes to permit it. She appealed the ruling to the U.S. Supreme Court. That Court, in the *Slaughter-House Cases* (1873), narrowly construed a citizen's privileges and immunities under the Fourteenth Amendment, and the very next day, largely on the basis of the decision in *Slaughter-House*, upheld the Illinois court in the Bradwell case. According to the U.S. Supreme Court, the Fourteenth Amendment had no bearing on women's admission to the legal profession.[19]

White women's entry into the legal profession in Virginia can usefully be compared with their access to other professions, as well as with black men's entry into the legal profession in the Commonwealth and with white women's entry into it elsewhere. Rosamond M. Scott, a Virginian herself, wrote in 1893 that Virginia women had recently entered "fields of employment hitherto monopolized by the opposite sex."[20] Nonetheless,

TABLE 1. Lawyers in Virginia by race and gender, 1880–1990

Year	Black men No.	Black men %	White women No.	White women %	Black women No.	Black women %	Aggregate
1880	7	0.5	0		1	0.1	1,355
1890	38	2.3	1	0.1	0		1,650
1900	53	2.6	7	0.3	0		2,032
1910	37	2.0	0		0		1,809
1920	52	2.6	6	0.3	0		1,981
1930	57	2.4	27	1.1	1		2,419
1940	44	1.4	51	1.6	3	0.1	3,206
1950	54	1.2	197	4.5	3	0.1	4,398
1960	59	1.1	158	2.8	0		5,600
1970	44	0.5	394	4.6	14	0.2	8,643
1980	311	1.7	2,359	12.9	100	0.5	18,253
1990	526	2.0	6,203	23.9	356	1.4	25,928

SOURCES: U.S. Census Bureau, *Compendium of the Tenth Census: 1880* (1888), pt. 2, 1383; *Report on the Population of the United States at the Eleventh Census: 1890, Part 2* (1897), 618; *Compendium of the Eleventh Census: 1890* (1897), pt. 3, 433; *Twelfth Census: 1900, Special Reports: Occupations* (1904), 402, and *Population*, pt. 2 (1902), 541; *Thirteenth Census*, vol. 4, *Population, 1910, Occupation Statistics* (1914), 526; *Fourteenth Census*, vol. 4, *Population, 1920, Occupations* (1923), 125, 1033; *Fifteenth Census of the United States: 1930*, vol. 4, *Population* (1933), 1662, 1671; *Sixteenth Census of the United States: 1940, Population*, vol. 3, *The Labor Force*, pt. 5, *Pennsylvania—Wyoming* (1943), 766, 770; *Census of Population: 1950*, vol. 2, *Characteristics of the Population*, pt. 46, *Virginia* (1952), 229, 238–40; *Census of Population: 1960*, vol. 1, *Characteristics of the Population*, pt. 48, *Virginia* (1963), 447–49; *Census of Population: 1970*, vol. 1, *Detailed Characteristics*, pt. 48, *Virginia*, chap. D (1972), 765; *Census of Population: 1980*, vol. 1, *Characteristics of the Population*, pt. 48, *Virginia*, chap. D, *Detailed Population Characteristics*, sec. 1 (1983), 427–42; 1990 Equal Employment Opportunity File.

NOTE: The census category is "lawyers and judges." The 1880 figure for black men is my estimate. The women lawyers in 1900 may not all be white. Known black women lawyers are missing from 1930 and 1960. The 1950 figure for "Negro" may include "other nonwhite." Figures beginning in 1970 can also be found for a category "Asian and Pacific Islander" (the 1980 figures indicate 51 men but no women in this category) and another for people of "Spanish origin." All figures for the more recent censuses are official projections from census samples.

she might have noted, men retained their monopoly on legal careers in Virginia. Women—in the Old Dominion and in other states—found the barriers to becoming lawyers even more difficult to overcome than entry into such other professions as teaching or even medicine. The notion of separate spheres for the sexes could be stretched sufficiently to accommodate women whose new activities might be perceived as consistent with traditional nurturing or caregiving functions. The law, by contrast, seemed quintessentially the public sphere, reserved by men for men.

Convicted of Being a Woman

In March 1894 Belva Lockwood packed her bag and boarded a train that would take her from Washington, D.C., where she carried on an extensive law practice, to Richmond, Virginia. There she hoped to become the first woman to be admitted to represent clients in the Virginia courts.

It was no idle quest. A widowed single parent, she had moved in 1866 from her native New York State to Washington, D.C., where she taught school and began her struggle to break into the legal profession. She gained only rejection, on the grounds that she was a woman, before being admitted in 1871 to a new institution, the National University Law School. She finished the program two years later, and then had to lay siege to President U. S. Grant, ex-officio president of the school, to get her degree.[21]

At no time in her long life did she abandon her legal practice or her commitment to opening the profession to women. Getting admitted to the bar in the nation's capital proved no problem; at about the time of Lockwood's admission to law school, the rules had been changed to permit women to practice in the District. Yet within a year she had been refused permission to argue a case before the U.S. Court of Claims, and in another two years she found herself similarly banging with futility on the door of the U.S. Supreme Court. As she recalled later, she had "pleaded guilty" to the charge of being "a woman" and then found herself charged with "being a married woman." The nation's highest court declared in 1876 that, "as this court knows no English precedent for the admission of women to the bar, it declines to admit, unless there shall be a more extended public opinion, or special legislation." She turned her energies to Congress, which in 1879 approved a bill to permit women to practice before the U.S. Supreme Court.[22]

Thus in March 1879 she became the first woman to be allowed to argue before the nation's highest court, and the barriers fell in the lower federal courts as well. She proceeded to say about herself in the next Washington city directory that she "practices in the United States Supreme Court, and Court of Claims." Just as proudly, in 1894, the year of her mission to Virginia, she announced the law firm of Belva A. Lockwood & Co.—"(Belva A. Lockwood and Lura M. Ormes), attorneys-at-law"—at her capacious home at 619 F Street Northwest. Ormes was her daughter.[23]

At least since 1867 Lockwood had been actively engaged in the call for women's voting rights. That year she was one of the founders of the Universal Franchise Association in Washington, which demanded the right to vote regardless of race or sex. A group of women meeting in California nominated her in 1884 to run for the U.S. presidency under the banner of the National Equal Rights Party, and she ran again in 1888.[24]

Belva Lockwood embodied a dual effort by some late nineteenth- and early twentieth-century women, focusing on entry into and advancement in the professions, to renovate the structure of opportunity in American society. Other examples from around the country are Florence Ellinwood Allen (in Ohio), Jennie Loitman Barron (Massachusetts), Mary Margaret Bartelme (Illinois), Helen Douglas Mankin (Georgia), and Lena Madesin Phillips (Kentucky).[25]

For these women, feminism had two aspects, one individual, the other collective. On the one hand, women as individuals sought to enhance their occupational options. On the other, collectively they sought to change the legal status of all women. They demonstrated that they saw the quest for the vote as fundamentally related to such other dimensions of American citizenship and equal opportunity as access to higher education, entry to the professions, and leverage on public policy—acting as subjects in making laws and applying those laws, not solely as objects on whom the laws acted.

A scene from Georgia in 1916 offers an example of the dual effort by many American women. That year the governor signed a bill to permit Georgia women to practice law. Among the women clustered around him as he signed the bill, one was Minnie Hale, who had brought a lawsuit that lost in the Georgia Supreme Court earlier that year but led to the legislature's passage of the bill. Another of the women was described as "Mrs. Mary L. McLendon, president of the Georgia Woman Suffrage association, who for twenty-five years has battled for the woman lawyer bill and woman suffrage."[26]

Women sometimes found, as Lockwood had, that completion of law school did not necessarily bring a law degree, nor did certification to practice law in the local courts—problematic as that was—necessarily lead to being permitted to argue cases in appellate courts. They found, too, of course, that winning a victory in one state did not translate directly into winning a similar victory in another state, though each victory made it easier to argue that the old norms were outmoded and need not control another outcome.[27]

In the twenty-five years before Lockwood made her way to the state capital of Virginia, at least some women had gained admission to the bar in most states in the North and West. Except in the District of Columbia, however, women were practicing nowhere south of the Mason-Dixon

Line at the time Lockwood took the train to Richmond in 1894. (Tabitha A. Holton, who had studied with her lawyer-brothers in North Carolina, was admitted to the bar by that state's supreme court in 1878, but she died in 1886.)[28]

Thus Lockwood's trip. She had a mission to break the male monopoly on the legal profession in Virginia. It probably came as little surprise to her that she first met failure, though a Virginia statute detailed how "any person" must qualify to practice in Virginia. It specified the principle of reciprocity, that only a simple procedure separated someone already licensed to practice law in another state from a license to practice, too, in Virginia.[29]

Rebuffed by a local judge, Lockwood appealed to the Virginia Supreme Court of Appeals, which (with one of the five judges absent) upheld the judge on a vote of 2–2. She took her case to the U.S. Supreme Court, whose members surely knew her as an accomplished attorney, but that court, too, turned her away. The justices told her that the Fourteenth Amendment had nothing to do with her case and that only Virginia could address her demands: the state legislature in enacting Virginia's laws, the state courts in interpreting and applying those laws—determining whether the meaning of the word *person* in such laws might be "confined to males."[30]

Back in the state supreme court, she gained a 3–2 victory and was admitted to the bar of that court in June 1894 when the absent judge, Robert A. Richardson, returned and sided with her. In October 1894 she obtained her license to practice law in Virginia. The *New York Times* reported on its front page that Lockwood had "won a signal victory in Virginia today for women" and later that year declared her "the only woman ever licensed to practice law" in that state.[31]

Thus she triumphed and became a "first"—or so she thought until six months later, in April 1895, when she brought a case to the court that had admitted her to practice the previous year. In 1895, however, the Virginia Supreme Court of Appeals had five new judges. All five of the men who had ruled on her application in 1894 had been elected by the legislature in 1882 when the Readjuster Party controlled the state, and their twelve-year terms ended on New Year's Day in 1895. When the time came to fill the vacancies, Democrats controlled the legislature and, by electing an entirely new slate of judges, revamped and "redeemed" the court.[32]

The new court undid the innovation. It ruled unanimously that under the statute (despite its phrasing), Lockwood had to be a man to practice law in that court. It refused to permit her to represent her client and argue the case. The city newspaper the next day reported that "she was much surprised and disappointed at the court's action. She said she had supposed that the decision of the old court was final, and she had no idea that this new court would reverse it." [33]

Little had changed since Annie Smith's failed efforts after all. Lockwood wanted to become a lawyer in Virginia, and she had all the training asked of any man. Because she was not a man, however, she could not practice as an attorney. Edward C. Burks—a former member of the Virginia Supreme Court of Appeals (dislodged by the Readjusters), compiler of the Code of 1887, author of a book on the property rights of married women in Virginia, and editor of the *Virginia Law Register*—observed that "it would be remarkable, that a Virginia woman should be denied the privilege of becoming a practising lawyer in the courts of this State, and that a non-resident woman should be accorded that privilege. If Mrs. Lockwood ever expects to practise law in the State, she must prevail on the Legislature to give her the status of a *man*." [34]

As Belva Lockwood well knew, the legislature had already seemed to close off that avenue in its response to Annie Smith, and neither the state nor the federal courts had answered her quest with the response she had sought. In 1896, at the next session of the legislature, the Virginia General Assembly revised the statute on the admission of lawyers. Section 3191 of the Code, which related to citizens of Virginia, was amended to read "any male citizen." No change was made in Section 3192, which continued to state that someone already licensed and practicing "in any state or territory of the United States, or in the District of Columbia, may practise as such in the courts of this State." [35] Yet in light of Judge Burks's statement that if Virginia women could not become lawyers in Virginia, surely women from elsewhere should not have the privilege, the legislature had closed the loophole through which Lockwood had sought to squeeze. The entire episode demonstrated that change might not ratchet in only one direction.

A Tale of Two States

The U.S. Supreme Court clearly had left the matter up to state courts and state legislatures to determine. For its part, Virginia had employed its discretion to decide the matter both ways in short order. The legislature maintained the exclusion in the early 1890s. The Supreme Court of Appeals upheld the exclusion in April 1894, overturned it later that year, and revived it in April 1895. The legislature ratified it again at its next session.

The neighboring state of Maryland—the other state bordering on Washington, D.C., where Belva Lockwood practiced law—supplies an alternative story line of women's efforts to join the legal profession. The Maryland Court of Appeals demonstrated a full awareness of the Supreme Court's narrow interpretation of the Fourteenth Amendment. In fact, the Maryland court applied the restriction to race long before applying it to gender.

Charles Taylor had practiced law for several years in Massachusetts before he attempted to gain admission to practice before the Maryland Court of Appeals, having already been admitted to practice in U.S. District Court in Baltimore. Maryland's high court unanimously rejected Taylor's petition, as he failed to meet the test that the Maryland statute, as late as 1876, specified regarding "any white male citizen of Maryland." The Maryland court relied on the *Bradwell* decision (which related to gender) and applied it to race. "In our opinion," said the court, *Slaughter-House* and *Bradwell* "are conclusive of the present case. They determine that the 14th Amendment has no application. It follows that the provisions of the [Maryland] Code are left in full force and operation, and must control our action; we cannot set aside or disregard the provisions of the statute; the Legislature alone can change the law. . . . The power of regulating the admission of attorneys in the Courts of a State, is one belonging to the State and not to the Federal Government." Change came only in the 1880s. After a favorable local court ruling, the first successful effort by a black lawyer to be admitted to practice in any Maryland court came in 1885, and in 1888 the legislature changed the statute's phrasing from "any white male citizen of Maryland" to "any male citizen of Maryland."[36]

Thus, according to the Maryland court as well as to the Virginia court and the federal courts, the matter was legal, not constitutional, and state, not federal. Thus, too, although black men moved into the legal profession in Virginia in the 1870s, their counterparts were thwarted in Maryland until well into the next decade. Even in Maryland, nonetheless, black men met with success years before white women did.

Etta H. Maddox, a Maryland woman who had graduated from law school in Baltimore, acted much as Belva Lockwood had in 1894. She appealed an adverse local ruling to the state's highest court. In November 1901 the Maryland judges upheld the traditional exclusion. They ruled that the statute governing admission to the legal profession, as amended only three years earlier, had continued to use phrasing that permitted only men to be admitted to the bar. Yet, by no means committed to the proposition that no Maryland woman could ever be a lawyer, the court invited the legislature to reopen the question: "If the General Assembly thinks, at its approaching session, that females ought to be admitted to the bar[,] it can so declare. Until then we have no power to admit the applicant[,] and her request to be allowed to stand for examination must be denied." Indeed, the legislature moved directly to end the exclusion. Beginning in April 1902, Maryland law provided that women "be permitted to practice law" on the "same terms" as men.[37]

Lawyers as legislators took the question to be one on which they could decide either way, even if lawyers as judges often felt bound to traditional ways in the absence of state legislation clearly to the contrary. In state after state—and eventually in Virginia—it was lawyers in legislatures who changed the law to permit women to join the profession.[38]

Comments in the *Virginia Law Register* took the Maryland court to task for poor judicial reasoning but not for the decision itself. "At the same time, we repeat, we do not regret the result of the decision," said an editorial. Regardless, it continued, "We know of no demand whatever in this State for legislation of this nature."[39] Virginia led Maryland on race, but Maryland took the lead on gender.

Woman Suffrage and Women Lawyers

Though the Maryland legislature in 1902 ended that state's ban on women lawyers, the Virginia legislature took no further action on the question until 1918. That year the Senate approved but the House of Delegates failed to pass a bill that would have ended women's exclusion from the legal profession. The Senate also considered a bill to direct the University of Virginia to admit qualified women to that school's graduate and professional programs.[40]

In 1920 three things happened almost simultaneously to change the political and legal status of women in Virginia. One was ratification in August that year of the Nineteenth Amendment, which eliminated gender as a basis for excluding Americans from voting. A majority of Virginia legislators, though voting against ratification, recognized that the amendment would soon become effective whatever Virginia did, and thus they enacted contingent legislation to accommodate the change. Second, at the same time—recognizing a relationship between exercising the franchise and practicing law—the General Assembly moved to open the legal practice to women. In doing so, it emulated recent action by such other southern states as Georgia and South Carolina. A change in the statute governing admission to the Virginia bar proved neither ambiguous nor sexually exclusive. A 1920 act changed the phrase "all male persons" to "all male and female persons," recast in 1922 to "all persons, male and female."[41]

Third, also in early 1920, the University of Virginia Law School ended its ban on female students. The university's decision appears better characterized as a compromise than as a pathbreaking initiative. The school had steadfastly fought full coeducation, and one view had been that the best way to prevent such an outcome would be to accept a proposal by Mary-Cooke Branch Munford and other Virginia women to establish a coordinate college in Charlottesville for white women. University alumni scuttled that proposal. When Munford urged, as a middle-ground resolution, the admission of white women to the graduate and professional schools, the board of visitors, at a meeting on January 12, 1920, adopted that approach and ordered the change in policy.[42]

Women could at last practice law, and the state university law school began to offer white women the training to prepare for that practice. The first women to be "licensed to practise law in all the courts of this State" under the new statute were Rebecca Pearl Lovenstein of Richmond and Carrie M. Gregory of Lynchburg, both of whom passed the bar exam in the summer of 1920. Within a year Annie M. Brown and Dorothy Powell joined them, and others soon followed. By 1923, moreover, Delaware and Rhode Island each also had a female lawyer, so women had entered the legal profession in every state in the Union.[43]

Not until January 7, 1925—thirty years after Belva Lockwood's failed effort—did any woman represent a client and argue a case before Virginia's highest court. At that time Lockwood's earlier success at being licensed, as well as her failure at being permitted to argue a case before the state supreme court, went unnoticed. So, for that matter, did Carrie Gregory's admission to the Virginia bar in 1920. A newspaper account on January 8, 1925, reported only that "Mrs. Rebecca Lovenstein, . . . who in 1920 was the first woman to be licensed to practice law in Virginia, has the distinction of being the first Virginia woman attorney to argue a case before the Supreme Court of Appeals of Virginia."[44]

The paper went on to tell how, together with her husband Benjamin Lovenstein, another Richmond attorney, she had presented the case and had presented it well. "Following her argument Mrs. Lovenstein was complimented for her able presentation of the facts in the case and members of the court shook her hand." Her life in the domestic sphere also evoked comment. "Mrs. Lovenstein, besides being a lawyer," the paper observed, "is a mother" with three sons, "directs the household affairs," and "finds some time for social and club affairs."[45]

"These New and Strange Beings"

William M. Lile, the dean of the law school at the University of Virginia, shared with many Virginians a profound doubt about the wisdom and propriety of admitting women students to the state's law school. At the end of the year 1920, he noted in his report to the university president, Edwin A. Alderman, that the most important change during the past year, what he called a "radical departure from the traditional policies," was the admission of three women as students. Dean Lile described the "conditions under which these new and strange beings" had been admitted. "With what reception they might have met had women suddenly invaded our lecture rooms in force, it is not possible to say," he conceded, but "I made occasion, at the very beginning, to appeal in their behalf to the chivalry of the young gentlemen of the several classes, and the response has been all that could be desired."[46]

A year later the dean reported with relief that little had changed. "There were no additions to the three women matriculates of last year," he wrote. "These three are enrolled again this year. They continue to maintain excellent records of scholarship." After still another year had gone by, the dean stated that both of the women admitted as regular students in 1920 had passed the bar. One, Rose M. Davis, had begun practice in Norfolk, while the other, Elizabeth N. Tompkins, returned to complete requirements for the degree. (The third woman, a special student, was Catherine R. Lipop, the law school librarian, who later observed that her course work had enabled her to be "of considerably more service to the [male] students in the library.") No additional women had entered the school, he noted, despite "the clamor for the admission of women to the Law School, so vociferous two years ago."[47]

Two other law schools in Virginia began admitting women at about the same time. Richmond College, which became the University of Richmond in 1920, had given consideration to admitting women law students for several years before 1920 and enrolled four that year, among them Rebecca Lovenstein. The College of William and Mary did not have to address the question directly, since white women undergraduates were regularly admitted beginning in 1918, and the policy seems to have been automatically applied to the law program that began to emerge in 1921.[48]

At the time of the University of Virginia's 1923 graduation, Lile recorded in his diary: "We had 71 graduates in the Law School this session, made up of an unusually fine body of *men*, with one exception—that of our first *woman* graduate. The exception applies to her sex and not to her capacity, for she is an unusually capable person and stood very near the top of the class. She is Miss Elizabeth Tompkins of Richmond. I predict that in spite of her legal ability, however, it will not be long before she deserts the profession of the law and takes up that of wife and mother, rolling a baby carriage instead of wrangling in court." Such "rolling a baby carriage" would be, he said, "a much more suitable and seemly occupation" for a woman.[49]

As it was, Elizabeth Tompkins, unlike Rebecca Lovenstein, never married. She did her share of "wrangling in court," and she practiced law for more than half a century, at first in Charlottesville and later in Richmond.[50] By the time she died in 1981, many more female law graduates had joined her in the legal profession in Virginia. Even if they never knew her name, they benefited from the path she blazed.

Thus, beginning in the 1920s, small numbers of women attended law school in Virginia. In 1923 Jane Brown Ranson became the University of Richmond's first female graduate in law, and in 1937 Virginia Mister Walker became the first at the College of William and Mary.[51] By the 1930 U.S. census, twenty-eight Virginia women identified themselves as attorneys, up from six a decade earlier (see table 1).

"The Glue That Held It Together"

Race ceased being a prohibitive criterion for admission to the Virginia bar nearly a half century before gender stopped, yet in terms of access to law school in Virginia, race proved the more insurmountable obstacle. In the parallel worlds of black and white after slavery, black men, like white, might enter the profession, though Virginia had no law school that they could attend. At the time of the statutory change in 1920, and for many years afterward, the state constitution insisted that "white and colored children shall not be taught in the same school," and the practice characterized schooling at all levels.[52] Elizabeth Tompkins and her fellow "new and strange beings" were women, to be sure, but they were white women. Inez C. Fields had had to go outside the state to study law, and other black women did the same.

L. Marian Fleming Poe worked for a time in the Newport News office of black attorney J. Thomas Newsome before she decided that she, too, would be a lawyer. She had been learning by watching and by doing, and she knew that she might enter the profession under the 1920 statute. Though married and the mother of two young children, she moved to Washington, D.C., graduated from the Howard University Law School, and then returned to Newport News to run her own law office. In 1925 she became the first black woman to be licensed to practice law in Virginia, and probably the third anywhere south of the District of Columbia. (Lutie A. Lytle was admitted to the bar in Tennessee in 1897, and Estelle A. Henderson in Alabama by 1919.) By 1927 Marian Poe had qualified to appear in the Supreme Court of Appeals. Among black residents of the Newport News area, she functioned as a one-woman community center for nearly a half century until her death in 1974.[53]

In ways that reflected both her race and her gender, Poe participated in the profession outside Newport News, even outside Virginia. A member of the Old Dominion Bar Association, a group of black lawyers in Virginia, she served as its secretary for many years. Roland D. Ealey, another member, observed long afterwards that she was "the glue that held it together." As a woman, she was a member of a national—and biracial—group, the National Association of Women Lawyers, whose conventions she attended as the state delegate from Virginia, once at midcentury and twice in the 1960s.[54]

Marian Poe did not long remain the only black female attorney in Virginia. In 1929 Norfolk's black newspaper announced that Poe, "Virginia's only Negro woman lawyer," would be giving a local talk. Bertha L. Douglass, concerned "because my profession is a means of livelihood to me, and not that I took offense," wrote the paper to correct its error. Douglass had joined the Virginia bar in 1926 and was practicing right there in Norfolk. In 1928, moreover, Inez C. Fields had moved to Hampton from Massachusetts. These three women from tidewater Virginia continued active in the profession through the 1960s, during a time when very few black women practiced law anywhere in the South.[55] Black women lawyers often perceived their gender to be an even greater impediment to their professional advancement than their race.[56]

"No Longer an Oddity"

Martha Bell Conway, too, was a Virginian who successfully pursued a career in law from the 1940s through the 1960s. While working for a blueprint company, she took a course in business law taught by David J. Mays. From Mays she began to see law as "covering everything you do every day," she later recalled. "It didn't quite hit me what I wanted" to be doing, she said, until she took that course. She decided against "staying downtown starving to death making nothing." She recalled the Great Depression as "so severe" that it was a great "Motivator." In 1937, at the age of twenty, she entered what is now the T. C. Williams School of Law at the University of Richmond. Conway never married. "I attended to my career as if I was going to be with it for the rest of my life, and that's fortunate," she told an interviewer, "because that's the way it happened." From 1952 to 1970 she served as secretary of the Commonwealth of Virginia. She later observed, "I really didn't know I wasn't supposed to be doing all these things, so I did [them]." She added, "Now we've got scores of [women lawyers] in Richmond and I'm glad of it. I think it's the perfect career for women."[57]

With reference to the licensing of attorneys, the Virginia Code of 1950 reverted to the phrase "any person," but by then one could safely infer that female persons were included.[58] Nonetheless, according to census figures (see table 1), the number of black female lawyers first exceeded three only in the 1960s; black male lawyers in Virginia numbered precisely the same in 1970 as in 1940; and white female attorneys declined in numbers in the 1950s. As late as 1960, fully 96 percent of all the lawyers in Virginia were white men. Nothing in the enrollment figures in Virginia's law schools suggested imminent change; not even 2 percent of law students were women. Yet change came, as the figures for black men, black women, and white women eventually displayed sharp rises.[59]

The enrollment of black female law students in Virginia could occur only when the racial barrier, like the gender obstacle, came down. When T. Ione Diggs completed her law degree at Howard University in 1948, she returned to Norfolk, where she joined forces with her father, J. Eugene Diggs, and with Bertha Douglass. No black applicant had ever been accepted at a white law school in Virginia. The next year, however, her classmate at Howard, Gregory H. Swanson, applied to take courses as a graduate law student at the University of Virginia. When that school rejected his application, he challenged the constitutionality of the school's action. In 1950, under federal court order, he started classes there, and token desegregation began at Virginia's largest public law school (see chapter 4).

At the end of World War II, none of Virginia's law schools admitted black students. By the late 1960s, all did. Litigation in the federal courts, followed by federal civil rights legislation, accounts for the timing of the changes, if not their magnitude. The College of William and Mary soon followed the University of Virginia and admitted its first black law student, Edward A. Travis, in 1951; he graduated in 1954.[60] Sometime later, Virginia's private schools began admitting black students. Washington and Lee University, a laggard on both race and gender, graduated its first black male law student, Leslie D. Smith Jr., in 1969, three years before admitting its first female students.[61]

By 1969 all of Virginia's law schools except for Washington and Lee had long been admitting at least some women students, and that year they had a combined female enrollment approaching 5 percent.[62] In 1972 Washington and Lee enrolled 7 women among its 81 law school freshmen, or 8 percent.[63] By that time, all of Virginia's law schools had admitted their first black students and their first female students as well.

At the end of the 1960s, a newspaper writer wrote that in 1968, at age twenty-seven, Gail Marshall had become "the first full-time professor of law in Virginia" at the University of Virginia, shortly after graduating there. He concluded with the observation that as of 1969 "Virginia still holds far more challenges untapped and waiting for the women lawyers of both today and tomorrow," all the way "to the office of the attorney general."[64] Years later, Marshall herself served as deputy attorney general while Mary Sue Terry headed that office.

By the mid-1980s women comprised at least one-third of freshman law classes at every one of Virginia's five law schools. Even Washington and Lee University's figure reached 37 percent, and Virginia's newest law school, at George Mason University, had more women students than men (66 out of 124). As the placement director at the University of Richmond's law school, a woman, put it, "Women in law school are now no longer an oddity." Every one of the five schools also had at least one woman on the law faculty, though the female faculty were concentrated in the lower ranks and among the adjuncts. There the changes were still at an early stage.[65]

Several factors in the late 1960s and early 1970s have been identified as promoting the sudden rise in the number of female law students, and thus of lawyers and potential law professors and judges in the years to come. For one, the advent of the birth-control pill gave women in their twenties and thirties much greater control in their reproductive lives and thus in their professional lives, and many chose to exercise that control. For another, many of the young men who might have been attending law school were, instead, in Vietnam. The war that so many women of that generation were protesting is sometimes seen as an event that brought women more professional opportunity than might otherwise have been the case.[66]

Other things were at work as well. As for national domestic policy, the Civil Rights Act of 1964 offered a beginning, but that measure (in Title VII) banned discrimination on the basis of sex only in employment. That it banned sex discrimination at all resulted from actions taken by Alice Paul and other members of the National Woman's Party, survivors from the feminist generation of the 1910s and 1920s. Eight years later Title IX of the Educational Amendments of 1972 extended the federal ban on sex discrimination to higher education. It made federal aid to education programs contingent on those programs' not discriminating on grounds of gender.[67]

Asked in 1985 to account for the surge of women law students in the years after 1970, Sylvia Clute, herself one of that group, pointed to

Title IX of the 1972 provisions.[68] Not only did Title IX supply incentive for holdout schools like Washington and Lee to admit women students. It also encouraged women to attend law school, for it applied equal employment opportunity provisions to law schools' placement offices by banning recruitment by law firms that refused to interview or hire women law graduates. The annual number of female law graduates at the University of Virginia, after first reaching double digits (or 5 percent) in 1969, hovered at 20 from 1971 through 1974. In 1975 the figure exceeded 30 (10 percent), graduates who had entered law school after the passage of Title IX. It reached 50 by 1977 and exceeded 100 (29 percent) beginning in 1981.[69]

Though Sylvia Clute was surely right that changes in federal policy promoted the rise in the number of female law students, and thus of female law graduates, she herself had entered law school before the enactment of Title IX. She earned her law degree from Boston University Law School in 1973, the same year that Mary Sue Terry earned hers at the University of Virginia. Another woman lawyer in Virginia offered an alternative account of opportunity and perceptions. Randy Parris, president of the Virginia Women Attorneys Association at the time, insisted that "just as important as Title 9 is the mind-set that women carry in their own heads."[70] Surely she was right that, even if federal policy led to new opportunities, people still had to choose to take advantage of them. Moreover, even before Title IX, women had turned their ambitions toward the legal profession, and some among those who did so later moved into highly visible public offices.

A new wave of feminism, reminiscent of the turn-of-the-century phenomenon, was sweeping across America. As in that earlier time, a feminist "mind-set" was at work. Two related things had changed, however, since that earlier wave. During the rise of the new feminism, much larger numbers of women sought entry into the law and other professions, and public policy supplied encouragement to them rather than obstruction.[71] As in 1920, a transformed federal policy brought change to every state, including Virginia, regardless of whether such change could have been enacted in that state. Feminists worked to achieve alterations in policy, and those alterations had wide effect, as the policy changes and the mind-set interacted to reinforce each other.

Gender and Law School: Enrollment and Graduation

At the University of Virginia, the number of women law graduates rose by about 100 between the mid-1970s and the mid-1980s, while the men's figure held at about 250. By the late 1980s women routinely made up about one-third of each graduating class at the school. In 1990—one hundred years after Annie Smith's failed efforts to be admitted to the bar—the University of Virginia Law School graduated 145 women, or 36 percent of a class of 398, and women graduates from other law schools in the Old Dominion that year constituted even higher percentages. Moreover, the female percentages tended to edge up in the 1990s. Even at the beginning of the twentieth-first century, though, men constituted small majorities at each law school in Virginia. The imbalance was actually a bit larger among Caucasians than the overall data indicate; among African Americans and Asian Americans, at all five law schools analyzed here, women outnumbered men.[72]

One scholar, Richard Abel, made the point in the late 1980s that women supplied the entire net increase in law school enrollment after 1973. It is an astute perception, and one that actually understates the phenomenon. National figures show that men's law school enrollment peaked in the first half of the 1970s and then dropped off, while women's enrollment continued to surge. Male enrollment in law schools topped 80,000 every year from 1971–72 through 1978–79, with 1972–73 the highest single year, just at the time that Title IX went into effect. Male graduation from law schools peaked in the years 1973 through 1979, with 1977 the highest year. Never again through the end of the century did male enrollment or graduation figures reach such numbers (table 2).[73]

In sum, across the nation in general and at the University of Virginia in particular, the rising number of women law students and graduates

TABLE 2. U.S. law school enrollment by gender, 1966–67 to 2001–2

Year	Men		Women		Total
	No.	%	No.	%	
1966–67	56,716	95.7	2,520	4.3	59,236
1971–72	82,658	90.6	8,567	9.4	91,225
1976–77	83,058	73.9	29,343	26.1	112,401
1981–82	77,634	64.2	43,245	35.8	120,879
1986–87	69,893	59.3	47,920	40.7	117,813
1991–92	74,470	57.5	55,110	42.5	129,580
1996–97	71,500	54.5	57,123	45.5	128,623
2001–2	65,134	51.0	62,476	49.0	127,610

SOURCES: *ABA Approved Law Schools: Statistical Information on American Bar Association Approved Law Schools*, 1998 ed. (1997), 451; *Official Guide to ABA-Approved Law Schools*, 2003 ed. (2002), 820.

came at a time of stagnation in enrollment and graduation by their male counterparts. Thus women comprised a growing percentage of law school students and graduates. In fact, national figures put female enrollment in law school at 49.0 percent in 2001–2 (see table 2).

The overwhelming numerical preponderance of men entering the legal profession through the 1960s and even the 1970s meant that the female percentage in the profession lagged far behind the female percentage of law school graduates. Yet, longer term, one could project an approach to parity—in the profession as a whole, as well as in law school enrollment and graduation—in the twentieth-first century.

From the 1890s to the 1970s

By the early 1990s some very prominent lawyers in Virginia were women. Elizabeth B. Lacy was a member of the Virginia Supreme Court, and Rebecca Beach Smith held a seat on a federal court, while Mary Sue Terry was in her second term as the state's attorney general (see chapter 8). Even as late as the mid-1980s, by contrast, no woman had ever held any such position in the Old Dominion. Until many years after the Civil War, in fact, Virginia had no female attorneys at all, not merely because no woman wished to become a lawyer or none had the training required of men but because the law itself was employed to prevent it.

The decade of the 1920s brought new beginnings in educational, professional, and political opportunities for white women and, to a degree, black women. Federal court orders in the middle years of the twentieth century, followed by civil rights legislation in 1964 and 1972, transformed the professional environment, first on race, then on gender. By the late 1960s all of Virginia's law schools were admitting students more or less regardless of race, and by 1972 all were admitting students more or less regardless of gender. Thus by the mid-1970s all of Virginia's law schools, the private ones (the University of Richmond, Washington and Lee) and the public ones (George Mason University, the University of Virginia, and the College of William and Mary) had at least some female students as well as at least some black students. Bridging the two breakthrough eras— the 1920s and half a century later—Elizabeth Tompkins and Marian Poe continued into the 1970s to practice the skills they had learned in the 1920s.

The pioneers pointed the way. It could well be said that by the 1990s the major barriers had been toppled. Certainly Belva Lockwood, whatever her thwarted hopes in the 1890s, would have had no trouble getting admitted to the Virginia bar in the 1990s. Then again, she would have felt no compulsion to take that train to Richmond to challenge a male monopoly on the profession in the Old Dominion. The exclusion that she contested in the 1890s had vanished by the 1920s, and it was so much a thing of the past by the 1990s that few people could recall that earlier time.

Since the Seneca Falls Declaration of Sentiments in 1848, much had changed: in voting rights, access to higher education, and claims on a place in the professions. For women in particular, little changed along these lines in the years immediately following 1848, either in Virginia or elsewhere in America. Yet by 1920 Virginia exemplified the beginnings of widespread change. Although Belva Lockwood's efforts in the 1890s proved unavailing, a second wave of American feminism crested in the next generation, as women in every state gained the right to vote. The single year 1920 brought Virginia women's entry into law school, the legal profession, and the voting booth.

After still another half century had passed, a third feminist wave swept more restrictions aside. The enrollment of women in law schools surged, as did the number of graduates. In Virginia, from among those graduates came a state attorney general and one state supreme court justice, then another, and yet another (see chapter 8). By the 1990s great changes had taken place in American law and the legal profession—since 1848, 1920, or even 1972.

4

The Siege against Segregation

Black Virginians and the
Law of Civil Rights

B ETWEEN THE END OF SLAVERY IN THE 1860S AND THE CIVIL RIGHTS laws of the 1960s, the world of "Jim Crow" racial discrimination characterized much of America. With even greater force it characterized the South. Black southerners everywhere were subject to the various dimensions of racial segregation: limited access to, even utter exclusion from, many places and opportunities. Especially between the 1890s and the 1940s, black southerners almost everywhere were subject to political disempowerment, whether through terror, the poll-tax requirement, a fraudulent count, or black exclusion from primary elections. The world of "separate but equal" proved far less equal than separate, and threats of economic reprisals or physical violence underlay and reinforced the entire structure of discrimination.

Relatively powerless—at some times and places completely powerless —in electoral politics, African Americans sometimes fought effectively through the courts to change prevailing practices. Particularly between the 1920s and the 1960s, black southerners in general and black Virginians in particular went to court to challenge a wide range of racial laws and practices. Within that context, this chapter emphasizes Virginia's civil rights lawyers and the civil rights litigation that they brought in the 1940s. Many of these court cases related to public transportation or public education—elementary, secondary, or even higher education. Some cases were Virginia versions of precedent-setting cases elsewhere. Other Virginia cases set such precedents. Together, the litigation of the 1940s set the stage for the assault on segregated schools in the 1950s and for a collection of final challenges to legal segregation in the 1960s.

Howard University Law School and Civil Rights

One of Virginia's great civil rights lawyers, Samuel W. Tucker, often said about his lifelong motivation to destroy Jim Crow, that his father always spoke of a golden age, of a time, as the senior Tucker put it, "before they Jim Crowed us." The younger Tucker, who grew up in Alexandria, was born in 1913, so he had never known that world. But his father had. He could have been referring to political disfranchisement, which took place under the Virginia Constitution of 1902. Or he could have had in mind transportation segregation (the "back of the bus"), which originated at the same time: in Alexandria in 1902 and through much of Virginia two years later.[1] Something of a golden age existed before Jim Crow segregation—on public transportation, in particular—and disfranchisement. There had been a time, many black Virginians knew, before segregation solidified. Some dreamed that it could be undone.

For a generation after the end of slavery—the last third of the nineteenth century—segregation did not yet systematically govern black life and race relations. The dictator Jim Crow had not yet ascended to the power that soon became his, had not yet tightened his grip on black southerners and squeezed out much of the black freedom that had flourished for a time. Yet public education for black Virginians was born "Jim-Crowed." It had no other history, no golden age before Tucker's lifetime. Segregated schooling replaced a regime of no schooling at all.[2]

Virginia's Constitution of 1902—at the same time that it greatly cut back on the numbers of black voters—incorporated the segregation language of the 1870 law that had inaugurated a public school system in Virginia: "White and colored persons shall not be taught in the same school but in separate schools." In the next quarter century, the state hugely increased the amount of money going to public schools, and it hugely increased the disparity between expenditures on black schools and white ones.[3] Through those years "separate but equal" remained entirely separate, and it became ever more unequal. Much of the civil rights litigation from the 1930s on was directed toward "separate but equal" public education, first to secure more "equal," then to reduce the "separate." But there was much else to fix as well.

In the early 1930s Howard University Law School inaugurated an enhanced push to train civil rights lawyers. At about the same time—when Oliver Hill and Thurgood Marshall, to take two notable examples, began their studies there—it changed from a part-time night school to a full-time day school, and it gained accreditation. Charles Hamilton Houston,

dean of the school and leader of the initiative, wrote at the time: "The social justification for the Negro lawyer as such in the United States today is
the service he can render the [black] race . . . as a social engineer," especially in the South, to "fight for true equality before the law." The civil
rights attorneys in Virginia had their counterparts in other southern
states. One was A. P. Tureaud, who finished at Howard in 1925 and then
for many years spearheaded civil rights litigation in Louisiana. Another
was Conrad O. Pearson, who earned his law degree at Howard in 1932 and
then did much the same in North Carolina.[4]

Into the 1930s, when Howard University began producing an appreciable crop of black civil rights attorneys, white lawyers handled much of
the civil rights litigation in the South, and their importance should not be
understated.[5] In a successful constitutional challenge to Virginia's white
Democratic primary in 1929 and 1930, black lawyer Joseph R. Pollard
teamed with white lawyer Alfred E. Cohen in federal court (see chapter 7).
Also in federal court, and at about the same time, Pollard and Cohen successfully took on a Richmond city ordinance that zoned black and white
residential areas.[6] But the Howard law graduates of the 1930s made vividly
clear, in the decades that followed, the impact that racial diversity in the
profession could make.[7]

Band of Brothers

Oliver W. Hill, a native of Richmond who grew up in Roanoke, Virginia, earned his law degree from Howard in 1933. So did Thurgood Marshall, Hill's classmate from Baltimore, Maryland. That same year, Hill's
lifelong friend and ally Samuel W. Tucker completed his undergraduate
degree at Howard. Tucker and Hill studied together for the Virginia bar
exam, and both of them passed it in late 1933. The state did not require a
law degree or even attendance at a law school to be licensed, so the major
impediment to Tucker's successful entry into the legal profession was that
he did not turn twenty-one until June 1934.[8]

By then, Hill and Tucker had completed their basic training for a war
on many fronts against Jim Crow, a war they waged mostly in the courts.
Aside from Hill and Tucker, some of the leading black civil rights lawyers
to begin practice in Virginia in the years around 1940 were Martin A.
Martin, a 1938 law graduate of Howard from Danville, and Roland D.
Ealey, who earned his law degree from Howard in 1939. Spottswood W.
Robinson III, the son of a Richmond lawyer and businessman, completed
law school at Howard in 1939, taught there for several years, and then also

participated in the siege against segregation in Virginia before being appointed a federal judge in the 1960s.

Oliver Hill and Samuel Tucker are best understood as belonging to a third generation of black attorneys in Virginia. They did not step into a world that had never before encountered black lawyers, though they brought new tools to the encounter and did their civil rights work in a new context. The first two generations (see chapter 3) had been significant in many ways, but it was the third generation that engaged Jim Crow between the late 1930s and the mid-1960s. It was the third generation that targeted the walls of racial discrimination under the law and used the law to bring those walls—eventually—tumbling down.

Barely a hundred miles—by auto, bus, or train—separated the state capital from the nation's capital. Without too great an expenditure of time or money—and facing less violence and intimidation than they would have in the Deep South—professors at Howard University Law School could make their way to Virginia courts, and black lawyers in Virginia, typically recent graduates of Howard, could go to Washington, D.C., to consult with their mentors, try out their strategies and concepts on current students, or even argue a case before the U.S. Supreme Court. It was not so very far for Thurgood Marshall to make his way from New York, the National Association for the Advancement of Colored People (NAACP) headquarters, back to Washington or even on to a meeting or a courtroom in Norfolk.

It was a small world in some ways, and it was a vibrant time and place. Black lawyers in Virginia—alumni of Howard, members of the NAACP, agents of change—were learning how to work with new tools and in new arenas to achieve change—change that their fellow black Virginians urgently needed. Their basic tools, along with their commitment and connections, they had imbibed at Howard. The more sophisticated work, and an enhanced chance of winning, depended on experimentation, as they tried out various ideas and approaches.

"I Went to Law School to Fight Segregation": Oliver Hill Emerges as a Civil Rights Attorney

At Howard University Law School, as Oliver Hill later remembered, their teacher Charles Hamilton Houston "hammered at us . . . that a lawyer had to be a social engineer or else he was a parasite." Hill never exhibited much tendency toward being a parasite. Whether at Howard Law School in the 1930s or in courtrooms in the 1940s, Hill and his colleagues knew they had a mission. Hill later reported a "tremendous esprit de corps among faculty and students" at Howard. As Samuel Tucker once explained, during the "early days of the civil rights struggle, litigation was the key." As another Howard alumnus, Roland D. Ealey, liked to say about himself, he went to law school "to save the world." Hill himself told an interviewer, "I went to law school in order to fight segregation."[9] And fight it he did; fight it they all did.

Hill emerged only gradually in the 1930s as a force in the siege against Jim Crow.[10] After passing the Virginia bar exam in late 1933, Hill tried to get a practice started in Roanoke, where he had lived as a child. But he was only a beginner, he was black, and the Great Depression was on. So, after a year or two of what he felt was futility, he returned in 1936 to Washington, D.C., where he took back his old job waiting tables at O'Donnells, a downtown seafood restaurant. Among his activities, he involved himself for a time in an effort to unionize waiters in the city.[11] Through those years and beyond, his wife, Beresenia "Bernie" Walker Hill, taught in the Washington public schools, supplying the couple with a regular income and subsidizing Hill's efforts.[12]

In 1939 Hill returned permanently to Virginia, this time to Richmond, his native city. Two black lawyers there, J. Byron Hopkins and J. Thomas Hewin Jr., asked a member of the law faculty at Howard, Leon A. Ransom, for some help on a murder case, and Andy Ransom drew in Hill. Then Hopkins, Hewin, and Hill decided to form a law firm. "That brought me to Richmond," Hill recalls. "By the time I got here they had split up so we never formed a law firm. [Laughs.] But it got me in Richmond anyway."[13]

Hill remembers, "I got involved in civil rights cases from the very beginning." There was another murder case. Then came a series of black teachers' salary equalization cases. Also in 1939, Spottswood W. Robinson finished law school, and in 1943 they formed a law firm, Hill and Robinson. World War II interrupted Hill's work in Richmond by taking him to Europe in the army. In the meantime Martin A. Martin, a Danville native, joined the firm: "So, the firm was Hill, Martin, Robinson when I came back."[14]

Hill and the others worked to build and maintain overlapping networks that might help them fulfill their mission. Their membership in the NAACP, and their efforts to foster local branches of that organization, provided one means. Their relationship with Howard Law School, and Charlie Houston's continuing mentoring, supplied another. And in 1942 the new generation of black lawyers in Virginia revived the Old Dominion Bar Association. The thirty charter members included Spottswood W.

Robinson III and Roland D. Ealey. Oliver Hill served as the group's first president; Martin A. Martin, its vice president; and L. Marian Poe, one of the earliest black female attorneys in any former Confederate state (see chapter 3), its secretary.[15]

Hill determined early on that he would not defer to Jim Crow's regulations in his daily life. "Commencing . . . around early 1940, I had made up my mind that I wasn't going to ride Jim Crow, I wasn't going to ride in segregated trains. . . . I always went in the white section. . . . I had no problem riding trains and . . . worrying about being arrested. As a matter of fact, I wanted to be arrested . . . to challenge the blame law."[16] The law requiring segregated seating on trains was unjust, Hill believed, and he would not validate it by obeying it. Challenging the law's enforceability, he would testify against segregation and embody an unsegregated alternative world. Moreover, in going about his everyday business, he would seek to occasion a court case to contest the law's constitutionality.

Hill managed to combine commitment, anger, playfulness, and optimism. He could be gritty. He could be gleeful. Hill has told of one time in a courthouse where

> they had a sign "gentlemen" [for the restroom] on one side of the hall and on the other side "colored men." Well, I knew I was a gentleman, so I went into the gentlemen's side. As I was about to start out, a white fellow started in. He saw me wiping my hands, so he figured this must be the Negro side, so he went rushing into the other side. When he opened that door, . . . he saw the mops and all the various paraphernalia you usually see in those kinds of places . . . and I, as I walked out I could see this look of astonishment on his face . . . when he saw me over here and he assumed that was what he was supposed to have over there. And I laughed and went right on down the hall. I don't know what he finally did.[17]

Hill and his colleagues always knew that they courted danger in their work. That awareness framed a story about an event in August 1939, only a short while after Hill began practice in Richmond. He and J. Thomas Hewin Jr. had gone to the Southside's Greensville County to see what they could do to curtail obstacles to black residents' voting in the Democratic primary there (see chapter 7). After they had argued their case in local court, the judge concluded, "Well, I'm not going to assume that the public officials won't perform their duty. But I'll be here in court on Tuesday, election day, and if you find any Negroes are not being permitted to vote who are qualified, then let me know, and I'll take some action."[18]

On election day, as Hill later recalled the incident, "Tom and I decided we'd ride all around the county and make sure there wasn't anything happening in the outlying districts. So we came around this old country road" at the top of a hill, where "there was a sharp turn and a steep down grade and . . . at the bottom of this hill was a one-way bridge" across a river.

> Tom had an old 1936 Ford with a rumble seat, I'll never forget this car, and we turned around this corner and all we could see was a large crowd of white folks, men, with poles and ropes and all kinds of tackle and stuff. I said to Tom . . . looks like this is it and he said it sure enough does. But it was a little narrow road and there was no place to turn around so we just kept on down and drove on through it. We got mid-way across the bridge, and we looked over and saw there was an automobile down in the river and these folks were out there trying to get the automobile. But it had all the appearances initially of a lynching party. I think that was the biggest fright I ever had.[19]

Samuel Tucker in the 1930s

While Hill was making his way through the 1930s, trying to get established, Tucker was trying to get launched in Alexandria. For two years, though, he was away, working with the Civilian Conservation Corps as a reserve army officer. In summer 1936 President Franklin D. Roosevelt directed an end to black exclusion from serving as commanding officers at black CCC camps. As a consequence, Second Lieutenant Tucker served in Pennsylvania under another black officer, Captain Frederick Lyman Slade, the new commanding officer of CCC Camp No. 2 at the Gettysburg National Military Park.[20]

In August 1939—the same month that Hill and Hewin made their way through Greensville County and had their scare there—Samuel Tucker engineered a pioneer sit-in. He and his brother Otto were returning to Alexandria from Richmond, where they had been visiting Oliver Hill, and the two were musing on the library situation in Alexandria. Two years earlier the city had opened a public library, open to whites only. Tucker pondered the matter. If someone had stolen my bicycle, he asked his brother, and I came across it on the street, should I just take it back, or must I go to a policeman about it? They agreed that the direct approach would be appropriate. And they considered how to deal with the segregated library that refused black citizens access.[21]

Some days later a young black man, well dressed and well mannered, entered the library, took a book to the circulation desk, and asked to take it out. He was politely refused. Thank you, ma'am, the man said, and he took a seat at a table and began reading. Five minutes later another young man repeated the ritual. Soon five tables were taken. A policeman was called, and he made his entrance but, declining to approve the manner in which the bicycle was being reappropriated, felt forced to arrest the young men—William Evans, Edward Gaddis, Morris Murray, Clarence Strange, and Otto Tucker.

Meanwhile, Samuel Tucker, who had been running the show, had alerted the media, and the next day the *Washington Post* published a photograph along with a story about the encounter at the library. It was called a "sit-down strike." Tucker and his colleagues, among them his brother Otto, did not manage to extract the privilege of using the public library.[22] As a result of their efforts, however, some months later the city made good on the "equal" in "separate but equal," and a black library was opened. Today it is the home of the Alexandria Black History Resource Center, at which one can watch a short video, narrated by Julian Bond, about the incident.

Salary Equalization: Aline Black, Melvin Alston, and the City of Norfolk

Beginning in the 1930s, black teachers and black attorneys in Virginia and elsewhere attacked "separate but equal" on the question of equality within segregation—not, as would come later, segregation itself. Thurgood Marshall took the lead in Maryland, where a victory in federal district court in *Mills* v. *Anne Arundel County Board of Education* in November 1939 brought an order to equalize salaries, subsequently extended by the legislature to the entire state.[23] Marshall's colleagues replicated the experiment in Virginia. They began with teachers' salaries in the public schools of Virginia's cities.

Aline Elizabeth Black and Melvin O. Alston played key roles in a challenge by black teachers in the Norfolk city public schools to the racial discrimination they suffered in their salaries. In 1937 the all-black Virginia Teachers Association (together with its local branch, the Norfolk Teachers Association), representing black teachers in the public schools, joined forces with the NAACP to organize a joint committee to pursue salary equalization, by which they meant having all teachers paid according to the white teachers' salary schedule rather than the lower schedule for the black teachers. The NAACP supplied legal assistance, and the VTA established a $1,000 fund that could indemnify against salary loss any teacher who was fired in retribution for serving as plaintiff in a court case.[24]

Aline Elizabeth Black initiated a case in state court in 1939 to achieve salary equalization. She was the ideal plaintiff. A graduate of Norfolk's black high school, Booker T. Washington High School, she was a member of the NAACP and the Norfolk Teachers Association. Having earned an undergraduate degree at Virginia State College in 1926, she also had a master's from the University of Pennsylvania (1935); was certified to teach English, Spanish, science, and chemistry; and had a dozen years of teaching experience at Booker T. Washington. Not yet married and still living at her parents' home, she was not very vulnerable in economic terms. Her professional qualifications were clear, so she could certainly lay claim to the higher pay that her white counterparts were receiving. As she later explained, "A teacher who was about to retire was to be named in the suit but at the last minute wouldn't do it, so I volunteered."[25] Black's lawyers were the NAACP's big guns—Thurgood Marshall, Leon A. Ransom, and William H. Hastie—together with Virginia attorney J. Thomas Hewin Jr.

At trial in local court in May 1939, Assistant City Attorney Jonathan W. Old argued that, while the school board had responsibility for providing equal educational opportunities, employment opportunities were something else. Liberty of contract ruled: "The only thing the board says is that, 'we will employ you and we'll pay you so much and no more; you can take it or leave it.'" The board had absolute discretion in hiring matters. Thurgood Marshall countered that nothing in the U.S. Constitution required states to supply anyone an education, but as soon as a state acted to support education, the Fourteenth Amendment came into play: "We submit that the entire discretion of the School Board of the City of Norfolk goes no further than the 14th Amendment allows it to go, and that amendment allows no discrimination on account of race."[26]

Aline Black lost, and before her case could be appealed to the Virginia Supreme Court, the school board declined to renew her contract. When she lost her job, her lawyers concluded that she no longer had standing to sue. The joint committee paid Black her salary for the school year, and she went to New York. There, for two years, she taught school and took classes at New York University toward a doctorate.[27]

After Aline Black lost her case in Norfolk, Marshall won the Anne Arundel case in Maryland. Although with some reluctance, Black's colleague Melvin Alston took her place in the litigation, with a similar guarantee of an indemnity of a year's salary if he lost his job as a consequence. Following the successful model in the Anne Arundel County case, Marshall and his colleagues took Alston's case to federal court, rather than state court. Alston's lawyers were the same as Black's, with the addition of

Oliver W. Hill (for whom Thomas Hewin had become something of a mentor and partner); Hill later called *Alston* "my first really important case."[28]

As a teacher Alston sought a permanent injunction against the school board's continuing to discriminate in its salary schedule on racial grounds. As a taxpayer he challenged the city's discriminatory allocation of the state school fund. He and his attorneys lost the case in February 1940 in federal district court but then took the case to the fourth circuit court of appeals.[29] Pending a decision there, the appeals court directed the school board not to distribute contracts for the coming year until July, so Alston could not be denied his job and no teachers could be required to waive their rights for that year.

In June 1940 Alston won. The appeals court determined that the Norfolk School Board had denied equal protection of the laws by paying black teachers lower salaries than white teachers solely on the basis of race. The court rejected the school board's contention that teachers, once they had signed contracts for the year, could not contest the terms to which they had agreed and, if they failed to sign, had no standing to sue. The court ruled that such waivers could not extend beyond the single year of the contract. Moreover, the appeals court overruled the district judge in the matter of whether the case concerned only Alston; rather, it was a class action suit that affected all black teachers in the Norfolk system.[30]

In October 1940 the U.S. Supreme Court let the decision stand. After difficult negotiations, and just before the case would have returned to district court, the Norfolk School Board and the black teachers agreed to a three-year, phased-in salary adjustment to eliminate race as a criterion for teachers' pay.[31]

Alston's case proved one of the NAACP's more important victories in its campaign in the courts for equalization of salaries, as it supplied a powerful precedent, both in law and in strategy, for similar suits in other cases, in Virginia and in various other southern states.[32] The *Alston* case led to litigation designed to achieve progress on other fronts in the public schools of the South, too—equal busing, equal facilities, and equal curricula—and black Virginians achieved victories regarding each of those in the 1940s.

Aline Black, no longer in litigation against the school board, retrieved her old job. As she later explained, "I came back to Norfolk because my roots are here and I felt I owed something to the people who had fought [alongside] me and who felt that the victory would be complete if I came back." Melvin Alston earned a doctorate at Columbia University and, finding himself still paid too little to support his growing family, soon left to teach at Florida A&M College. The local community, largely forgetting Alston's role, celebrated Black as the champion in the litigation. She taught at Booker T. Washington High School until 1971 and then, before retiring, taught for two years at the new Jacox Junior High School, whose principal, Charles S. Corprew Jr., had studied with both Black and Alston at Booker T. Washington High School in the 1940s.[33]

Variations: Richmond and Newport News

By the time Alston began his action, Oliver Hill had moved to Richmond and had begun to practice law there. After *Alston*, Hill became involved in various actions across the state, each designed to exploit the victory in that case. In Richmond, as attorney for Antoinette E. Bowler and the Richmond Teachers Association, Hill challenged the school board to equalize teachers' salaries. The maximum salary for a black teacher there was one dollar less—substance is important; symbols are, too—than the lowest salary of any white teacher. The black teachers' proposal called for equalization within five years. When the school board rejected that plan in favor of one that would take ten to fifteen years to secure parity, Hill filed suit in U.S. district court. Settling out of court in February 1942, the school board accepted a plan similar to the one it had previously rejected. Other such developments unfolded elsewhere in Virginia.[34]

Oliver Hill has described the tactics of pursuing salary parity. "The equalization process was a matter of litigation . . . [after] direct appeals to the school boards failed. Then, with the precedents in hand, it was a matter of personal appearances in front of boards, letters threatening legal action, with the whites agreeing in principle but always trying to delay by making the black teacher increments over five-seven-ten-year schedules. We finally got it down to three-year cycles of equalization."[35]

In the first half of the 1940s, black teachers' salaries across the state moved much of the way toward parity from what had been a big deficit compared with whites' salaries.[36] But the process could prove slow, even in the cities. One case that dragged on for years was in Newport News, where Dorothy Roles and the Newport News Teachers Association filed a suit in federal district court in 1942 against unequal salaries. Despite a court order in January 1943, shortly before Hill left for the army, she had yet to obtain her equal pay when VE-day came in 1945. Finally, in August 1945 Judge Sterling Hutcheson of the federal district court directed the school board to raise the black teachers' salaries, give thirty-nine of them a total of $22,000 in back pay, and also pay the teachers' lawyers.[37]

Beyond Salaries: Newport News and Norfolk County

Salaries were not the only item on the agenda, even in the early 1940s. They were the main item, and *Alston* pointed the way, but in Newport News, for example, facilities and the curriculum were important as well. Black citizens there sought an increase in the minimum salaries from $600 to $750 per year. They called, as they had for a dozen years, for vocational training at Huntington High School. During the time that officials had rejected pleas for trade courses at Huntington High, the *Norfolk Journal and Guide* noted, "funds have been found to improve and modernize vocational facilities and equipment at the Newport News High School for white pupils where trades are an integral part of the curriculum."[38]

The victory in *Alston* might prove a good beginning to build on, or it might prove only a fleeting promise. Norfolk County supplied a compelling example of how little the *Alston* decision would mean over the near term in some jurisdictions, even in tidewater Virginia. There the school board responded to black teachers' petition for salary equalization by firing three black principals, planning instead to have white principals supervise black schools.[39] Oliver Hill went into action as spokesman for the teachers.

Hill conveyed to the school board the opposition among Norfolk County's black citizens to the dismissal of the three black principals. He declared, "We know that the three principals . . . are fully qualified, capable, and efficient." Superintendent James Hurst retorted: "That is your opinion." About the board's plan, Hill declared that "it is a vicious system intended to intimidate the [black] citizens of Norfolk County." Rather than white supervisors, "we want progressive people at the head of our schools." In language that resonated to world events at the time, he asserted that "anything short of equal opportunity for all is not democracy, but the most vicious kind of Nazi-Fascist system."[40]

Hill's rhetoric suggested an agenda far more extensive than pay parity. He told the board, "If you are interested in the welfare of Negro children, give us better bus transportation, consolidated schools, and other improvements." Pointing out that the flow of events had been replacing white principals of black schools with black principals, not the other way around, he declared, "We object to having white principals over Negro schools." He pointed toward an entire constellation of role models, motivation, job opportunities, and public schooling: "What good does it do to educate Negro children and then take away their economic opportunity?"

It was the school board's turn to speak. "We have always tried to be fair with the Negro children of Norfolk County," the school superintendent said. "We believe that the colored schools of Norfolk County will measure up to any in Virginia."

Hill retorted, "That's not saying anything." He let that sink in, then elaborated. For him, the appropriate measure of the quality of the black schools in a Virginia county was the white schools there, and certainly not the black schools in some other county. Like the school board, he knew that far more was at issue than teachers' salaries. "I have visited the colored schools in practically every county of the state," he explained, "and none of them compares in any way with the white schools."

The struggle in Norfolk County dragged on for many months. Hill inspected the school board's records, and he took direct action to drama-tize the inadequacies of public school funding in the county. On one oc-casion he led a group of black students to the white high school, Church-land High, where they attempted to register for subjects unavailable at any black school in the county. On another, he accompanied students who stopped a white school bus and sought rides when none was available for black students. Both efforts, of course, were rebuffed, but each generated further evidence against local practices, and Hill explained them as "lay-ing ground work" for possible legal action.[41]

Many county residents, growing impatient with the pace of progress, decided to go ahead without the NAACP. T. H. Reid and Robert F. Mc-Murran, two local black attorneys, took up the case. In January 1942 county citizens filed a petition in Norfolk County Circuit Court. As the *Norfolk Journal and Guide* stated the matter, "This suit against the school board" had come "as a climax to months of petitioning and protest meetings."[42]

The Norfolk County suit addressed more than salaries or even the dis-missal of the three black principals. As taxpayers, plaintiffs alleged that in per capita terms the school board had allocated "more funds for the edu-cation of the white race than for the Negro race," that it had "permitted" the buildings at black schools "to become dilapidated and unfit," and that neither the facilities nor the curricula at the black schools were equal to what white students enjoyed. Thus they sought a court order to require "suitable facilities," an allocation of school funds between black and white systems on an equal per capita basis, and a "uniform" curriculum that ap-plied to black and white schools alike.[43] Even in the early 1940s, then, black Virginians sought more than equal salaries in their public schools.

Yellow Buses and Black Schools

Yellow buses took white children to white schools. Why not black chil-dren to black schools? In March 1941 a team of lawyers that included Mar-

shall, Ransom, Hastie, Hill, and Martin filed suit in federal district court
on behalf of Ollie Mae Branch against the school board and school superintendent of Greensville County, where fifteen buses took white children
to school but none was available to black children. A year later, in the
spring of 1942, on behalf of Lula Winn and all other black students in
Nottoway County, Oliver Hill filed suit in federal court for equal free
school bus transportation. As a result, the state superintendent of education, Dabney S. Lancaster, came out against racial discrimination and
urged that equal busing "be established as soon as possible."[44]

Some months later, early in the school year that began in the fall
of 1942, some black residents of Fauquier County refused to send their
children to school. White children rode school buses into Warrenton.
Black children walked—until some stopped walking. Walking to school
was more than inconvenient or unjust. The traffic along U.S. Route 29, in
particular, made it dangerous. For some years black parents had asked the
school board to end the disparity and permit their children to ride, too.
Always rebuffed, at least two families finally decided that their children
would stay home. But that raised questions of truancy and violations of the
state's mandatory school attendance law, and two fathers, Wade Foster and
Braxton Porter, were fined $10 each. In December 1942, when they ap-
pealed in circuit court, the judge refused the instructions that their attorney urged, and the jury convicted them. Porter was fined $50, and Fos-
ter $75.[45]

The parents persisted. Their attorney, Oliver Hill, told the school
board members that he planned to take them to federal district court for
their discrimination against black citizens in providing school bus transportation. That secured the board's attention, and it began to provide busing for black school children in Fauquier. Not only that, Foster and Porter
appealed their convictions to the Virginia Supreme Court. With Hill in
Europe in the army, his colleague Spot Robinson took the case. But when
it came before Virginia's highest court in October 1943, the state attorney
general, Abram Penn Staples, declined to press it. He told the court that
the Fauquier County Circuit Court was in error, that it should have instructed the jury to acquit each man "if evidence showed that the lives of
his children were in danger if they walked to school along a highway [he]
contended was dangerous." Thus, the *Richmond Afro American* reported in
triumph, the cases would go back to circuit court, which was expected to
dismiss all charges. The challenge had, as the newspaper observed, "ap-
parently ended with victory for the parents."[46]

In September 1942, at about the same time as the Fauquier County litigation regarding bus transportation to black schools, Oliver Hill filed a

suit in federal district court on behalf of five black high school students in
Sussex County seeking their admission to white schools. Hill argued that
though they lived within a few miles of white high schools in the county,
they were denied admission "solely on account of race and color." They
lived from thirty to forty-five miles from the Waverly Training School,
the only black school in Sussex County that offered classes above the seventh grade.[47]

Hill's complaint reached still further. It charged that the county provided free bus transportation for the white high school students but none
at all for black students. It pointed out that the black school-age population numbered three times the 1,000 white students in the county, yet only
whites enjoyed access to "four modern, fully staffed and well equipped
schools." Hill described the county's black schools—Waverly and the elementary schools alike—as "small, antiquated and of the one and two-
room variety; poorly equipped, poorly heated and badly ventilated."[48] In
short, access had to do with more than merely equal separate transportation to patently unequal segregated schools.

Judge Robert N. Pollard stated that—assuming "some of the charges
to be true"—he would allow the school board "a reasonable time" to prepare "equal facilities in separate institutions." If such were not provided,
he suggested, he would have no choice but to order the admission of the
black students to the white schools.[49]

Oliver Hill was prodding Virginia down the road toward equality
within segregation. He was doing what he could to seize the "equal" in the
hoary old formula of "separate but equal." Already in 1942 "separate but
equal" appeared to be moving toward a point at which the "equal" would
be insisted on, and with some effectiveness. Equality might at last be
urged, even mandated—in school bus transportation, even in the schools'
facilities and curricula. Moreover, if the effort failed to secure objectively
equal schools, then segregation itself might be in jeopardy.

Segregated Seating in Interstate Travel

By no means did all the civil rights litigation in Virginia in the 1940s
involve schools, and some of it challenged segregation directly. Interstate
transit offers an exemplary image of segregation and the challenges to it at
that time. It also highlights the difficulties of mounting such challenges.
Four cases will serve to illustrate. In June 1942 a black woman, Mrs. Addie
Jordan, was charged with violating Virginia's segregation statutes when,
on her way by train from her home in New York City to her mother's home
in Petersburg, she refused to move to the Jim Crow car when she got to

Virginia. Here was a citation based on the segregation laws, rather than the routine charge of disorderly conduct that seemed to supply no basis for testing segregation's constitutionality. Would Jordan consent to be a plaintiff in a test case? No. She rebuffed Oliver Hill's offer of aid, said her "only interest was in getting out of jail," paid her fine, and went her way.[50]

A more promising case developed two years later, in July 1944, after Irene Morgan climbed aboard a Greyhound bus in Gloucester County, Virginia. She had a ticket to Baltimore, Maryland, the bus's destination. A short while later the bus driver ordered her and another African American woman to move two rows back to the last row so that some new white passengers could be seated. A Virginia state law required seating segregation by rows, whites forward and blacks to the rear, and it required the bus driver to take the action he did. When Morgan chose to remain in her seat, she was forcibly removed and subsequently convicted of violating the segregation statute and resisting arrest. She paid the $100 fine for resisting arrest, but she was committed to appealing her conviction and $10 fine for violating the segregation law.[51]

In Baltimore she contacted the NAACP, which put her in touch with Spottswood Robinson in Richmond. Robinson later recalled, "When Irene Morgan told me that she had been charged with violation of the segregation ordinance, I couldn't believe my ears." In state court Robinson took the approach that states had no authority to regulate interstate commerce in this manner. Nonetheless upholding the statute and the conviction, a unanimous Virginia Supreme Court determined that the statute met the test of "separate but equal," so the policy was a legitimate exercise of the state's police powers to limit friction between the races.[52]

On to the U.S. Supreme Court, where Robinson and Morgan achieved victory. Determining that the Virginia segregation law conflicted with the Constitution's commerce clause, the high court overturned Morgan's conviction.[53]

As Hill later recollected, "Spott had the Morgan case going when I came back."[54] That the war was over, black lawyers were back from Europe and the Pacific, and the siege against Jim Crow was once again fully under way became increasingly evident.

On October 28, 1946, Hill's friend and fellow attorney Sam Tucker boarded a Trailways bus in Washington, D.C., to return to his home in Emporia, Virginia. Much of the bus was empty, and though the company required black passengers to occupy seats as far back as possible and whites as far forward as possible, Tucker took a seat in the fourth row from the front and seventh from the back, and there he sat, unchallenged, all the way to Richmond. In Richmond, however, a number of white passengers boarded, and one had already taken a seat behind Tucker, with others waiting to board, when the bus driver ordered him to move back two rows. Tucker declined to comply, and he was arrested. State law required segregated seating, gave bus drivers authority to direct passengers where to sit, and made it a misdemeanor to "cause" a "disturbance" by refusing to obey such direction.[55]

Oliver Hill and Martin Martin represented Samuel Tucker in Richmond Police Court. Tucker was convicted. His lawyers vowed to take the case, if necessary, to the U.S. Supreme Court, but the next step was Judge John J. Ingram's hustings court in Richmond. There, Martin took the position that the bus company's rules endowed bus drivers with arbitrary powers to force passengers to move and that, moreover, enforcement of those rules would convert "the disorderly conduct statute into a segregation statute." The prosecution side, by contrast, pointed out that the *Morgan* decision had outlawed state laws that required racial segregation on interstate carriers but had not ruled on the right of private companies to make and enforce their own seating regulations. The Virginia statute required that all passengers move when ordered to do so; "the color of the defendant . . . is utterly immaterial." Moreover, the refusal to move constituted the misdemeanor, and thus the state need prove no other act of disorder, for any person who refused to move would be guilty "even if he smiles and blows kisses" at the driver.[56]

Judge Ingram ruled in Tucker's favor. Refusing to distinguish the *Morgan* case, the judge declared that to enforce the statute in this manner would be "doing indirectly what you couldn't do directly."[57]

In 1948 Norvell Lee—a World War II veteran, electrical engineering student at Howard University, and a recent alternate on the 1948 U.S. Olympic boxing team—was convicted on the charge that he "did unlawfully fail to take a seat assigned to him, pursuant to the segregation law of the State of Virginia." The Chesapeake and Ohio train on which he had been riding was a local train, but he was riding with an interstate ticket. The firm of Hill, Martin, and Robinson took the case to the Virginia Supreme Court. That court, which had been reversed in *Morgan*, ruled about Lee—on the basis of *Morgan*—that "it is the character of the journey, not the character of the train, which determines his status." It overturned his conviction.[58]

Judicial Enforcement of Segregated Housing

Oliver Hill saw residential segregation as one wall in the fortress of Jim Crow, and in 1947 he took an opportunity to attack that side of the fortress. That year a black couple purchased a home from a white couple in a Richmond area where, since 1900, deeds carried a restrictive covenant stipulating that "the premises hereby conveyed shall never be used or occupied by any other than a white person." Some among the black couple's new neighbors went to court to prevent the change in occupancy.[59]

Judge William D. Miller decided to hold off on the petition for a temporary injunction against the black family's occupancy of their new property. As all parties knew, a case already before the U.S. Supreme Court, *Shelley* v. *Kraemer*, would address the question of whether restrictive covenants might any longer be enforced in American courts to buttress segregation.[60] Accepting NAACP attorneys' arguments in that case, the Supreme Court decided some months later that restrictive covenants were no longer to have that power. It was a landmark decision that enlarged the definition of *state action* to include judicial enforcement of such private agreements.[61]

The decision differed from Judge Ingram's opinion in Tucker's case not only in that it related to housing rather than transportation but that it hinged on the Fourteenth Amendment rather than on the commerce clause. The two resembled each other, however, in their conclusions that state action to enforce private efforts to achieve racial segregation no better met the test of constitutionality than did direct state efforts to achieve the same ends.

Virginia Civil Rights Organization

The courts were not the only avenue taken by the proponents of change in the law of race in Virginia. Oliver Hill was among the organizers in December 1947 of a new entity, the Virginia Civil Rights Organization, designed to push for change through legislative and executive channels, at both the state and national levels. In part, the group sought implementation of the report *To Secure These Rights*, issued two months earlier by President Truman's Committee on Civil Rights. The timing seemed right to broaden the effort beyond the courts.[62]

The group emphasized segregation on public carriers and in public assemblies. Jim Crow public transit continued to embody the most irking of day-to-day mandated segregation, though the report used broader language to attack segregation: "We believe that segregation is utterly inconsistent with American ideals and that it invariably produces hardships or inequalities and that it constitutes a barrier to mutual understanding and respect." Taking issue with white southerners' conventional argument that racial separation curtailed racial friction, the report declared that "it is the firm conviction of this organization that if segregation enforced by law or custom is abolished it will definitely improve race relations."[63]

The Virginia Civil Rights Organization pointed a finger at segregated higher education. One resolution committed members to "work for the opening of the doors of our public institutions of higher learning in Virginia for graduate and professional study to all citizens regardless of race, creed or color." According to that resolution, segregation at elementary and secondary schools could remain intact, as the quest for equality in salaries, facilities, and curricula continued within the old formula of "separate but equal." Most undergraduate programs could remain segregated, too. But such entities as the law schools of the College of William and Mary and the University of Virginia, for which there were no black counterparts, would be required to end their policies of excluding all African Americans.[64]

A little over two years later, in February 1950, the Courts of Justice Committee of the Virginia House of Delegates held a hearing on some of the matters that had been raised in December 1947 by the Virginia Civil Rights Organization. A newspaper account reported that "an unsegregated crowd packed the House floor and galleries and overflowed deep into the corridors outside." Speakers—both black and white and representing business, churches, professions, and education—advocated bills that called for establishing a state commission on race relations and repealing Virginia laws requiring segregation in intrastate transit on buses and railroads.[65]

Armistead L. Boothe, a white moderate representing Alexandria in Northern Virginia, was the legislation's chief sponsor. He noted that change was coming and that it was overdue. Federal action might well force the issue, and Virginia should act first. A white bank officer characterized most whites and blacks alike in Virginia as moderates, and he noted —with relief and reassurance—that the proposed legislation would not in any way attack bans on segregated education or interracial marriage.[66]

Black speakers at the hearing voiced related concerns and hopes. Dr. W. L. Ransome, the minister at a black church in Richmond, noted that black Virginians "look to Washington," or more particularly to "the federal courts," for improvements on the racial front. He pointed to "three great human rights" of black southerners that had recently been recognized by federal courts: voting rights, equalization of teachers' salaries, and an end to the segregation of interstate travel. An officer of a company operating buses between the nation's capital and Northern Virginia testified in favor of ending segregation in in-state travel. After the Supreme Court handed down its decision in *Morgan* v. *Virginia* in 1946, his company had stopped its practice of requiring segregation across the Potomac River, and things had gone smoothly. Not only had the old court cases (about one a month) come to an end, but there had been "not a single complaint or incident," he said.[67]

Such appeals did not obtain the legislature's support. Even such moderate change in public policy proved more than could be made through conventional legislative politics. Black Virginians would continue to "look to Washington," especially, into the 1960s, to "the federal courts."

Criminal Justice

Never was it true that the only significant civil rights work that Oliver Hill and his colleagues did was related to "separate but equal" education, segregated housing, or Jim Crow transportation. There was always work to be done regarding political rights in a poll-tax world. And there was always the matter of black Virginians' encounters with the criminal justice system. Oliver Hill recalled that it was murder cases that drew him back to Richmond in the late 1930s and then kept him there long enough to settle in. Two felony cases, one from the early 1930s, the other from mid-century, illustrate the matter of civil rights attorneys' involvement in the criminal justice system.

In 1933 a black man named George Crawford went on trial in Loudoun County (a short distance west of Washington, D.C.) for the murder in January 1932 of two white women, Agnes Boeing Illsley, a wealthy widow, and Mina Buckner, who lived with her. Although every lawyer in the county was white, and all the grand jurors who indicted Crawford were white, Crawford's lawyers were all black men. Howard University's Charles Hamilton Houston led the defense team, which also included Edward P. Lovett and James G. Tyson, both of them Howard law graduates working in Washington, D.C., as well as Howard law professor Leon A. Ransom. As they worked on the case, Houston ascertained that grand jurors in the county were always drawn from the property tax lists; the lists were divided between white and black; and only the first list, the white list, was drawn from. Much the same seemed true of trial jurors.[68]

Whether Crawford was guilty or innocent of the charge, it was widely expected that he would be convicted and executed. As it happened, considerable evidence was developed that indicated his guilt, and yet, though he was convicted, he was sentenced to life in the penitentiary rather than death. His defense team had saved his life. The state's leading white newspapers all commented on the extraordinary competence and demeanor of the defense team, especially Charles Hamilton Houston.[69]

A shift toward reliance on black lawyers was clearly under way. Howard University School of Law was putting in place—through its faculty and its alumni—a cadre of attorneys who would bring training and experience to their work and who could and would challenge such matters as the systematic exclusion of black citizens from juror pools in criminal proceedings.

At mid-century another high-profile criminal proceeding unfolded. In January 1949 Ruby Stroud Floyd was raped by several men in Martinsville, Virginia. In criminal proceedings that stretched over the next two years, seven black men were convicted and sentenced to die for the crime. There was reason to believe that some of the seven men had participated in the crime. There was also reason to believe that others had not, though their presence subjected them to the same prosecution.[70]

On appeal to the Virginia Supreme Court, the lawyers for the "Martinsville Seven" were Oliver W. Hill, Samuel W. Tucker, Martin A. Martin, and Roland D. Ealey. Whatever the culpability of one defendant or another, the appeals lawyers developed a battery of evidence that the death penalty for rape was reserved in Virginia for black men. Never in the twentieth century had a white man been executed for such a crime. Whites went to the penitentiary; blacks went from there to the electric chair. Oliver Hill voiced the perspective of white Virginians he saw embedded in the formal procedure: "We don't need to lynch the niggers. We can try them and then hang them."[71]

Just as Charles Hamilton Houston had challenged the systematic exclusion of black men from the pool of grand jurors and trial jurors in the George Crawford case, the defense lawyers in the Martinsville Seven case challenged the historical disparity in sentencing black defendants far more severely than white defendants for the same category of crime. In the case of the Martinsville Seven, the defense team could show no gain from their efforts. In February 1951 all seven were executed. But the use of historical evidence proved an important step in developing a civil rights attack on racial discrimination in criminal cases.

Black Virginians and Electoral Politics

Oliver Hill was a central participant in the efforts in Virginia in the 1940s to promote black participation in the electoral process. As Samuel Tucker put it, an important part of the civil rights struggle back "in the days of the poll tax" was "overcoming the barriers between black people and the ballot box." Part of that effort, of course, was reflected in the trip by Hill and Hewin to Greensville County to joust with the ghosts of Virginia's white Democratic primary (see chapter 7). Increasingly, however, it became clear that the major obstacles lay elsewhere.[72]

A historian at Virginia State College, Luther Porter Jackson, did what he could across the 1940s to persuade black Virginians to pay their poll taxes and go to the voting booths. Oliver Hill, for his part, ran for public office four times between 1947 and 1955: twice for Richmond City Council, twice for the state legislature. Luther Porter Jackson characterized Hill's first attempt—a 1947 campaign for the House of Delegates, when he was narrowly defeated in the Democratic primary—as "the most significant advancement in the citizenship aspiration of southern Negroes . . . in the past half-century."[73]

The next year Hill did better. In 1948 Oliver Hill became the first black member of the Richmond City Council in the twentieth century. Fifty years earlier, in 1898, city councilman Henry Moore had been defeated in a bid for reelection. When he left his post, it was the first time since 1871 that Richmond had had no black member of city council. But then came the long dry spell when black Virginians were largely excluded from electoral politics. When Hill took his seat, ninety-year-old Edward R. Carter was the only living black former member.[74]

By appealing to white as well as black voters, Hill later observed, "I had demonstrated that a black could . . . get elected." As he explained, "To run for office you go to where the people got the votes." Hill's victory revealed a renovated political world in which black voters as well as white voters picked officeholders, and a world in which some white voters were prepared to consider voting for a black candidate. Through electoral politics he brought to an end a longtime pattern in which the city council of Virginia's capital was segregated, always exclusively white.[75]

By the end of his term, Hill had been selected by reporters who covered local politics and government as one of the two most knowledgeable, most effective members of that body.[76] He wished to demonstrate to his fellow black Virginians that voting was possible, that it could make a difference, that running for public office was no pipedream, that winning election was possible, and, for that matter, that they had an interest in political battles that took place in legislatures as well as in courtrooms.

But, though Hill took seriously his responsibilities in city council and no doubt took pleasure in such victories as he experienced, such venues never attracted his primary interest. One reason, to be sure, was his narrow defeat for reelection in 1950. A few years later Hill ran again for the state legislature, but he remembers that in the aftermath of the *Brown* v.

Board of Education decisions in 1954 and 1955, "I ran for the House of Delegates in '55 because I wanted somebody to be able to present . . . the situation from our point of view, but of course, I couldn't have been elected dog catcher at that time."[77]

Regardless of the electoral outcome, to Hill's mind the courtroom strategy would remain for some time the more promising one, and his legislative responsibilities had interfered with his courtroom tasks.[78] Into the 1960s Hill and his partners continued their aggressive pursuit of the courtroom strategy. In that decade, however, the time for electoral politics would return, as was demonstrated by some of Hill's colleagues in the siege against segregation (see chapter 8).

Back to School: The Emphasis Shifts to Facilities and Curricula

Salary equalization, achieved or not, never constituted the final goal in the early 1940s for Hill or his colleagues regarding public schools in Virginia. But a lull occurred in the mid-1940s, while Oliver Hill and other black Virginia lawyers (among them Samuel Tucker and Roland Ealey) were away in Europe or the Pacific fighting World War II. Fuller activity resumed after they returned, and by the late 1940s real results could be seen.

A concerted effort in 1948 and 1949 made considerable progress in squeezing greater equality out of the old "separate but equal" formula. Spottswood Robinson and the Virginia NAACP's executive secretary, W. Lester Banks, drove thousands of miles around the state. They compiled information about the public schools and did the groundwork to nurture potential plaintiffs and massage potential cases.[79] In some jurisdictions, disputes reached the federal courts.

These cases went well beyond the earlier primary concern with salary equalization or school buses. They also transcended concern with physical facilities. The prevailing image of the formula that litigation followed in the 1940s—from salary equalization to bus transportation to physical facilities (or simply from salaries to facilities)—supplies a convenient shorthand way of getting at the shift in major immediate objectives. But it severely oversimplifies the story. For example, equality in physical facilities might be achieved, as Hill later mused, "brick for brick," but what about the schools' curricula? Such questions as this loomed large in the late 1940s. Hill had eventual desegregation in mind, but "right now," he said, "we want the brick for brick." He also wanted bus for bus, dollar for dollar, and class for class.[80]

The new wave of litigation struck pay dirt in federal district court. There, following up his rulings in the Newport News case, Judge Hutcheson ratcheted up the level of equality of segregated schooling that would be required in Virginia. The first victory in the surge of the late 1940s came in a case from Surry County. In March 1948 Judge Hutcheson determined that the school board in Surry County was discriminating in teachers' salaries, bus transportation, and physical facilities. Moreover, black children there were being denied an accredited high school and an equal curriculum. In a wide-ranging decree, Judge Hutcheson demanded that school officials demonstrate progress in narrowing the substantial disparities between the opportunities of black and white children to obtain high school educations in Surry County.[81]

The firm of Hill, Martin, and Robinson was on a roll. The *Surry* decision proved as important in the postwar surge as the *Alston* decision had been in the earlier effort. It supplied a precedent to build on, to take to other school boards, and it energized teachers and other black Virginians to take action to redress ancient inequities. The next month, moreover, Hill and his partners gained another major victory in Judge Hutcheson's district court. That decision governed three different cases, one each from Chesterfield, King George, and Gloucester Counties. The statewide black teachers' association exclaimed, "Thank God for the Federal Courts!"[82]

School boards could prove recalcitrant, but Hill and his partners proved tenacious, and Judge Hutcheson sided with the black plaintiffs, not the white defendants. Hutcheson was even prepared to declare those defendants in contempt of court. When he found the members of the Gloucester County School Board in contempt, the *Richmond Times-Dispatch* editorialized that "it was the sort of thing, which if carried out to its logical conclusion, might find nearly all the Virginia jails choked with its school boards and superintendents, because it is well understood that nowhere in Virginia are colored school facilities quite up to the standards of the white schools, nor could the situation be swiftly remedied."[83]

But the returns could surely be mixed. For example, the King George High School, a white school, offered a number of courses not available at the King George Training School, its black counterpart. Under court order to remedy the deficiency, the county school board sought to comply by dropping four courses at King George High: chemistry, physics, biology, and geometry. As a result, white high school students and their parents, like their black counterparts, found themselves protesting the actions of local authorities.[84]

Next came such considerations as extracurricular activities, where equalization would force either the termination of such activities at white schools or the expansion of opportunities at black schools. The squeeze was on.

Beyond *Alston*, beyond *Surry:* Christiansburg and Arlington

Yet another case came not from the eastern half of the state, where most black Virginians lived, but from the west, in Pulaski and Montgomery Counties. Christiansburg Industrial Institute, founded in 1866 as a Freedmen's Bureau school, had been adopted by local officials as a regional high school for black students. Parents of some Pulaski students filed suit to force the Pulaski County School Board to provide facilities closer to home. Though rebuffed in the U.S. District Court for the Western District of Virginia—Hill and Robinson had finally lost a case in federal court—the parents won in the fourth circuit court of appeals in November 1949. Busing itself could be unconstitutional if students had to travel sixty miles each day to segregated schools; their health, their safety, and their time for recreation and study all were compromised.[85] Here the problem was not the poor quality of a black school—its facilities or curriculum—but the imposition of such a long commute to reach it. Here the problem had not been posed as one of low teachers' salaries or a lack of busing, but the reliance on long-distance busing to achieve segregation.

In a case in Arlington County, lawyers for the school board argued that the limited opportunities, curricular and extracurricular, at the black high school resulted not from the students' racial identities but from the fact that there were so many fewer black students than white. Black plaintiffs lost the case in federal district court, but the fourth circuit court of appeals declared in May 1950 that it found all kinds of "unlawful discriminations against pupils of the colored race; and it is no defense that they flow in part from variations in size of the respective student bodies."[86]

Segregation itself began to appear in jeopardy. For one thing, Hill and his colleagues often proposed desegregation as a means of resolving disputes about unequal educational opportunity. Moreover, a white newspaper writer noted in June 1950 that "the seeds are there, in the appellate court decision [in the Arlington County case], for a future demand for entrance of Negroes into white high schools of counties where the Negro population is so small that a court may find 'substantial compliance' cannot be met." Meanwhile, Oliver Hill and Spottswood Robinson continued to crisscross the state on these and other cases.[87]

Black Exclusion and Higher Education

Segregation itself came under attack in higher education at this time in Virginia, where the two public law schools (and the two private ones as well) excluded all black students. Gregory H. Swanson—who graduated in 1948 from Howard Law and then worked for a time for the firm of Hill, Martin, and Robinson—applied in 1949 to take classes as a graduate law student at the University of Virginia. The Supreme Court had recently handed down a decision, in *Sipuel* v. *Oklahoma*, that severely narrowed states' ability to maintain segregated law schools; and by June 1950 the Court had ruled against segregation in a follow-up case from Texas, *Sweatt* v. *Painter*.[88]

It was hard to see how the University of Virginia had a legal leg to stand on should it choose to turn Swanson down. The faculty and dean of the law school supported Swanson's application, but they did not have final say within the institution. In a special meeting in June 1950, four days after the U.S. Supreme Court decision in *Sweatt* v. *Painter*, the university's board of visitors decided to get a formal ruling from the state attorney general, J. Lindsay Almond Jr. The board of visitors displayed concern about what laws should regulate its behavior, and it also worried about the loss of support among university alumni and state legislators. In view of the Virginia state constitution and laws, it asked, did university officials have a "legal duty" to reject Swanson? Almond advised the board that if it turned Swanson down, he was sure to appeal its decision in federal court and it could not win such a case.[89]

When the school nonetheless rejected Swanson in July 1950, he went into federal court to challenge his exclusion. Representing him were Oliver Hill, Martin A. Martin, and Spottswood Robinson, with Robinson arguing the case before a special three-judge federal panel. The judges— John J. Parker, Morris A. Soper, and John Paul—ruled that since Virginia had only one state-supported law school offering graduate work in law, Swanson could not be rejected solely on the basis of his racial identity. In September 1950, under federal court order, Swanson began classes at the University of Virginia. Token desegregation there had begun.[90] Dr. J. M. Tinsley, the president of the NAACP's Virginia branch, offered his opinion that the state should stop waiting for citizens to go to court and for the courts to act. Rather, the state should just open its public institutions of higher education to "all citizens."[91]

Indeed, in light of the court's ruling, Virginia's other public law school, at the College of William and Mary, admitted its first black student,

Edward A. Travis, the next year. Also in 1951, William and Mary admitted Hulon Willis as a graduate student in physical education. Moreover, since black students could not obtain an undergraduate education in engineering at a black school in the state, Virginia Polytechnic Institute admitted Irving L. Peddrew III in 1953 and a few other black engineering students through the rest of the 1950s. Similarly, the University of Virginia admitted its first black engineering undergraduates in 1955. Yet black applicants to white schools for programs available at Virginia State College continued to be rejected, directed instead to seek the program they wanted where they could get it without enrolling in a nonblack program. For the most part segregation in higher education persisted.[92]

Assault against Segregation

As the 1950s began, lawyers Hill, Martin, and Robinson continued to pursue the kind of public school litigation that had taken so much of their energy in the late 1940s. Yet the case against the University of Virginia hinted that a change of strategy was under way.

In April 1951 Hill and Robinson were preparing to take a trip west from Richmond to look after the case in Pulaski and Montgomery Counties. That same month Barbara Johns, together with her classmates at Robert R. Moton High School in the town of Farmville in Prince Edward County, went on strike against the poor physical facilities at their school. Before long they had contacted Oliver Hill and Spottswood Robinson in Richmond to request their support. Hill and Robinson promised to stop off in Farmville on their way to Christiansburg, and they did so.[93]

The previous summer, however—weeks after the Supreme Court handed down its decisions in the *Sweatt* case—the national NAACP had made a strategic decision to mount a direct attack against segregated public schooling, and in October 1950 the Virginia State Conference of the NAACP agreed to that policy.[94] Not all NAACP lawyers were certain that this was the way to go. Hill recollects that Martin A. Martin "was not enthusiastic about fighting the per se fight; he was something of a separatist anyway."[95] But the decision came that it had become time to gamble, to challenge the "separate" rather than only insist on the "equal" in "separate but equal."

Thus Hill and Robinson advised the black community in Prince Edward that they would take the case only if, instead of merely seeking improved facilities of the sort that white schoolchildren in that county enjoyed, they contested the segregation itself. Agreement was reached. The Virginia case began that, together with cases from Delaware, South Carolina, and Kansas, went to the U.S. Supreme Court, which handed down its decision in *Brown* v. *Board of Education* in May 1954. According to *Brown*, segregated public schooling could not meet the standard that the Supreme Court's interpretation of the Fourteenth Amendment's equal protection clause had come to demand. A second decision in *Brown*, in May 1955, provided for implementation of the 1954 decision.[96]

The Struggle to Litigate Social Change

When Oliver Hill, Thurgood Marshall, and Samuel Tucker finished their studies at Howard University in 1933, the Supreme Court had supplied favorable rulings against Jim Crow in voting rights and in housing access—as had lower federal courts in cases that arose in Virginia—but not in transportation or education. Even after World War II, when Hill returned to Richmond from Europe, they still had few useful precedents to build on, few proven weapons in their arsenal.

Nonetheless, across the 1940s Virginia's civil rights attorneys won important skirmishes on various fronts: in the *Alston* case, in *Morgan*, in *Surry*, and in *Swanson*. Two of those court decisions constituted victories against segregation itself, and in areas that had yet to supply useful precedents before the late 1930s: *Morgan* (interstate transportation; on commerce clause grounds) and *Swanson* (higher education; based on equal protection). With respect to elementary and secondary schools, the strategic shift—from siege to assault, for the NAACP in general and the firm of Hill, Martin, and Robinson in particular—came in 1950.

But no victories seemed final. Despite *Brown* v. *Board of Education*, no elementary or secondary public school anywhere in Virginia was racially integrated in 1954 or 1955 or, indeed, before 1959, and most remained fully segregated into the mid-1960s. U.S. district judge Sterling Hutcheson, for one, proved obstructionist. Oliver Hill, who had spent a great deal of time in Hutcheson's court, would later characterize the judge as "exceptionally fair" in the equalization cases of the late 1940s, "as long as we were talking about equality." That is, Hill explained, "as long as we were [working within the framework of] 'separate but equal,' . . . we got tremendous, tremendous support from the federal courts. It wasn't until we hit the segregation head on, then there was a different story."[97]

Outside the courts, meanwhile, the environment proved even more hostile, as Virginia adopted a policy of Massive Resistance. The state came up with one approach after another to postpone desegregation, and the starting point was a pledge—a state policy—to close a school before permitting it to be desegregated. Massive Resistance not only caused years of delay before any—let alone much—desegregation could take place but also contributed profoundly to limiting the impact that desegregation could have when it finally did happen. Oliver Hill and his colleagues struggled for years, for example, to achieve desegregation in the Richmond city public schools.[98]

Indeed, the state engineered another variant of Massive Resistance, specifically targeting the NAACP and its ability to bring litigation in quest of obtaining implementation of the apparent victory in *Brown*. Beginning with the same special session in which Massive Resistance was inaugurated, 1956, the legislature attempted to put an end to the NAACP's operations in Virginia and thus bring an end to the litigation. The organization had to fight for its life, in the process tying up its resources defending itself rather than fighting segregation.

The NAACP itself called the anti-NAACP legislation "part of the State's massive resistance plan, as they called it, to desegregation in Virginia," a characterization that appears entirely appropriate. In *NAACP v. Button* (1963), a Supreme Court case that finally brought an end to a very dangerous period for the organization, the NAACP explained that the behavior to be curtailed under the anti-NAACP laws was "inherent in litigation in which Negroes resort to the courts in an effort to free themselves and the country of the burden of racial discrimination."[99]

One reason the NAACP adopted the go-for-broke strategy of the early 1950s was the great difficulty it had experienced in its piecemeal litigation, issue by issue and city by city, county by county, in the 1940s. Despite hopes for a smooth desegregation after *Brown*, the NAACP replicated its 1940s experience, as it had to go back into court in countless jurisdictions in the late 1950s and the 1960s. (A clear rebuttal might be that *Brown* led quickly to racial desegregation in parks and other public facilities; *Brown* was, whatever else, and whatever anyone's intent or expectation, the crucial precedent in areas other than education.)

The years of the late 1950s and early 1960s looked remarkably like the years of the late 1940s, except that in the earlier period Hill and his colleagues were laying the foundation for such an attack as the Prince Edward case represented. The later period came after they had "won," yet Hill and the others had cases in the courts all over the state—dozens of cases, everywhere.

The granddaddy case was the one in Prince Edward, where the county simply closed the public schools for five years. The policy of Massive Resistance, in its original form, lost in both state and federal court in January 1959. Later that year, when a federal court directed Prince Edward County to desegregate, the county instead adopted a local version of Mas-

Congress of Racial Equality and in Washington, D.C., by Howard University students. Young people in Oklahoma City engaged in sit-ins beginning in 1958.[1]

In 1960, however, the tactic became widespread. On Monday, February 1, 1960, four young men, students at the North Carolina Agricultural and Technical College, staged a sit-in at a Woolworth's lunch counter in Greensboro. Between then and the passage of the Civil Rights Act of 1964, sit-ins took place across the South. Some led to desegregation without arrests. Yet arrests were made in every former Confederate state and in Border South states, too, and dozens of cases made their way to the U.S. Supreme Court.[2]

Most studies of the Civil Rights movement of the 1950s and 1960s have focused on Deep South communities: Montgomery, Alabama, for example, with such individuals as Rosa Parks and Rev. Dr. Martin Luther King Jr. and such institutions and organizations as Dexter Avenue Baptist Church and the Montgomery Improvement Association. By contrast, this chapter highlights an Upper South community, Richmond, Virginia, from early 1960 through mid-1963.

At issue were property rights, the relevance of such concepts as equal protection and state action, and—in Virginia—a state law requiring segregation in "public assemblages."[3] Opponents of change insisted that lunch counters, in particular, were private and therefore immune to the Fourteenth Amendment. Protest demonstrators and their lawyers drew upon the logic of *Shelley* v. *Kraemer*, a 1948 Supreme Court decision that banned judicial enforcement of private agreements that promoted racial segregation in housing.

Planning the Richmond Sit-ins

Virginia Union University is a small, private, black institution of higher education located several miles northwest of downtown Richmond. In 1960 it was the center of the Richmond sit-in movement. On February 6, the Saturday after the Greensboro sit-ins began, three friends met and discussed the recent events. Two of them, Frank Pinkston and Charles Sherrod, were graduate students at Union Theological Seminary. The other, Woodrow Grant, was a senior at Virginia Union. Grant later recalled that they "reflected" on the events in Greensboro and "the possibility of doing the same thing in Richmond."[4]

In that meeting the three men discussed how to mobilize the campus and the wider community. They also planned a meeting to be held two days later, on Monday, February 8, on the Virginia Union campus. At the

Monday meeting students readily agreed to the proposal that nonviolent direct action should govern their protest. The leaders reminded the group of a talk by Martin Luther King at Virginia Union the year before, and they pointed to the sit-ins at Greensboro as exemplifying the approach. The students discussed how to prepare for the demonstrations they had in mind. By the end of the week, they had begun training in nonviolent direct action and had held mock demonstrations. Taking turns playing all the roles—protesters, store personnel, police, hecklers—they acted out various scenarios that they might confront.

Moreover, they reached out to the wider community for support. Seminary students Pinkston and Sherrod saw as their best opportunity working through area ministers and addressing black congregations. The next Sunday, February 14, students addressed black congregations throughout the Richmond area to explain the protest and seek support. If store managers did not immediately agree to change their policies, the success of the protest would depend on picketing and boycotting. Picketing would draw attention to the stores, their policies, and the protests. Boycotts would bring economic pressure to bear.

The group made contact with Nat Eggleston, owner of the Eggleston Hotel, who offered his establishment as a meeting place for the protesters. Eggleston also took the lead in rallying other black businessmen in support of the protest. Students engaged in the sit-ins would need transportation back and forth between campus and downtown. When the protests began, black taxi drivers supplied transportation for many students, who signed tickets for their fares. The taxi drivers or companies covered some of the costs, and so did various other black businessmen.

The NAACP and Richmond's black lawyers—especially Martin A. Martin, Oliver W. Hill, and Clarence W. Newsome—teamed up to supply legal counsel. Martin, in particular, gave the kind of advice that, from the beginning, the three organizers had known they would need. He schooled them on the law in Virginia as it might apply to demonstrations. He went over for them the process of arrest and police procedures they might encounter. And because of the success in raising funds from business people and others in the community, Martin was able to assure the students that if arrested, they would be able to meet bail and thus need not stay in jail.

During the week that followed the mock demonstrations on campus and the addresses to black congregations, the students fine-tuned their plans. They continued to rehearse, and they decided on tactics. They would target four downtown stores, among the larger and more visible department stores in the city, each with eating facilities, the point of the intended demonstrations: Murphy's, People's Service Drug Store, Thalhimers, and Woolworth's, all of them on Broad Street between Fourth Street and Sixth. In the days before the protests began, some students went to each store to familiarize themselves with the places they would soon be disrupting.

The group selected Saturday, February 20, as the first day of their sit-ins. Classes were not held on weekends, so no one would have to miss class to participate. And the stores would be busier than during the week, so that anything the students did would prove more disruptive and would gain the attention of more people.

The Richmond Sit-ins Begin

On Saturday, February 20—nineteen days after the North Carolina sit-ins began—students at Virginia Union University launched their protest demonstrations, as approximately 200 students converged at about 9:00 A.M. on downtown Richmond. A group of protesters went first to Woolworth's store at Fifth Street and Broad, where they ignored the small counter at the back of the store set aside for black customers and occupied the thirty-four seats in the larger section to the front reserved for whites. Store officials quickly closed the counter. The students continued to sit, talking among themselves or reading. Meanwhile, when a small group entered Grant's Department Store, the manager closed the lunch counter even though the students had not attempted to sit there.[5]

About 9:30 a larger group went into nearby Murphy's. They took all seventy-four seats in the whites-only section, and it too was closed. Questioned about the demonstration, students explained that they had come as individuals, although two, Charles Sherrod and Frank Pinkston, identified the others as classmates at Union. The two leaders took pains to characterize the demonstration as "spontaneous," that is, not in any way sponsored by the university, but they conceded strong sympathy with similar demonstrations elsewhere. Richmond was just one of many offshoots of the Greensboro original.

At about 1:00 P.M. managers at Murphy's and Woolworth's both announced they were closing the stores, and the demonstrators left. Soon afterwards, the group moved into Thalhimers, at Sixth and Broad, and tried to take seats at all four eating places there. At the restaurant on the fourth floor, they had to wait in line, but they took seats at the soda fountain in the basement and at the lunch bars on the main floor and the mezzanine. All four places were immediately closed. Thalhimers personnel urged the demonstrators to leave the store, and after perhaps forty-five minutes they did so. William B. Thalhimer Jr. announced that the store would remain open but the eating places would all remain closed for the rest of the day.

The group moved up Broad Street to People's Service Drug Store, where they took all the available seats at the counter. Service was halted immediately. The manager announced that the store would close for ten minutes, and when it opened it would be for prescription business only.

As to whether the protests might end anytime soon, Charles Sherrod spoke for the students in indicating a willingness to speak with retail merchants in the downtown area. But he made it clear that the group had no intentions of backing away from its objective: "Our aim is to end segregation, period." The reporter for the *Times-Dispatch* saw only one older person, he said, who remained the entire day with the demonstrators. This was Clarence W. Newsome, an attorney and the executive secretary of the Crusade for Voters in Richmond, who claimed to be present not as a demonstrator but as an "observer."

Dr. Samuel D. Proctor, the Virginia Union president, found himself in a different situation than did some of his Deep South counterparts. Virginia Union, as a private school, did not depend on state appropriations for its survival, and officers of the school were not public appointees, subject to dismissal. Distancing the institution from direct responsibility, Proctor noted that any Union students present were acting only as individuals. The demonstrations were not some kind of class project sponsored by the school. But Proctor planned no disciplinary actions against participating students as long as they remained orderly, he said, and indeed he spoke out in favor of the demonstrations. "We look at this as part of a total protest on the part of the Negro people against the whole pattern of segregation," he was reported as saying. "This is one fragment of the total protest. I suppose we can expect one form of protest or another perpetually until racism is gone."[6]

The Thalhimers Thirty-Four

Demonstrators stayed away on Sunday—Thalhimers was closed Sundays—but Monday morning, February 22, they returned for a second day of lunch counter protests. This time there were perhaps 500. They did not sit at the lunch counters at Woolworth's or Murphy's: both places kept their eating places closed all day. But about thirty sat at the lunch counter at Grant's. The counter then closed. After a half hour the students left, and the counter was reopened. Another group went to the lunch counter at People's. They also were refused service, and again the counter was closed for a time.[7]

Some groups went to Thalhimers. Seventy-five people attempted to enter the Richmond Room, a tea room on the fourth floor. Others went to the lunch counter on the first floor. Refused service and asked to leave, they remained, some of them holding textbooks and notebooks, a few holding small American flags. The counter was closed for a while, though the Richmond Room remained open for white guests, while store officials called for city magistrates and again requested that the students leave.

At each of the two places—the tea room and the lunch counter—seventeen arrests were made. As the *Times-Dispatch* reported, there might have been many more, but not all the students stayed. Some Union faculty members suggested that many students leave. Dr. E. D. McCreary Jr., a theology professor at Union, explained: "We're just advising the students to leave because we believe we have the case."[8]

Those who left mostly walked over to the police lockup, on Sixth Street at Marshall, where they waited for their classmates to complete the process of being booked and then released on $50 bond. Each time some of the thirty-four exited the lockup, the group clapped and cheered.

The thirty-four included Charles Sherrod and Frank Pinkston as well as twenty-two other men and ten women. Among them were Woodrow Grant, one of the original organizers; Raymond Blair Randolph Jr., a student from New Haven, Connecticut; and eighteen-year-old Ford Johnson and his nineteen-year-old sister, Elizabeth, the children of a Richmond dentist, Dr. Ford Tucker Johnson Sr.

The Thalhimers Boycott

Students returned the next day—Tuesday, February 23—a little before 11 A.M. But the numbers were smaller this time, and the eating facilities at the places that had been targeted on Saturday and Monday—Grant's, Thalhimers, Woolworth's, People's, and Murphy's—remained open. The protesters focused on Thalhimers, the scene of the arrests the day before. Rather than sitting in again, they remained outside and picketed the store. They distributed a leaflet urging black Richmonders not to enter the store and certainly not to buy there. It explained: "Thalhimers had our Negro youths arrested because they tried to exercise their constitutional rights to eat in a public place. Don't buy in this store!" Among the slogans on the pickets' placards was: "Can't eat . . . Don't buy."[9]

Pickets made it clear that they planned to keep coming back to Thalhimers. No mass marches would be needed now, and perhaps no more sit-ins would take place, but for the indefinite future downtown merchants could expect the demonstrators to keep up the pressure. Only about ten students at a time were needed for picket duty, and from time to time others arrived to take their places. They paced the sidewalk in front of Thalhimers, some chatting and cheerful, others more somber. The vigil had lasted most of the business day, as the last picket did not leave until after 5 o'clock.

During that day the students and their supporters acted to broaden their support in the black community. They and their supporters announced a mass meeting for 8 o'clock that evening at the Fifth Street Baptist Church.

Community Support

On February 23, the day after the thirty-four arrests, black Richmonders—in a group estimated at 3,000—gathered in support of the demonstrators. As the *Afro American* reported in its next issue, they jammed the church's auditorium, its balcony, and a downstairs meeting room. The church could not contain them all: "Loud speakers carried the message to hundreds who filled the outside pavement, sat on the church steps, on the neighboring porches and in cars double-parked for blocks around." [10]

The reporter turned his readers' attention to the inside of the church, where the crowd "cheered the arrested students and signed pledges of 'moral, active, physical and financial support and participation until our objectives have been achieved.'" They cheered when Oliver Hill suggested that picketing should be "extended to the General Assembly," which Hill termed "one of the most undemocratic institutions in the state of Virginia." And they made clear their support of boycotts of Thalhimers and, in fact, all downtown stores that "deny equal dining services to all patrons."

Oliver Hill had some things to say to his fellow Afro-Richmonders. After two decades of pushing for change through actions in the courts (see chapter 4) and the legislature, he articulated the critical need for direct action. "It was back in 1954 that the Supreme Court said that segregated schools are unconstitutional. Yet today, in 1960, the School Board is still trying to establish new jim-crow schools." And he attacked the Virginia legislature for its inaction, for it "has not done one thing to bring about orderly desegregation."

It was time for a different approach, Hill told the crowd, and the Virginia Union students had shown the way. "We are not going to accomplish our human rights by litigation," he declared in a remarkable statement from someone who had engaged in civil rights litigation for two decades, "but by a determination to make the sacrifices necessary. We intend to assert those rights." And, he exhorted, "If the new trespass laws mean sacrifice and jail for us, then more and more colored people ought to go to jail."

"If necessary," Hill continued, "we'll put on an austerity campaign in this town. Boycott the stores and wear threadbare clothes. We must hold fast until the powers that be approach this situation in a sensible fashion. Until they intend to do right—and move toward the end of segregation. Nothing short of that is right. We must be willing to do picket duty, not leave it to just these students. Everybody must help keep the spotlight on this Capital of the Confederacy until it becomes a part of the United States."

The pastor of the Fifth Baptist Church, Rev. Robert S. Anderson, declared: "I sat at the lunch counters with the students. We were not hungry for the potato chips they moved off the counters. We were hungry for liberty and our human rights." [11]

Before the meeting was over, three specific things had been accomplished. The crowd approved a proposal to boycott stores in Richmond whose eating facilities discriminated against blacks. By the hundreds they signed up to join picket lines at such stores. And they set up a fifteen-member steering committee to guide the movement. Among the members were student leaders Frank Pinkston and Charles Sherrod; civil rights attorneys Oliver Hill and Clarence Newsome; Dr. J. Rupert Picott, executive secretary of the all-black Virginia Teachers Association; W. Lester Banks, executive secretary of the NAACP's Virginia State Conference; and Dr. Felix Brown, Dr. C. C. Scott, and Rev. Wyatt Tee Walker. [12]

Perspectives on Segregation, Protest, and the Law

Black and white Richmonders tended to display starkly contrasting views of the legitimacy of what was going on. Martin A. Martin, attorney for the Thalhimers Thirty-Four, offered his observations about the validity of the charges of trespass. The thirty-four were not trespassers, he maintained, but "business invitees." He explained: "Colored persons are invited into this store to shop. The store may perhaps not choose to serve them but the state has no right to jail them as long as they are orderly." Public authority had no place in supporting private discrimination. And he warned that civil suits might well result from the arrests for trespass. [13]

Elizabeth Johnson, one of the Thalhimers Thirty-Four, spoke to nationwide audiences about developments. She and Lacy Streeter, an Air Force veteran studying at a black college in North Carolina, spoke to a group of newsmen at a press conference, at which Roy Wilkins, executive secretary of the NAACP, introduced them. The next day (Monday, February 29), the two students appeared on the Dave Garroway television show. Johnson, a junior at Virginia Union, described fellow student Frank Pinkston as the group's leader. She explained that they had been inspired by the North Carolina students. "We wanted to do our part," she said, so "we went out and tried to get served" at drugstores and at Woolworth's, Kress, and Thalhimers.[14]

Veteran journalist Virginius Dabney offered a white Virginian's assessment in an editorial in the *Richmond Times-Dispatch* titled "Who Is Defying the Law Now?" For Dabney, the questions were also very clear, but the answers very different. "Store proprietors in Virginia have every legal right to serve any type of customer they wish, and to refuse to serve any customer. Privately operated establishments are not subject to constitutional mandates or to court rulings which apply to tax-supported agencies or institutions."[15]

Dabney stretched to validate the arrests of the thirty-four: "Arrests of Negroes who seek to enter restaurants reserved for whites are in accordance with recent court rulings. The latest such ruling was in the Delaware Supreme Court on January 11. It dismissed a suit brought by Negroes demanding service in a Wilmington restaurant. The United States Circuit Court of Appeals for this circuit on July 16, 1959, dismissed a suit by a Negro attorney against an Alexandria restaurant which had denied him service." Then he turned the question of moral right against the protesters. They were "trying to enter establishments where they have no legal right to go," he wrote. "In trying to enter restaurants in Richmond and other Virginia cities from which they have been banned by the proprietors, Negroes are wide open to prosecution. Other Negroes who back them up by picketing establishments which do not serve Negroes in their restaurants are in the position of lending moral support to law violators."

"The people of the Old Dominion"—as Dabney termed white Virginians—had a legal right to resist desegregation. Black Virginians, it seemed, did not have the same right to resist segregation: "The Virginia state government and the people of the Old Dominion were severely assailed for years by the NAACP for 'defying the law,' when they exercised their *legal* prerogatives in connection with the Supreme Court's school decision of 1954. They were not defying the law at all, but that is exactly what the Negroes who are entering white restaurants are doing. Will the NAACP tell them to stop, or will it encourage them and thereby convict itself of rank hypocrisy?"

White Richmonders expressed various kinds of discomfort at the way things were going. They didn't like the sit-ins, they didn't necessarily like the official response to the sit-ins, and they didn't at all like some other things. While rejecting the students' constitutional argument, "whatever grievances they may have on the grounds of custom," the editorial page of the *Richmond News Leader* observed:

> Many a [white] Virginian must have felt a tinge of wry regret at the state of things as they are, in reading of Saturday's "sitdowns" by Negro students in Richmond stores. Here were the colored students, in coats, white shirts, ties, and one of them was reading Goethe and one was taking notes from a biology text. And here, on the sidewalk outside, was a gang of white boys come to heckle, a ragtail rabble, slack-jawed, black-jacketed, grinning fit to kill, and some of them, God save the mark, were waving the proud and honored flag of the Southern States in the last war fought by gentlemen.[16]

New Antitrespass Legislation

Governor J. Lindsay Almond Jr. himself was no mere onlooker. On February 24 he recommended new antitrespass legislation to the General Assembly, which was in session at the time and took prompt action. The governor signed the three bills into law the next day, and they took immediate effect.

The laws provided penalties of up to a year in jail and a $1,000 fine for criminal trespass, including inciting or conspiring to trespass in a building from which the owner had given "proper notice" against the trespass. Almond might have been tentative in anticipation of judicial rejection of the laws, or perhaps he was simply emphasizing their immediate availability for stifling demonstrations against segregation, when he observed, "As of this moment, they are the law of the land."[17]

Legislators had read or heard about the meeting at which Oliver Hill and others had raised the possibility of picketing the General Assembly. As they acted, therefore, they were half expecting that demonstrations might take place at any time at the State Capitol itself. Until the Senate convened at noon, its gallery remained closed. And all day long, reported a newspaper, "as an extra security precaution, uniformed state troopers stood guard near the House and Senate doorways and galleries." No demonstrators appeared, however.[18]

The events in Richmond resonated in Prince Edward County. There, Rev. L. Francis Griffin, community leader in the fight against school segregation (see chapter 4), attacked the antitrespass legislation that the Virginia General Assembly had hastily adopted to deal with sit-ins. "The natural outcome of a totalitarian government," he said, "is to put people in jail who do not agree with the dictators." [19]

Don't Shop Where You Can't Eat

On Thursday, February 25—the morning after the big rally at the Fifth Street Baptist Church—the protests continued. Outside of the Thalhimers store, the pickets walked. Rain fell much of the day, and most of the protesters carried umbrellas. Students continued to urge black patrons who approached the store to "turn in their credit cards and stop shopping there." [20]

That same day the new committee met and named Rev. P. B. Walker, pastor at the Third Street Bethel A.M.E. Church, the temporary chairman. Speaking for the committee, Pastor Walker explained that the group had no intention of taking the movement over. The protest against segregated eating facilities had begun with the students, he said, and it should remain with them. Keep up the protest, he said, though be sure to "be orderly and respectful of other people."

Pickets were back on duty Friday. In the afternoon they were joined by Rev. Wyatt Tee Walker, pastor at the black Gillfield Baptist Church in Petersburg, and 'his wife. Walker explained that "I'm here because I'm in sympathy with the students." He further explained to the predominantly white readership of the *Times-Dispatch* that he believed in this kind of protest, nonviolent direct action, as a means of achieving social change. It provided a means, he said, for blacks to draw attention to their struggle, to the discriminatory conditions that they experienced and their intent to change those conditions. [21]

On the same day a four-hour meeting took place at the Central YMCA among about twenty-five Richmond leaders—retail merchants, black preachers, and white ministers—to discuss the developments. The white ministers had taken the lead in organizing what the *Times-Dispatch* reporter called "the peace move, which went on behind the scenes for most of this week." One minister explained, "We want to see what we can do to bring good out of this situation."

That evening, plans were announced for another mass meeting. This one would take place at 12:45 Sunday afternoon at Cedar Street Memorial Baptist Church, and Oliver Hill would be speaking. Dr. Benjamin W. Robertson, pastor of the host church, explained that the meeting would give people in the Church Hill area "an opportunity to better understand the plan of the Negroes regarding the sitdowns and the picketing."

On Saturday, February 27, Virginia's NAACP leaders demonstrated their solidarity with the student protesters. The day began like any other that week, with students from Virginia Union showing up at Thalhimers at midmorning to begin picketing. Meantime, about sixty presidents of local branches of the NAACP met for about three hours at the state headquarters in Richmond to discuss the demonstrations. Around 4:30 that afternoon, about twenty of them walked down Broad Street to Thalhimers, where they worked their way into the picket line and took the students' places. Robert D. Robertson of Norfolk, the state president of the NAACP, led the twenty. He carried a large sign that said, "We are in full support of the students," and he explained to a reporter that their action was intended to display "our support and solidarity" with them.[22]

After the march the twenty returned to the NAACP headquarters. Asked there about the new antitrespass laws, Robertson answered that he did not see any effect on the demonstrations: "I don't think the new laws are going to stop Negroes from seeking their constitutional rights." And a black minister stated his expectation that the new laws were headed toward an early test in the courts.[23]

The Thalhimers Thirty-Four Go on Trial

The first contingent of the Thalhimers Thirty-Four to go on trial— Marise L. Ellison, Gordon Coleman, Milton Johnson, and Frank Pinkston —faced Judge Harold C. Maurice in police court on Friday, March 11. Their lawyers were Oliver W. Hill, Martin A. Martin, and Clarence W. Newsome. The defendants and their attorneys tried to show that race had been the governing consideration behind the arrests. Judge Maurice sustained Commonwealth's Attorney James B. Wilkinson's objections and prevented any such testimony from being introduced. As the *Afro American*'s headline put it, "'Why?' Is Touchy."[24]

The principal witness against the four was Newman B. Hamblett, vice president and operating manager at the Thalhimers store. He testified that the students had been in the restaurant area on the fourth floor and that after asking them to leave the store, he had authorized trespass warrants to be issued against them. He conceded that the store had been open at the time and that when the arrests took place, there had been at least fifty other patrons on that floor.

Attorney Martin asked, "Well, what was this particular person doing that was different from any other patron?" The prosecution objected. "What he was doing is irrelevant. He is not charged with disorderly conduct, only with trespassing. Testimony is that he was asked to leave the premises of a private corporation and he refused to do so, which makes him guilty of trespassing under the Virginia code. No reason for his being asked to leave is required." Judge Maurice sustained the objection.[25]

Martin tried again. Was he doing "anything" in any way "disorderly"? "No." "Then why did you ask him to leave?" Objection. Sustained. "Did you ask any other person to leave?" Objection. Sustained. "Did you ask any white persons to leave?" Objection. Sustained. "Were all the persons you asked to leave colored?" Now the judge objected. "This is not a racial issue." At such a preposterous notion, as it seemed to them, a number of African Americans in the courtroom laughed.

Unable to get answers on the record to these and similar questions, Martin argued that "the store was open for public business, and this man was a business invitee." He was only doing what other such business invitees were doing in the store, and "no one had any business inviting him out." Martin concluded the thought and established the point that he anticipated would be the basis for an appeal of his clients' convictions: "And just because he failed to leave, being ordered to without rhyme or reason, he was arrested. I maintain that this is a violation of his legal and constitutional rights, and that he is being denied equal protection of the law."

Martin's colleague, Oliver Hill, elaborated the argument and pointed toward another clause in the Fourteenth Amendment. "We are not attacking the constitutionality of the trespass statute. If someone goes into a store and does something that he should not do, something that affects the operation of the business, certainly the law is applicable." That, Hill contended, was not the case here. "What action of this defendant," he wanted to know, "was different from the action of other customers there at the time? I submit that in denying us development of that situation, you are denying him due process."

The trials of the Thalhimers Thirty-Four continued. On Tuesday, March 15, for example, another six Virginia Union students were convicted and fined $20 each. The ritual unfolded much as the earlier rendition had, with the students' lawyers seeking to introduce race as the reason for the arrests and the judge upholding the prosecution's objections that the only reason relevant to the proceedings was that they had failed to leave the store when asked to do so. Seven more students faced charges on March 24. These seven—among them Woodrow Grant, Elizabeth Johnson, and her brother, Ford T. Johnson Jr.—had been at the soda fountain and lunch counter on the first floor, not the restaurant or tea room on the fourth floor.[26]

The Thalhimers Thirty-Four appealed their convictions to the Virginia Supreme Court. Not for many months would they learn the results. In the meantime, sit-ins persisted in Richmond and in many other communities across Virginia. When and where might actual desegregation take place? The demonstrators' main objective, after all, had been to change the ways business was conducted and life was lived in Virginia, not spend time in court, pay fines, or go to jail.

The Virginia Supreme Court

On April 24, 1961, the Virginia Supreme Court upheld the convictions of Raymond B. Randolph Jr., Ford Tucker Johnson Jr., and the other thirty-two people who had been arrested on February 22, 1960, for sitting in at the Thalhimers store in downtown Richmond. Proprietors could decide, "on purely personal grounds," whether to accept or reject customers. Writing for the court (and quoting with approval from a previous statement), Chief Justice John W. Eggleston declared, "It is 'well settled that, although the general public have an implied license to enter a retail store, the proprietor is at liberty to revoke this license at any time as to any individual, and to eject such individual from the store if he refuses to leave when requested to do so.'"[27]

The Virginia Supreme Court said, on one page, about the Thalhimers Thirty-Four, "Because of their race they were refused service at these facilities." It then said, on the next page, about Raymond Randolph: "There is no evidence to support his contention that he was arrested because of his 'race or color.' On the contrary, the evidence shows that he was arrested because he remained upon the store premises after having been forbidden to do so by [Ben] Ames [the personnel manager], the duly authorized agent of the owner or custodian."[28]

Refusing to leave when asked to, Randolph violated a state trespass statute. "It would, indeed," the court concluded, "be an anomalous situation to say that the proprietor of a privately owned and operated business may lawfully use reasonable force to eject a trespasser from his premises and yet may not invoke judicial process to protect his rights." State action had in no way, therefore, been employed in violation of Randolph's constitutional rights under the Fourteenth Amendment. In refusing to serve him and then refusing to permit him to stay on the premises, Thalhimers had "violated none of his constitutional rights," and thus the lower court's judgment was "plainly right."[29]

By April 1961 Thalhimers had for some time been seating customers at its eating facilities without regard to race. The Thalhimers Thirty-Four had achieved their objective in desegregating those facilities. But according to the Virginia Supreme Court, they remained guilty of trespass. They planned an appeal to the U.S. Supreme Court.[30]

Sit-in Cases and the U.S. Supreme Court

The U.S. Supreme Court faced dozens of sit-in cases in the early 1960s. The first wave preceded the case of the Thalhimers Thirty-Four. In *Garner* v. *Louisiana* and two other cases from Louisiana, decided in December 1961, the Supreme Court overturned all the convictions. Trespass was not at issue, and property rights remained secure; a police officer had arrested the students without any request from the drugstore owner, who simply declined to serve them. Chief Justice Earl Warren wrote the opinion of the Court, that there was not enough evidence to convict the demonstrators.[31]

Though there were no dissents from Warren's opinion, the Court's apparent unanimity masked a divergence in perspectives that made the decisions in subsequent sit-in cases by no means certain. Justices William O. Douglas, Felix Frankfurter, and John Marshall Harlan concurred in the outcome, but each for a different reason and with a separate opinion. Justice Frankfurter saw no evidence of a crime, for the protesters' "mere presence" could not justify a guilty verdict for "disturbing the peace." Justice Harlan saw an issue of demonstrators' First Amendment freedom of political expression, provided they had the owner's consent to be there. Justice Douglas thought that, given the degree of whites' commitment to segregation in Louisiana, the demonstrators surely threatened the peace by their peaceful action, so there was sufficient evidence to sustain the convictions. Yet he insisted that the protests had occurred in places of public accommodation; the sit-in participants had a right to be there to seek and get service; and the actions of the police in arresting them, and of the courts in convicting them, constituted state action in violation of the equal protection clause of the Fourteenth Amendment.

The early cases supplied straws in the wind, but no conclusive direction that the Court might follow in *Randolph* v. *Virginia*. Would the Court even take the case of the Thalhimers Thirty-Four? If it did, how would it rule? Those questions remained hanging, for the answers did not come until much later: the ruling was handed down in June 1963. In the meantime, participants in the Civil Rights movement in the Richmond area pushed ahead both in their civil rights activities and in their daily lives.

Courtroom Segregation: *Wells* v. *Gilliam* (1961)

Black Virginians, like their counterparts across the South in the early 1960s, targeted racial segregation wherever they encountered it in public places, whether in public schools, on public transportation, or at lunch counters. In some cases they took legal action against segregation. In other cases they took direct action, were arrested, and ended up in court anyway.

In court they often encountered segregation yet again in the racially separate seating arrangements that characterized many southern courtrooms. If they challenged the legitimacy of such arrangements, they raised new questions of what the Constitution, particularly the Fourteenth Amendment, permitted or required in the administration of justice.

One such case came out of Petersburg, Virginia. In 1961 George Wells and other black residents of Petersburg brought action in federal court against Judge Herbert B. Gilliam. They sought a declaratory judgment and a permanent injunction against a requirement that the spectator area be segregated during court proceedings in the Petersburg Municipal Court. Their case was heard in Richmond in the U.S. District Court for the Eastern District of Virginia.[32]

The district court concluded that there was "no separation of the races in the area before the bench or the bar of the Court." To the contrary, litigants, lawyers, and witnesses alike sat in an unsegregated manner when their case was before the court. By contrast, in the area of the courtroom "reserved for spectators and those awaiting the call of their business before the court," seating was assigned on the basis of race. Blacks sat on one side, whites on the other, with equal space on each side.[33]

George Wells and his fellow plaintiffs knew that this rule was enforced. More than once, Judge Gilliam had had occasion to order them to move out of the section reserved for whites. The district court found that whites, too, were subject to such orders. "Separate but equal" was alive and well in Petersburg. "The same order and requirement has been enforced in the case of all other citizens, white and Negro alike."[34]

All parties recognized that not all judges and courtrooms in Virginia required segregated sitting. Nothing in the laws—the statutes of Virginia or the ordinances of Petersburg—required segregated seating in courtrooms. In fact, many courts in the Old Dominion, including the Virginia Supreme Court, did not require such segregation. According to the district court, however, "whether other courts of Virginia deem it necessary or unnecessary to promulgate a similar order is immaterial." Arguments that a requirement of segregation constituted a "mockery of justice" or was "degrading and shameful" did not move the federal judges from their conviction that they had no call to interfere in Judge Gilliam's courtroom.[35]

The district court remained unimpressed with the arguments against the way Judge Gilliam ran his court. Nothing the judges heard convinced them that they should reconsider their assumption—they considered it "axiomatic"—that "a judge has control of his court room and the conduct of those attending his court." Regarding people who attended court as spectators, the court concluded, "If they have the right to determine where they sit, they have the right to applaud, the right to take pictures, and many other similar rights; carried to the extreme, proper court room decorum and order would be non-existent." The judge was captain of his ship, and—as of June 1, 1961, according to the U.S. District Court for the Eastern District of Virginia—the Fourteenth Amendment had no power to govern such matters.[36]

To Sit? Where to Sit?

Ford T. Johnson Jr. was living at home in Richmond and was in his final term at Virginia Union University in the spring of 1962 when he went for a drive one day in the family car. He had no idea that he was about to be arrested. He did not know, he later said, that the license tags had expired or that the new tags were in the car waiting to be put on; his sister later razzed him for being arrested for not having something on his car that was sitting there in the car with him.[37] Nor did he then know that in the next two years, his name would reach the U.S. Supreme Court in two separate cases.

Ford Johnson was cited by a police officer that day for driving with expired tags and without a driver's permit. Johnson appeared in traffic court, at Eleventh Street and Broad, on the afternoon of April 27. Traffic court took place in the same building, even the same room, as police court, but in the afternoons rather than the mornings, so it was Johnson's second time in that room, two years after his trial as a member of the Thalhimers Thirty-Four.[38]

Hoping to "get the thing over with" with as little fuss as possible, he later recalled, he took a seat near the back, on the window side of the courtroom. "I just sat down," he says, "in the first available seat." But then "this entire situation occurred." He noticed that court officials seemed troubled about something, though he could not tell what. The bailiff came over and asked him to leave his seat and move to the other side of the courtroom.

When Johnson did not immediately respond to this directive, the judge, Judge Herman A. Cooper, himself took action and called him to the front of the courtroom.[39]

Still unclear as to what he was doing that could be the cause of any concern, Johnson left his seat and went to the front of the courtroom. Judge Cooper then directed Johnson to "take a seat," more specifically to take a seat in the section of the courtroom reserved for African Americans. Directed to the other side of the courtroom from where he had been, Johnson began to realize that he was being asked to do something that he could not, and would not, do. For one thing, Ford T. Johnson Jr. had been one of the Thalhimers Thirty-Four, the students arrested two years earlier in the sit-ins in downtown Richmond. He was not primed to obey the order without putting up some kind of resistance, certainly not without hesitating, which itself could be, and was, construed as an offense against the authority of the court. Johnson was removed from the courtroom for about fifteen minutes before being brought back for trial on the traffic violations and the contempt citation. He was "summarily convicted of contempt," on the charge that he "would not be seated, but insisted on standing in front of the judge's bench so that other cases could not be heard." Judge Cooper imposed a $10 fine, which he suspended.[40]

Johnson has always held that he did not know, when he stepped into the courtroom that day, that the seating would be segregated. In his previous appearance in the same courtroom two years earlier, for his hearing on the Thalhimers sit-in, it had not been so. Moreover, while he understood the segregated ways of department stores and lunch counters, "it never occurred to [him] that the courtroom was segregated," too. In short, as he later put it, "There was no prior intent to go there and stage any demonstration" that day.[41]

But when he found out about the rules and was directed to follow them, he froze, caught between two impulses, "two sets of pressures." One was an inclination to do as he had been told, reinforced by any black southerner's education in the etiquette of segregation. Another, however, was a considerable emancipation from that ingrained tendency to follow the rules, "an interior propensity" according to which, especially "having been in court two years before," he "had clearly made the break from that world" of necessarily following the dictates of segregation.[42] He would not defy the court's authority by returning to the white section, but he could not submit to unrighteous authority and go take a seat in the black section. So he moved aside and then just stood.

Test Case?

The traffic violation could be handled in traffic court—he was fined $20 and that was that—but the citation for contempt lived on. The various NAACP lawyers in Richmond differed in their views as to whether this case could serve as the vehicle for a constitutional challenge. They needed a "pure" case, one that raised the constitutional question directly. The contempt citation satisfied one condition. Dr. Johnson later remembered that without that citation, "we would have had no leg to stand on." But was there anything about the encounter—anything about Johnson Jr.'s behavior, quite aside from his racial identity—that might have justified the citation? His son had not raised his voice, or kicked a chair, or done anything of the sort to register a challenge to the judge's authority, except to refuse to sit in the "colored" section. Yet, might the fact that he had folded his arms be construed in itself as an act of defiance? Roland D. Ealey later recalled that he had argued—successfully—that the case was clean enough and that, moreover, the Johnsons were willing litigants. The decision was made. Now was the time; this was the case.[43]

Not long after young Johnson's adventure in traffic court, W. Lester Banks, executive secretary of the state NAACP, called the Johnson household to express an interest in young Johnson's case. For one thing, the elder Johnson, a dentist in Richmond, had been actively involved with the local NAACP chapter. For another, courtroom segregation had long rankled black Richmonders. The previous year, in fact, a delegation among the Richmond lawyers in the Old Dominion Bar Association had requested an end to the practice. Moreover, the group had been considering the issue as one that might serve to recruit new members. Banks wanted to pursue the possibility that this particular case might prove the test case to challenge such segregation. He obtained the Johnsons' consent.[44]

Johnson appealed his conviction to the Hustings Court of the City of Richmond. In a written brief as well as in oral argument, his lawyers contended that Johnson's conviction in traffic court had violated his rights under both the due process clause and the equal protection clause of the Fourteenth Amendment. Johnson, it was claimed, was being "punished for violation of a racial segregation rule."[45]

At the hustings court on Monday, June 18, witnesses all agreed that Johnson had not been making any commotion. L. B. Turner, the bailiff who had asked him to leave his seat, explained: "I asked him to move. He wouldn't move so the judge told me to tell him to come forward. Then he refused to sit down where the judge directed, so the judge said to lock him up." As for Johnson, he testified that, yes, he had been told, more than once, to move to the other section and had failed to do so, but no, he had not continued to stand in front of the judge. Rather he had taken several steps away over "near the counsel table." The judge "told me again to sit down. I told him I preferred to stand. I stood there and crossed my arms, but it was not in any defiant manner."[46]

The hustings court determined that "the sole issue" was one of "contempt, and not whether the Traffic Court . . . was segregated." Johnson was again convicted.[47]

Johnson and his attorneys did not give up. Next stop was the Virginia Supreme Court. Johnson's lawyers, in their notice of appeal to that court, insisted that "there was no evidence of any misbehavior or disorderly conduct" by Johnson, that "he was requested to move his seat because of his race and color," and that "the real basis of the charge against him" was "his refusal to so move." In the petition for a writ of error, they again argued from both due process and equal protection that Johnson's Fourteenth Amendment rights were being violated. The state, on the other hand, relied in part on the federal court decision in *Wells* v. *Gilliam* to argue that Johnson's case had no merit.[48]

On October 5 the Virginia Supreme Court determined that the judgment of the hustings court was "plainly right." Johnson's petition for review was denied, his conviction affirmed.[49] The stops in June and October left intact the outcome back in April. Courts could segregate their courtrooms, and people in those courtrooms had to obey the orders of court officers enforcing such segregation.

Would the U.S. Supreme Court agree to review the case? Johnson's attorneys hoped so. Advised that they planned such an appeal, the Virginia Supreme Court stayed the enforcement of its ruling for three months, until January 3, 1963.

Johnson v. *Virginia* (1963)

On January 2 Ealey filed an appeal. In his petition for the nation's highest court to review the actions in the Virginia courts, he wrote, "This is a very plain and simple case of a criminal conviction based upon petitioner's refusal to obey a racial segregation rule in a city courtroom." Under the Fourteenth Amendment, he argued, a state could not enforce racial segregation on government property. The action of the courts surely qualified as "state action" under the Fourteenth Amendment. "Indeed," he continued, "racial distinctions in courts of law are particularly inimical to the American ideal of equal justice for all which is embodied in the equal protection clause of the Fourteenth Amendment." Johnson's "refusal to take a seat in the Negro section of the courtroom was justified since petitioner had a right to sit in a public courtroom on a nonsegregated basis. Therefore, petitioner's conduct could not be determined to be contempt of court except by the application of an unconstitutional segregation principle."[50]

Most of the justices agreed. Justice William O. Douglas's clerk summarized the state's argument:

> Resp. goes through all the motions of saying how important it is to maintain courtroom decorum etc. And how the Ct. was clearly exercising valid power etc. Then when resp. gets to the guts of the problem he reasons like this: 1) the 14th amend. gives citizens no rights, 2) thus pet[itione]r did not have the right to sit where he wanted to in the ct. 3) if he could sit where he wanted to he could clap—justice would then go to pot. 4) the ct. was merely keeping petr from doing what he had no right to do. To me, at least, it is obvious that the 14th amend. gives a person the right not to be discriminated against by the state on the grd. of race. Resp. concedes that the ct. here was merely upholding an old tradition of segregated cts.[51]

Justice Potter Stewart nonetheless wanted to deny the appeal. Johnson's case "involves internal arrangements in the courtroom," he said, and did not merit consideration. His eight brethren, by contrast, found Ealey's arguments compelling. On April 29 they announced their decision, which reversed the state courts and directed that Johnson recover $100 from the state of Virginia for his costs.[52]

After reviewing the uncontested facts about Johnson's behavior the previous year, the Court declared, "It is clear from the totality of circumstances, and particularly the fact that the petitioner was peaceably seated in the section reserved for whites before being summoned to the bench, that the arrest and conviction rested entirely on the refusal to comply with the segregated seating requirements imposed in this particular courtroom." Then came the conclusion, stated in sweeping language. "Such a conviction cannot stand, for it is no longer open to question that a State may not constitutionally require segregation of public facilities." With more specific reference to the facts in Johnson's case, the Court asserted that "State-compelled segregation in a court of justice is a manifest violation of the State's duty to deny no one the equal protection of its laws."

In the News

The *New York Times* announced the news—on page one, above the fold—the next day in a story by Anthony Lewis, "High Court Bars Any Segregation in a Courtroom." The *Richmond Times-Dispatch* did much the same, though below the fold.[53]

The *Richmond Afro American* was jubilant. In addition to a news story, it published an editorial, "The Court Shows Its Impatience." "Almost a year to the day after he was convicted for contempt in refusing to be seated in a segregated section of traffic court," it said, "a 20-year-old Freedom Fighter, Ford T. Johnson of Richmond, now a Peace Corps worker, saw his stand vindicated." The nation's high court "took only three sentences to declare this ancient Dixie custom 'a manifest violation of the state's duty to deny no one the equal protection of the laws.'"[54]

The black voice of Virginia's capital brought out what it saw as the larger implications of the court's decision, which it termed "a welcome and a historic decision, advancing by another giant step the century-old struggle to wipe out the terrible wrongs perpetrated under the legal illusion of 'separate but equal.' The decision is certain to have a widespread impact on police and trial courts in the belt of Confederate states from Virginia to Texas. But more important than the abrupt ruling against this long injustice practiced in what are supposed to be chambers of impartial justice, was the court's one-sentence death knell pronounced on all enforced segregation of public facilities." The paper went on to note that according to the Supreme Court, it was "no longer open to question that a state may not constitutionally require segregation of public facilities.' This clearly means that the nation's highest court has not only frowned upon segregated seating in courtrooms, but is serving blunt notice that such quaint Southern customs as racially separate drinking fountains, restrooms, tax windows and even prison cells stand in violation of the Constitution."

Black southerners could see that the tide of history had changed direction. What had been law for so long no longer was. The editorial writer raised his voice another octave: "That the court chose to hand down this sweeping decision buried in a bundle of orders was but one more indication of the high tribunal's growing irritation and impatience with the Southern refusal to accept as final its oft-pronounced new racial order of things. That impatience is likely to become shorter and shorter as these states continue their contemptuous practice of needless and endless appeals of cases where constitutional questions clearly are no longer at issue.

This Dixie game of delay by appeal is rapidly running out its course." Even white southerners, the paper concluded, "must finally realize that the United States Constitution must have as much meaning in Mississippi as it does in Minnesota or it has no meaning at all."

The stakes were high, the paper was saying. There appeared to be considerable grounds for optimism. Ford Johnson's victory had brought a good day to black southerners everywhere. His resistance had led to a pronouncement by the U.S. Supreme Court that went far to undercut segregation in all government facilities. The rationale of *Plessy* v. *Ferguson* and "separate but equal" had been rebuffed yet again. The logic of *Brown* v. *Board of Education* continued to rumble through time and space.

Randolph v. *Virginia*

On May 20, 1963, three weeks after the *Johnson* decision, the Supreme Court announced its decisions in a number of other civil rights cases. *Peterson* v. *City of Greenville* proved to be the key case in a cluster of sit-in decisions handed down in that spring.

On August 9, 1960, ten young African Americans had entered the S. H. Kress chain store in Greenville, South Carolina, and taken seats at the lunch counter. Police were called, the lunch counter was declared closed, and the ten were asked to leave. When they kept their seats, they were arrested. Subsequently tried and convicted of violating a state trespass statute, they had taken their appeal to the U.S. Supreme Court. There it was held that the Fourteenth Amendment rights of the ten had been violated. On account of their race, the authority of the state had been called upon to arrest them and remove them from the lunch counter. Thus, said the Supreme Court, they had been denied the equal protection of the laws.[55]

On May 20, the day the *Peterson* decision was handed down, the Court also issued rulings in a variety of similar cases. Three of these came from Birmingham, Alabama; New Orleans, Louisiana; and Durham, North Carolina. Another—*Wright* v. *Georgia*—related to six young black men who had been "convicted of breach of the peace for peacefully playing basketball in a public park in Savannah, Georgia, on the early afternoon of Monday, January 23, 1961," a park "owned and operated by the city for recreational purposes" and "customarily used only by whites."[56]

Each of the cases had local attorneys as well as national NAACP lawyers. Once the organization had decided to join in the litigation, the participation was vigorous and coordinated. In the case of the Thalhimers Thirty-Four, *Randolph* v. *Virginia*, the local attorneys were—as they had been from the beginning—Martin A. Martin and Clarence A. Newsome. They were assisted by national NAACP lawyers Jack Greenberg and James M. Nabritt III, who along with Constance Baker Motley all participated in *Wright* v. *Georgia* and *Peterson* v. *City of Greenville*.[57]

The various decisions in *Peterson* and the other cases elicited widely varying responses. The *Times-Dispatch* saw an ominous trend; the *Afro American* was, once again, jubilant.[58]

On June 10—six weeks after the Supreme Court announced its decision in *Johnson* v. *Virginia* and three weeks after *Peterson*—it did the same in *Randolph* v. *Virginia*. As with *Johnson* v. *Virginia*, the opinion was unsigned, and it was even shorter. In effect, the Court threw out the convictions of the Thalhimers Thirty-Four: "The petition for writ of certiorari is granted, the judgments are vacated and the case is remanded to the Supreme Court of Appeals of Virginia for reconsideration in light of *Peterson* v. *City of Greenville*."[59]

In Richmond the decision in *Randolph* came as less of a surprise than it might have had it come earlier and accompanied the cluster of cases that included *Peterson*.[60] Again, a black Virginian's name was on the title to a federal case of constitutional law in which the proponents of change in the racial order obtained a decision that upheld their right to act in the way they had.

Campaigning against Segregated Movies—and More

Sit-ins and other demonstrations rose and fell and rose again in the many months beginning in February 1960. After segregated lunch counters, segregated movie theaters were a central target, but there were others, too. By 1963 efforts in Richmond looked to secure the desegregation of two facilities that the city leased to an enterprise that enforced the state law requiring segregated seating: the Mosque, an auditorium and entertainment center in downtown Richmond, and Parker Field, a baseball field.

Those efforts revealed that sit-ins and picket lines were not the only ways to seek and secure desegregation. Two members of the group that had formed to support the Thalhimers Thirty-Four filed suits against segregation at the two facilities. J. Rupert Picott led the way on the Mosque, and Felix J. Brown did so regarding Parker Field.

Roland D. Ealey, who had taken Ford T. Johnson's courtroom segregation case to the U.S. Supreme Court, told the *Afro American* in May 1963 that he did not see how segregation could persist at the city facilities.

Ealey tied together the courtroom case, the sit-in cases, and a case regarding the Mosque. As he said, "In effect, the Supreme Court has ruled that race may not be a determin[ing] factor as to with whom anyone may associate at any cultural assembly. It said state powers may not be used to enforce segregation, the same thing it said in the restrictive covenant cases [*Shelley* v. *Kraemer*]. I think that the basis for the court ruling Tuesday was the Johnson versus Virginia case in which it spelled out the fact that in any situation where there is governmental control, there cannot be racial discrimination."[61]

Some people expected a decision on June 10 from the state supreme court in the cases involving segregation at Parker Field and the Mosque. But no decision in the cases came down that day. Impatient to finish the job, three black Virginians resorted to informal negotiation to spur the process along. The next day (Tuesday, June 11), Windred Mundle, Dr. J. Rupert Picott, and H. H. Scott met with the new owner of the Richmond Virginians baseball team, Romeo J. Champagne. At that meeting Champagne declared a new policy of open seating at the stadium. With that, Mundle and Picott bought tickets for a game that evening with Richmond playing Indianapolis.[62]

The *Afro American* was able to report, "The Parker Field baseball park is now desegregated." Desegregation came in time for much of the 1963 season, "with no trouble at all," according to a city official, and the anticipated court decision was handed down in September, invalidating segregation at the city's facilities. In reaching its decision, as Ealey had forecast, the Virginia court relied in part on *Johnson* v. *Virginia* as well as such cases as *Peterson* and *Randolph*.[63]

Throughout Virginia the efforts against segregation continued, sometimes with the results that had been sought, sometimes not. In Petersburg students demonstrated against segregated movie theaters and were arrested for it. The first three to be tried and convicted, fined $25, and given suspended thirty-day jail terms were high school student Roland L. Sherrod, younger brother of Charles Sherrod, and two undergraduates at Virginia State College. In the Lynchburg area a number of lunch counters began desegregated service in May, and a week later ten restaurants "opened their doors to all races for the first time." Even the city of Danville saw various drugstores and restaurants begin desegregated service, though Danville displayed in various ways the degree to which it was Virginia's nearest thing to Birmingham, Alabama, and violence was visited on demonstrators in mid-1963.[64]

Sit-ins and the Urban Upper South, 1960–63

The 1960s sit-ins reached back to the 1930s for one aspect of their inspiration. In the Great Depression decade, many American cities had witnessed black "Don't Buy Where You Can't Work" protests.[65] In the 1960 movement by the Virginia Union students in Richmond—and by their better-known counterparts elsewhere—the terms of the protest had changed from "Don't shop where you can't work" to "Don't shop where you can't eat."

The Civil Rights movement consisted of a host of people and events. Across the South in the early 1960s, people set out to "sit in" at various locations to challenge segregation laws and practices. Many of them found themselves arrested, and thus their cases came to court. Many cases that came before the courts in those years, in turn, led to decisions that changed the ways Americans lived their lives.

Ford Johnson's actions in the winter of 1960 were deliberate and collective, and they led to changes: in the ways Thalhimers (and other department stores as well as drugstores) did business; in the ways the U.S. Supreme Court interpreted the U.S. Constitution. Ford Johnson's actions in the spring of 1962 were more spontaneous as well as individual, and they, too, led to changes: in the ways the Richmond city traffic court did its business; and again, in the ways the U.S. Supreme Court interpreted the U.S. Constitution. Events that appeared mundane could have transforming consequences. As Ford Johnson Jr. later put the matter, his courtroom case was "just one piece of the puzzle" as black southerners went about the business of "desegregating a whole range of things."[66]

On the one hand, in no decision did the Court squarely face the central issues or declare a right to protest against segregation. On the other, in none of the cases that came out of the events of 1960 through 1963 did it uphold the prosecutions of sit-in demonstrators. Of course, nobody involved in the demonstrations could have known what would be the result, whether in terms of criminal prosecution or changes in segregation practices.

In the middle months of 1963, the demonstrators obtained one victory after another. Some came in such actions as the movie protests and led to "voluntary" desegregation of public establishments. Others, including Ford Johnson's two cases before the U.S. Supreme Court, brought court decisions that supported their actions. Many Virginians, white as well as black, went to the nation's capital in August 1963. There they presented a human petition on August 28 in the form of the huge "March on Washington for Jobs and Freedom," which gave a big push toward passage of the Civil Rights Act of 1964—which in turn largely ended the practices that had led to the sit-ins.[67]

Even before the march on Washington, Virginia's capital had undergone considerable change in the three years since February 1960. A wide range of actions by a myriad of individuals had led to major shifts in private behavior and public law. Ford Johnson's actions had contributed to two Supreme Court decisions during spring 1963 that pushed the process of desegregation along. As his father so proudly said three decades later, *Johnson* v. *Virginia* "desegregated the nation's courtrooms." Wherever the judicial captains of their ships had continued into 1963 to exercise the authority of law in separating people in a courtroom according to racial identity, they lost that authority.

As for lunch counters and similar establishments in the service sector of the private sphere, the 1964 Civil Rights Act changed the law of public accommodations throughout the South, and the season for sit-ins had largely passed. In a case in December 1964, a narrow majority on the Court ruled that convictions had to be thrown out if they could not have been secured had the new civil rights act existed at the time of the arrests. Writing for the Court majority, Justice Tom C. Clark noted that the 1964 Civil Rights Act had substituted "a right for a crime."[68]

Ford T. Johnson and *Johnson* v. *Virginia*

Ford Johnson was not in the country when the Supreme Court's decision came down. In between the original citation for contempt in April 1962 and the decision in hustings court two months later, he had graduated from Virginia Union University. The commencement speaker that year was black historian John Hope Franklin. And a new program, inaugurated the year before during John F. Kennedy's first year in the White House, drew Johnson overseas to Africa. On the same day in 1961 that the Virginia Supreme Court upheld Johnson's conviction for the Thalhimers sit-in, Peace Corps director R. Sargent Shriver said, while in Accra, Ghana, that he was finding so much demand for Peace Corps volunteers that the agency might not be able to meet the demand.[69]

Two years later, on the job with the Peace Corps in Ghana, Johnson was called by his supervisor and asked if he knew he was on the front page of the *New York Times*. Johnson figured that the case of the Thalhimers Thirty-Four had finally been decided, and evidently they had won their appeal to the nation's high court. As it happened, the Court had not yet decided that case.[70]

What had been decided was the case of the man who had refused to sit as directed in a segregated courtroom, not the case of the man who had refused not to sit in a whites-only cafeteria. Either way, Ford Johnson had declined the dictates of the practice of segregated seating. Either way, many months later, the U.S. Supreme Court was telling him he had had a constitutional right to do as he did.

In going to Ghana, Johnson had been, in part, buying time before making a final decision whether to head off to dental school. Not only was his father a dentist, but he himself "got caught up in the Sputnik thing," so he had studied math and science. But his father had said something to the effect that to be a dentist, he "had to learn all the bones before he could focus on the teeth," and increasingly Johnson Jr. knew that neither science nor medicine was what he wanted to do. The news about the Supreme Court and the *New York Times* made something click that changed his career course. Instead of going to medical school, he applied to law school, and it was in law school that he enrolled upon his return to the States.[71]

The time came when, as a student at Harvard Law School, he was asked in class by a professor to review the case of *Johnson* v. *Virginia*. The reported decision was brief and revealed little detail in fact or argument. Johnson's account went beyond the material available there; he was "bringing in some facts that were not apparent from the record," he has since recalled. Tell us, Mr. Johnson, he was asked, how do you know these other things about the case? Because, he replied, I am that Mr. Johnson.[72]

6

Racial Identity and the Crime of Marriage

The View from Twentieth-Century Virginia

ONE NIGHT IN JULY 1958, TWO NEWLYWEDS SUDDENLY AWOKE AT their home in Caroline County, Virginia, startled by the sound of men in their room and the glare of flashlights on their faces. One of the three intruders demanded to know who they were and what they were doing in bed together. Mildred Loving murmured, "I'm his wife," and Richard Loving pointed to a marriage certificate hanging on the wall. "That's no good here," retorted the trio's leader, Sheriff R. Garnett Brooks. The young couple were arrested and jailed.[1]

Mildred Jeter and Richard Loving had been seeing each other for several years, and during the spring of 1958 they determined that the time had come for them to marry. They had the impression that they could not have their wedding in Virginia, but he thought they would be all right if they went to the District of Columbia. They drove the hundred miles north to the nation's capital, where they had their ceremony; returned to the community where they had lived all their lives; and moved in with her parents.

The issue that had given him pause and led to their trip to the big city—and the problem that led to their arrest that summer night—was that Richard Loving was Caucasian, and Mildred Jeter was not. It was no crime in Virginia to be white or black, male or female. But it was a crime for two people to marry if one of them was white and the other not. Marrying in violation of Virginia's law against interracial marriage could bring a term in the state penitentiary for at least one year and for as long as five years.

Other Virginians had spent years in prison for breaking that law, and now it looked like two more people would join their ranks. The Lovings were terrified at the prospect. They were free while awaiting their trial, but a trial nonetheless loomed. Not only was there no way to turn the clock back to May, they would not have wanted to. They wanted to be married, and they wanted to live together in peace in their rural community. Richard Loving had thought they could do both if they went out of state to marry, but they discovered that the same law banning their getting married in Virginia also outlawed their living together there as an interracial married couple, expressly so if they had briefly left the state to evade the law that prevented their marrying each other in Virginia.

Virginia was by no means alone in maintaining a law—termed a "miscegenation" law—against marriages between people identified as white and other people, especially African Americans but sometimes also Asian Americans and Native Americans. From 1913 to 1948 thirty states had miscegenation laws on the books (map 1), and as late as 1958, when the Lovings were arrested, twenty-four of the forty-eight states retained such laws. The last of those states outside the South dropped theirs in 1965.[2] Retaining such laws were all seventeen states of the Deep South, the Upper South, and the Border South (map 2): all eleven states of the former Confederacy plus Delaware, Maryland, Kentucky, Missouri, Oklahoma, and West Virginia.

The prospect of successfully challenging the Virginia law's constitutionality was not bright, though court challenges had occasionally succeeded in other states. In the history of the Republic, four state supreme courts ruled against the constitutionality of a miscegenation law. During Reconstruction, in the 1870s, three states did so—Alabama, Louisiana, and Texas—before reversing themselves, restoring such statutes, and leaving them in place, where they remained until 1967. In 1948, by a 4–3 vote, the California Supreme Court did so, but no other state supreme court followed, in or out of the South.[3]

Before the Twentieth Century

The law under which the Lovings were charged in 1958 was called the Racial Integrity Act of 1924, but its antecedents reached back into Virginia's early years. As a colony Virginia enacted a law in 1691 that called for banishing any European American who married a Native American or an African American. The law was changed over the years, but penalties for black-white marriage persisted beyond the American Revolution, beyond the Civil War, and, indeed, as the Lovings found out, well into the twentieth century. The specific law that governed their behavior was enacted in 1878, long before they were born. As the Lovings' experience revealed, people did not always follow the law, but it had a way of being enforced.[4]

MAP 1. As late as 1948 thirty states maintained miscegenation laws. Eighteen states outside the South did not. (Courtesy John D. Boyer)

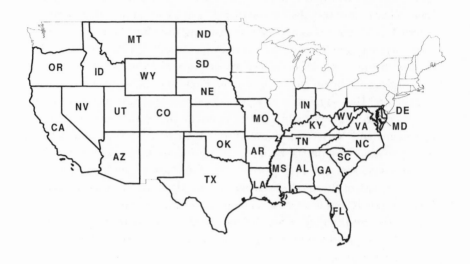

MAP 2. By 1966, on the eve of a Supreme Court decision overturning all miscegenation laws, only the seventeen southern states retained such laws. (Courtesy John D. Boyer)

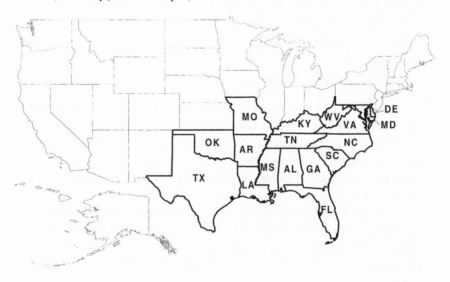

Before 1878 the Virginia law specifically targeted the white party to an interracial marriage. Since no black-white marriage could be valid, however, both parties to an interracial marriage could be prosecuted for living together outside marriage. The 1878 law made three major changes in the law of race and marriage in Virginia. It criminalized the behavior of both parties to a marriage between someone defined as white and anyone defined as black. And it converted the penalty from one taking property—the maximum penalty had been a $500 fine—to one taking liberty, with a term of two to five years in prison. Moreover, expressly going beyond criminalizing interracial marriages contracted in Virginia, the 1878 statute imposed the same new penalties on Virginians who went outside the state to evade the law and then returned to Virginia to live together as husband and wife.[5]

Prosecutions soon commenced under the new law. Edmund Kinney, a black man, married a white woman, Mary S. Hall, in Washington, D.C., in October 1878, and they then returned to their Virginia home in Hanover County. Convicted of violating the March 1878 statute against going out of state to get married, both parties were sentenced to five years at hard labor in the Virginia penitentiary.

Kinney petitioned U.S. district judge Robert W. Hughes for a writ of habeas corpus, but Judge Hughes rejected all constitutional grounds for intervention. What about the Fourteenth Amendment and its talk of privileges and immunities? Nowhere, declared Judge Hughes, did that amendment "forbid a state from abridging the privileges of its own citizens," a matter left to "the discretion of each state."[6]

Comity—one state's recognition of contracts entered into in another state—would require acceptance of most out-of-state marriages, but there were exceptions, said the judge: "marriages which are polygamous, incestuous, or contrary to public policy" and which had been "made the subject of penal enactments." Edmund Kinney was "a citizen of Virginia amenable to her laws." Though married in the District of Columbia, he brought back with him to Virginia "no other right in regard to the marriage which he made abroad than he took away. He cannot bring the marriage privileges of a citizen of the District of Columbia any more than he could those of a [polygamous] citizen of Utah, into Virginia, in violation of her laws."[7]

Judge Hughes also rejected the relevance of the Fourteenth Amendment's equal protection clause, which, he said, gave "no power to congress to interfere with the right of a state to regulate the domestic relations of its own citizens." He continued: "But even if it did require an equality of privileges, I do not see any discrimination against either race in a provision of law forbidding any white or colored from marrying another of the opposite color of skin. If it forbids a colored person from marrying a white, it equally forbids a white person from marrying a colored."[8]

"In the present case," Judge Hughes went on, "the white party to the marriage" was in prison, and so was "the colored person." Both had been prosecuted for the same crime, both convicted, and they had received equal punishment, so the judge saw no denial of equal protection. "I think it clear, therefore, that no provision of the fourteenth amendment has been violated by the state of Virginia in its prosecution of this petitioner."[9] It did not matter to the judge that their crime could just as well be seen as a consequence of their color, not their behavior.

Year after year, Virginia's penitentiary records showed the couple serving out their five-year sentences.[10]

The Supreme Court and Interracial Marriage

In a series of cases in the 1880s and 1890s, the U.S. Supreme Court made it clear that district judge Hughes had ruled in a way that would not be successfully challenged anytime soon.

In the early 1880s an Alabama court convicted Tony Pace and Mary Jane Cox, a black man and a white woman, for carrying on a sexual relationship, and the a statute made the offense far greater than if they had both been white or both black. (Had they married each other, they would have faced the same harsh penalty, a minimum of two years in the penitentiary system, as they did as an unmarried interracial couple.) They appealed their convictions, first to the Alabama Supreme Court and then to the U.S. Supreme Court, but they lost and then lost again. Writing for a unanimous U.S. Supreme Court, Justice Stephen J. Field rejected the argument that the Fourteenth Amendment's equal protection clause offered a shield against their being prosecuted under a law that made their racial identities a central part of the crime. The Alabama law treated the races in precisely the same manner, he said, in that it "applies the same punishment to both offenders, the white and the black," in an interracial relationship.[11]

The decision in *Pace* v. *Alabama* (1883) did not rule directly on a statute barring interracial marriage, yet its reasoning could have been applied —and was understood to apply—to such a statute. Nor was *Pace* the only decision by the U.S. Supreme Court in the 1880s that bolstered the constitutionality of miscegenation laws. In *Maynard* v. *Hill* (1888), a case that seemed to have nothing to do with race, the Court ruled that marriage "has always been subject to the control of the Legislature." Under the Constitution's full faith and credit clause, marriage might have qualified as a contract that could be safely transported across state lines—such as the marriage Edmund Kinney and Mary Hall thought they had imported into Virginia from Washington, D.C.—but the Court ruled otherwise. Regarding marriage, states ruled. There was no general law of the land, only what each state chose to recognize or reject, regardless of whether a marriage arose within its borders or elsewhere.[12]

Homer Plessy became famous to students of American constitutional history and American race relations as a result of his arrest for violating a Louisiana law, passed in 1890, that required African American passengers to take seats in a different passenger car than was set aside for whites when directed to do so by a railway conductor. Plessy challenged the Louisiana law, and his case went to the U.S. Supreme Court. In deciding *Plessy* v. *Ferguson* (1896), the Court took occasion to comment on the constitutionality of miscegenation laws. On the way to a conclusion upholding state authority to require "equal but separate" railroad facilities, the Court said: "Laws forbidding the intermarriage of the two races may be said in a technical sense to interfere with the freedom of contract, and yet have been universally recognized [here the Court ignored contrary state decisions on marriage] as within the police power of the State."[13]

Shifting the Color Line: 1910 and 1924

In Virginia the 1878 law remained on the books, and it was enforced against various couples over the years. Newspapers carried a story in 1909 about a couple convicted in Prince Edward County for violating Virginia's miscegenation law. Marcus Lindsay, went the report, "is the son of a white woman. He always accepted a story, however, that he had colored blood in his veins. Believing this, he had associated with Negroes from his infancy, lived with them, and attended their churches and schools. Some months ago Marcus was married to Sophie Jones, a Negress, and the widow of a Negro," and he "has since lived with her."[14]

Marcus Lindsay found himself migrating across the color line from black to white. More often in the twentieth century, the law pushed people in the other direction. A 1910 law redefined the races by adjusting the boundary that separated white from nonwhite. Virginia law had long classified as "white" anyone of European descent who was less than one-fourth African (a fraction that had shaped the outcome in a number of court cases). The new statute left the definition of an Indian unchanged:

"every person not a colored person" who had "one-fourth or more of Indian blood." But after 1910, the law insisted, "Every person having one-sixteenth or more of negro blood shall be deemed a colored person."[15]

Thus Virginia's quest for racial purity took it from a one-fourth fraction—the nineteenth-century standard—to one-sixteenth. Under the rule of one-fourth, three fully white grandparents sufficed to make a person white only if the fourth grandparent were part Indian or part white. Under a one-eighth rule, seven of eight great-grandparents would have been required in addition to whatever margin the eighth could offer. Now, under the one-sixteenth rule, fifteen white great-grandparents out of sixteen would fail to satisfy the definition of a white person unless the sixteenth was at least some fraction white. The intent, of course, was to make the definition of a white person more exclusive, making it ever more difficult for a person of both African and European ancestry to qualify for marriage to someone who satisfied the more stringent requirement as a white person.[16]

Indeed, any such modification in the law gave "interracial marriage" a new definition. Two Virginia lawyers wrote that the 1910 statute had "changed the status" of some mixed-race people "from white to colored." Regarding the marriage of a white woman named Lucy Grasty and a mixed-race man named John Moon, they observed that although Moon was "legally white" when Grasty married him, he was "now a negro under the law."[17]

After throwing out the old one-quarter rule by adopting a one-sixteenth threshold in 1910, the legislature went on to redefine "white" in 1924 to exclude anyone of any traceable African ancestry. With interracial marriage in mind, the 1924 Act to Preserve Racial Integrity required all Virginians to register their racial identities with a local registrar as well as with the state registrar of vital statistics. The process was cumbersome and designed to be fail-safe. Any trace of nonwhite ancestry whatever meant that a person was defined as nonwhite and thus incapable of marrying someone who still qualified as white. The sole exception related to the so-called Pocahontas defense, pertaining to the "white" Virginians who had long admitted, even celebrated, their descent from the seventeenth-century union between Pocahontas and John Rolfe. Any otherwise white Virginian, if possessing no African ancestry and no more than one-sixteenth Indian ancestry, would qualify as a "white person." The key people involved in passage and implementation of the new law were John Powell, whose Anglo-Saxon Clubs of America screamed about racial purity, and Walter Plecker, the hard-driving director of the Virginia Bureau of Vital Statistics.[18]

The 1924 statute listed any number of racial identities: "Negro, Mongolian, American Indian, Asiatic Indian, Malay, or any mixture thereof," as well as "Caucasian." Previously, legislators had been concerned with white, black, and Indian; now they included other racial categories. Previously, they had identified "white" in a way that permitted mixed-race people with limited African ancestry to qualify as white, but no more. Beginning in 1924, Virginia state law made whiteness an even more exclusive quality than ever before. In that sense, the 1924 law meant something new when it declared: "It shall hereafter be unlawful for any white person in this State to marry any save a white person." Interracial marriage had been redefined, but it still carried all the penalties that had been imposed in 1878: "All laws heretofore passed and now in effect regarding the intermarriage of white and colored persons shall apply to marriages prohibited by this act." [19]

The redefinitions of 1910 and 1924 each moved the boundary that determined racial identity under the law. Every time a state moved the boundary that separated one racial identity from another, it demonstrated how flexible the legal definition was, how arbitrary was the entire enterprise of legislating identity.

The 1924 law redefined race—supplied a new definition of "white"— as it related to marriage but otherwise left interracial marriage as it had been since 1878, a crime carrying a penitentiary sentence of two to five years. Virginia's laws specifying the boundary between white and black racial identities continued to have real consequences and to lead to real controversies. In the wake of Virginia's 1924 law on racial purity, the courts faced cases alleging hidden African ancestry in one partner to a marriage involving a Caucasian, and then Plecker went to work to maintain the color line in public schools by propelling some children out of "white" schools. [20]

In the summer of 1924, the clerk of court in Rockbridge County denied Atha Sorrells and Robert Painter a marriage license. Painter was white, it seemed, but was Sorrells? Told she could not marry Painter because she had some African ancestry, she sued. Walter Plecker was determined to win the case and see the racial purity act continue to do its work, and he expected to do so on the strength of testimony from local people who had known generations of the Sorrells family. He had recently won a similar case in the same county involving Dorothy Johns and James Connor. This time, though, a number of local people opposed Plecker and proved just as determined to win as he was. His main witness failed to show up at the trial to testify, "afraid that his barn will be burned or other injury done to him or his property." The presiding judge, Henry Holt, therefore ruled in favor of Sorrells and directed the clerk to issue the license.[21] The use of the courts could cut more than one way when it came to racial identity and marriage licenses.

In May 1928 an Amherst County jury convicted Mary Hall, a "white woman," and Mott Hamilton Wood, a mixed-race man who was reportedly one-sixteenth black and had lived all his life as a white man. The couple were each sentenced to the penitentiary for the minimum two years. He had been white at birth, but the law later rendered him black, and he paid a big penalty for marrying someone who had remained white. Some juries, though, failed to convict, given the two-year minimum sentence. Evidently for that reason, the 1932 legislature made one last change in Virginia's miscegenation law, reducing the minimum sentence for a violation to one year.[22] The new minimum remained in effect when the Lovings encountered Virginia's miscegenation law in 1958.

The Virginia courts faced a number of cases while Richard Loving and Mildred Jeter were growing up. For example, Clark Council Hamilton and Florence Madelon Hammond obtained a marriage license in Salem on May 22, 1948, and the pastor of the Riverdale Baptist Church, Rev. K. A. Painter, married them the same day. Hamilton claimed to be twenty-two years old and a native of California. He and Hammond, a "19-year-old country girl," each claimed to be white. After their wedding, a newspaper later said, they lived "in a white section of Roanoke for about two months before moving to Baltimore." In November the bride's mother obtained a warrant for the groom's arrest for the felony of breaking the Virginia law against interracial marriage, and in December her father filed a suit for annulment of the marriage.[23]

By late December, Hamilton had been brought back to Roanoke County, scene of the alleged crime, from his new home in Maryland. Back in Baltimore, his wife, who continued to work in a store there, answered all questions with "What do you want to know for?" At Hamilton's trial on March 4, the Virginia prosecutor claimed to have obtained a birth certificate that showed him to be a twenty-year-old native of Alabama whose race was listed as "colored." Hamilton pleaded guilty and received a three-year prison sentence. Circuit court judge T. L. Keister asked whether he planned to leave Virginia and was told "as soon as possible." The newspaper reported that "the short, light-skinned Negro," when his sentence was suspended "on good behavior," "left immediately, presumably for Baltimore."[24]

The racial purity act of 1924 intruded into various Virginians' lives. People could be denied a marriage license. They could be sent to the penitentiary. Or they might be exiled from the state. On into the 1950s and 1960s, Virginians ran into their state's law against interracial marriage.

Ham Say Naim's Quixotic Quest

On June 26, 1952, Ham Say Naim, a Chinese sailor, married a white woman from Virginia, Ruby Elaine Lamberth, in Elizabeth City, North Carolina, where they had visited briefly from Norfolk, Virginia. Like Virginia, North Carolina banned marriages between whites and blacks, but unlike Virginia, it permitted marriages between Caucasians and Asians. For some months the Naims made their home back in Norfolk, although he was often away at sea. Then she decided that she wanted out. On September 30, 1953, Ruby Elaine Naim filed a petition seeking annulment on grounds of adultery, and if that effort failed, she asked that an annulment be granted on the basis of Virginia's ban on interracial marriages.[25]

Judge Floyd E. Kellam of the Portsmouth Circuit Court ruled in Mrs. Naim's favor. The couple had gone to North Carolina in order to evade the Virginia law, as much a crime as having had the ceremony in Virginia. Of course the marriage was void, and he granted the annulment she sought. Her quondam husband appealed the decision to the Virginia Supreme Court. On the basis of his marriage to an American citizen, he had applied for an immigrant visa, and unless he remained married he could not hope to be successful. His immigration attorney, David Carliner, mounted a test case against the 1924 Racial Integrity Act.[26]

The constitutionality of Virginia's miscegenation laws had never been successfully challenged, and a unanimous Virginia Supreme Court revealed that nothing had changed. Justice Archibald Chapman Buchanan, writing for the court, relied on the Tenth Amendment to fend off the Fourteenth. "Regulation of the marriage relation," he insisted, is "distinctly one of the rights guaranteed to the States and safeguarded by that bastion of States' rights, somewhat battered perhaps but still a sturdy fortress in our fundamental law, the tenth section of the Bill of Rights."[27]

What about *Brown* v. *Board of Education* and its interpretation of the equal protection clause, that states could not constitutionally segregate their public schools? No problem, Justice Buchanan assured Virginia authorities: "No such claim for the intermarriage of the races could be supported; by no sort of valid reasoning could it be found to be a foundation of good citizenship or a right which must be made available to all on equal terms." He could find nothing in the U.S. Constitution, he wrote, that would "prohibit the State from enacting legislation to preserve the racial integrity of its citizens, or which denies the power of the State to regulate the marriage relation so that it shall not have a mongrel breed of citizens." Rather than promote good citizenship, he suggested, "the obliteration of racial pride" and "the corruption of blood" would "weaken or destroy the quality of its citizenship."[28]

Refusing to give up, Naim appealed to the U.S. Supreme Court. Unhappily for Naim, his case came to the Supreme Court in the aftermath of *Brown*, and the Court was unprepared to confront the issue. Law clerks for various justices saw the inauspicious timing. Justice John Marshall Harlan's clerk worried, "I have serious doubts whether this question should be decided now, while the problem of enforcement of the [school] segregation cases is still so active." Justice Harold M. Burton's law clerk struck much the same tone: "In view of the difficulties engendered by the segregation cases it would be wise judicial policy to duck this question for a time."[29]

The observations of the Court's justices and their clerks make it clear that a number of them, at least, were inclined to view miscegenation laws as unconstitutional. The Court ducked the Naim case, just as it had ducked a miscegenation case from Alabama the year before, a few months after the decision in *Brown* was handed down. No judicial reconsideration took place by the Supreme Court in the 1950s regarding miscegenation laws in Alabama, Virginia, or anywhere else. Prosecutions continued to take place under miscegenation laws—in Mississippi, Louisiana, and elsewhere.[30]

The biographer of federal circuit court judge Learned Hand credits Justice Felix Frankfurter with having "twice successfully persuaded his colleagues on the Court" to avoid cases that challenged the constitutionality of miscegenation statutes. Regarding the issue, Justice Frankfurter wrote Judge Hand in September 1957 that the Court had "shunted it away and I pray we may be able to do it again, without being too brazenly evasive." And again, "I shall work, within the limits of judicial decency, to put off [a] decision on miscegenation as long as I can."[31]

Hand, for his part, was convinced that although the states generally had jurisdiction over marriage, the Fourteenth Amendment's equal protection clause made an exception and required that "a state shall not make race—Negro race—one of those conditions." As it happened, Justice Felix Frankfurter left the Court in 1962 and took his opposition with him. Meanwhile, Justice William O. Douglas and Chief Justice Earl Warren— who had leaned toward taking Ham Say Naim's case[32]—remained on the Court.

Identity, Comity, and the Calma Couple

As the Naims' story reveals, Virginia courts faced an occasional case of an interracial couple that included a Caucasian and someone of Asian/Pacific ancestry. In the late 1950s Rosina and Cezar Calma were living in Virginia. The Calmas—she Caucasian, he Filipino—had married in New Jersey in 1954 and had relocated to Virginia.[33] Virginia authorities did not arrest them, yet the public law of interracial marriage nonetheless affected their private lives.

When Rosina Calma sought to end their marriage, Virginia courts refused to recognize its validity, and thus she and her husband could not terminate it through divorce in the new state of their residence. She took her case to the Virginia Supreme Court, where she argued that "the action of the lower court in failing to recognize the marriage performed in New Jersey as valid in Virginia was in violation of the full faith and credit clause of Article IV, Section 1, of the Constitution of the United States." She argued, too, that the refusal to recognize her marriage violated "the rights guaranteed to her by the equal protection and due process clauses of the fourteenth amendment."[34]

In December 1962 the Virginia Supreme Court—declaring that "we do not reach and decide the constitutional issues" Rosina Calma had raised—upheld the lower court's disposition of the case, on procedural grounds.[35] It seems improbable that she could have convinced any court in Virginia to recognize her marriage. Basing an argument such as Rosina Calma's on the full faith and credit clause—seeking validation of a marriage that violated state policy—held little promise of success. The U.S. Supreme Court had long ago, in *Maynard* v. *Hill*, ruled that marriage was not a contract in the sense that the Constitution's full faith and credit clause had any application to it. Rather, it was left to each state to devise the law of marriage as it applied to people within that state, even if they had moved there from elsewhere. It was up to each state whether to recognize out-of-state marriages that violated state policy. As for the Fourteenth Amendment's equal protection clause, it had taken shape by the early 1960s as a powerful tool in many cases of state action and racial discrimination, but its time had not yet arrived for being applied to the law of marriage.

Virginia versus the Lovings—Arrest, Trial, and Exile

Someone—the Lovings never knew who—complained to authorities in Caroline County, Virginia, who then took action against them. On July 11, 1958, Commonwealth's Attorney Bernard Mahon obtained warrants for the arrest of Richard Loving and "Mildred Jeter," each for a felony associated with their marriage on June 2 in Washington, D.C. Then, late at night, Sheriff Garnett Brooks and two officers went to make the arrests.[36]

The three law officers entered the Lovings' bedroom and awakened them that July night. "We were living with my parents," Mildred Loving would later recall, in "a guest bedroom downstairs." "I woke up and these guys were standing around the bed. I sat up. It was dark. They had flashlights. They told us to get up, get dressed. I couldn't believe they were taking us to jail."[37]

There was an interlude before they actually left the house. First, "I went upstairs, sat on the bed, talked with my mother," she remembers. "Make them go away," she pleaded to her mom. But the intruders had ascertained that the two were indeed living together as husband and wife. The couple did not share a racial identity, and yet they shared a bed. The men "explained we had broken the law," Mrs. Loving says, and "they took us to jail."[38]

Unlike a series of couples who were brought to court in the 1920s, 1930s, and 1940s under Virginia's Racial Integrity Act of 1924, there was no doubt in anyone's minds as to the racial identities, white and black, of the people who claimed to be Mr. and Mrs. Loving. They could just as easily have been charged under the 1878 law rather than under the more demanding racial definitions of 1910 or 1924. Certainly the statute that made an effort to evade the law—going out of Virginia to marry and then immediately returning to the state with a claim to being married—dated from 1878. The case against Richard Loving and Mildred Jeter started out in much the same way as the case of Edmund Kinney and Mary S. Hall eighty years earlier. The only way in which the Lovings' case was clearly affected by the twentieth-century changes in the law was in the minimum penalty they faced, one year in prison.

The Caroline County grand jury brought indictments at its October 1958 term. At their trial on January 6, 1959, the Lovings pleaded not guilty at first and waived a jury trial. At the close of argument, they changed their pleas to guilty, and circuit court judge Leon M. Bazile sentenced them to one year each in jail. In accordance with their plea bargain, the judge suspended those sentences "for a period of twenty-five years"—

all the way to 1984—provided that "both accused leave Caroline County and the state of Virginia at once and do not return together or at the same time to said county and state for a period of twenty-five years."[39]

The suspended sentence did not mean that after twenty-five years the Lovings could move back to Virginia. One of them, it seemed, could live in Caroline County, Virginia, with impunity. Or, after twenty-five years both could live there separately. As matters stood in 1959, if they ever attempted to live together in their native state, they faced trouble. If they were caught together in Virginia anytime during the next twenty-five years, they would each serve their suspended sentence. If they lived together in Virginia even after the twenty-five years had elapsed, they would face prosecution just as they had in 1958. If they were going to live together, it would have to be outside Virginia.

Richard Loving and Mildred Jeter, as the court knew them in Virginia, moved to Washington, D.C., where they resumed their identities as Mr. and Mrs. Loving. There they lived at 1151 Neal Street Northeast with Mildred Loving's cousin Alex Byrd and his wife, Laura. Either of the Lovings could visit Caroline County, but both could not legally do so at the same time. Nonetheless they returned home from time to time, and Mrs. Loving was in Virginia for the births of all three of their children: Sidney, Donald, and Peggy. But the family had to live and work outside the state, and the couple longed to live in Caroline County. As Mrs. Loving later explained, "I wanted to come home. My family was here, and my husband's family was here." She added, "I hate to live in the city."[40]

The Lovings versus Virginia

In August 1963 a reporter asked President John F. Kennedy whether, in his "crusade" against racial discrimination, he would "seek to abrogate" the miscegenation laws that were still on the books in some twenty states, and, if so, "how would you go about it?" The president did not bite. Kennedy's evident discomfort with the subject had primarily to do with his having to get legislation through a Congress dominated by southern members of his own party. "If" there was an interracial marriage, he posited, and "if any legal action was taken" against the couple, then presumably they would take their case, if necessary, all the way to the Supreme Court.[41]

Kennedy implied that the Court eventually would rule against such laws and thus put an end to them. Regardless, the Justice Department had no particular role to play in the matter. And in no way did he suggest that the civil rights bill then under consideration—which was enacted the next year as the Civil Rights Act of 1964—might address the question. The responsibility for changing the legal environment regarding race and marriage rested, it seemed, with some interracial couple who had been charged under a state miscegenation law—a couple like the Lovings in Virginia—and who took their case to the Supreme Court.

After four years of exile, the Lovings began to contest their fate. In 1963 Mildred Loving wrote Robert F. Kennedy, attorney general of the United States, for assistance. As she recalled many years later, "I told Mr. Kennedy of our situation" and asked "if there was any way he could help us." The Justice Department redirected her letter to the National Capitol Area Civil Liberties Union with the suggestion that, though the federal government could not help the Lovings, perhaps the American Civil Liberties Union (ACLU) could. That organization had been pushing litigation for years to rid the nation of miscegenation laws like Virginia's.[42]

ACLU member Bernard S. Cohen, a young lawyer practicing in Alexandria, Virginia, welcomed the opportunity to take the case. Years later he commented: How could he not? For one thing, he wanted to help make things work out for the young couple. For another, they were bringing the perfect test case for attacking the nation's miscegenation laws. Here were two people who clearly loved each other and wanted to live together and raise their family in familiar surroundings. The name of the prospective federal case itself enthralled him: *Loving* v. *Virginia*.[43]

Indeed, Cohen took the Lovings' case, and while their case went back to the courts, Mr. and Mrs. Loving and their three children returned to the Caroline County area. Because they faced uncertainty there, though, they actually stayed in an adjacent county, and they kept their sanctuary in Washington, D.C., at the ready.[44]

In November 1963 Cohen filed a motion in Caroline County Circuit Court to set aside the original convictions and sentences. Cohen knew that he would have to be creative to overturn a century's worth of adverse precedents. Of course he deployed the Fourteenth Amendment's equal protection clause to contest the constitutionality of Virginia's miscegenation statutes. He argued, too, that the suspended sentence "denies the right of marriage which is a fundamental right of free men"; that it constituted banishment and thus violated due process; that it also constituted "cruel and unusual punishment," in violation of the Virginia constitution; and that twenty-five years exceeded the "reasonable period of suspension" permitted by Virginia law.[45]

Judge Bazile was in no hurry to second-guess himself, so for some time nothing happened. In mid-1964 another young attorney, Philip J. Hirschkop, joined Bernard Cohen in the case, and no action having been taken

on the petition in state court, Cohen and Hirschkop began a class action
in October 1964 in the U.S. District Court for the Eastern District of Virginia. They requested that a three-judge court convene to determine the
constitutionality of Virginia's miscegenation statutes and to prohibit the
enforcement of the Lovings' convictions and sentences under those laws.
Pending a decision by a three-judge panel, they asked district judge John
D. Butzner Jr. for a temporary injunction against the enforcement of
those laws, which they said were designed "solely for the purpose of keeping the Negro people in the badges and bonds of slavery." Judge Butzner,
however, saw no "irreparable harm" to the Lovings while awaiting the
panel's decision and denied the temporary injunction. Recognizing that
the federal panel was due to meet soon, Judge Bazile finally set a date to
hear arguments on Cohen's motion.[46]

In January 1965, six years after the original proceedings, Judge Bazile
presided at a hearing on the Lovings' petition to have his decision set
aside. In a written opinion he rebutted each of the contentions that might
have forced reconsideration of their guilt. Pointing back to an 1878 Virginia Supreme Court decision, Bazile insisted that the Lovings' marriage
was "absolutely void in Virginia" and that they could not "cohabit" there
"without incurring repeated prosecutions" for doing so. Pointing to the
Virginia high court's 1955 decision in the case of Ham Say Naim, he noted
that marriage was "a subject which belongs to the exclusive control of the
States" and that the U.S. Supreme Court had done nothing to overturn
the Virginia decision or to undermine any other state's laws against interracial marriage. By way of conclusion, Judge Bazile wrote: "Almighty God
created the races white, black, yellow, malay and red, and he placed them
on separate continents. And but for the interference with his arrangement
there would be no cause for such marriages. The fact that he separated the
races shows that he did not intend for the races to mix."[47]

The Virginia Supreme Court

The Lovings' case moved on from Judge Bazile's court, for his was not
the last word. First, lawyers for the state convinced the federal court that
the case should next be heard in the Virginia Supreme Court. So the Lovings took their case to the state's highest court, and their lawyers and the
state's rehearsed arguments that, both sides well knew, were likely to be
heard again before long at the U.S. Supreme Court.

In mounting one of their arguments, Cohen and Hirschkop quoted
from *Perez* v. *Sharp*, the 1948 California Supreme Court decision against
the constitutionality of miscegenation laws, "If the right to marry is a fun-

damental right, then it must be conceded that an infringement of that right by means of a racial restriction is an unlawful infringement of one's liberty." They went on to assert: "The caprice of the politicians cannot be substituted for the minds of the individual in what is man's most personal and intimate decision. The error of such legislation must immediately be apparent to those in favor of miscegenation statutes, if they stopped to consider their abhorrence to a statute which commanded that 'all marriages must be between persons of different racial backgrounds.'" Such a statute, they claimed, would be no more "repugnant to the constitution"— and no less so—than the law under consideration. Something "so personal as the choice of a mate must be left to the individuals involved," they argued; "race limitations are too unreasonable and arbitrary a basis for the State to interfere."[48]

The Virginia Supreme Court's opinion rejected the Lovings' arguments and largely adopted the brief of the state of Virginia. Its reasoning and conclusion from a decade earlier in the case of Ham Say Naim remained, as the court saw things, entirely viable. A unanimous court declared on March 7, 1966, "We find no sound judicial reason . . . to depart from our holding in the Naim case."[49] As far as the court was concerned, the state law against interracial marriage was as sound in the 1960s as it been in the 1880s.

The Lovings had exhausted their appeals in the Virginia courts, and their convictions remained intact. They were still not allowed to "cohabit as man and wife" in Virginia, so they appealed their case to the U.S. Supreme Court.[50]

In the 1950s and 1960s, no southern court was going to do what three southern states had done nearly a century before. By the mid-1960s a serious campaign was under way to do away with all such laws. The defenders of the old regime fought back. In law journals and other publications, the two sides voiced their contrasting views of miscegenation laws and the Constitution. Each side hoped to sway the nation's highest court.

Dueling Histories

The matter of miscegenation's constitutionality made its way with some frequency into law review articles in the 1960s. Such articles have long served as a means for the best arguments to be expressed in a forum other than the briefs that argue specific cases before the Supreme Court.[51] Legal experts seeking to shape the discourse on an issue can press their arguments in law review articles. One representative article—published by a lawyer from Georgia a few years before the *Loving* decision, with a miscegenation case from Florida in mind that was then at the Supreme Court—appeared in the *North Carolina Law Review*.

R. Carter Pittman wanted it to be as absolutely clear as possible that the federal courts had no authority to rule any state's miscegenation statute unconstitutional. "From earliest colonial times," he insisted, "laws, customs, and court proceedings proscribing miscegenation were a fundamental part of the mores of the American people." Those laws, he warned, "are now under attack as in violation of the fourteenth amendment." But the framers of the Fourteenth Amendment had not meant to negate such statutes, he argued, and only a new constitutional amendment could reach them.[52]

Pittman's account of the past was full of passion, and in very broad outline it had merit, but it missed some essential facts. For one thing, by no stretch is it true that all states had ever—let alone "from the earliest colonial times"—sported such laws. For another, the story of what the framers had meant to do was more complicated than he wished it to be. And he seems to have had no idea that seven of the ten states that were the objects of Congressional Reconstruction had lifted their bans in some manner in the 1870s for periods averaging a decade or so.

Pittman's judicial history of miscegenation statutes and the Fourteenth Amendment was even more inaccurate. In *Pace* v. *Alabama* (1883) the Supreme Court had upheld a miscegenation law—one banning interracial cohabitation—against constitutional challenge, but it had not, Pittman to the contrary, directly addressed the question of interracial marriage. True enough, various other court decisions, state and federal, had upheld miscegenation statutes. But the fact that Americans across the nation in those early years raised the argument in the first place—insisting that the Fourteenth Amendment provided a shield against their prosecution—offered some evidence that a full consensus regarding the meaning of the amendment had not emerged. Perhaps more relevant, judges in a considerable number of states ruled against such statutes. Some were trial judges, whether in Indiana or North Carolina in the 1870s or Nevada and Arizona in the 1950s. Some were appellate judges—court majorities in Alabama, Texas, and Louisiana in the 1870s—who found miscegenation statutes unconstitutional, no longer enforceable.[53]

Pittman's penultimate paragraph bears quoting in full: "All court decisions on the question have upheld the constitutionality of anti-miscegenation statutes, with the exception of a split four to three decision of the Supreme Court of California. In order to find the California statute to

be in violation of the fourteenth amendment, the majority of that court relied principally on equalitarian propaganda, masquerading as scientific
authority, and the Charter of the United Nations." Pittman had no problem with arguing his case on the basis of inaccurate and incomplete history, any more than he had a problem with writing antiequalitarian propaganda masquerading as scientific authority.[54]

A year or two later, Alfred Avins published an article in the *Virginia
Law Review* that in many ways replicated Pittman's approach. Reviewing
several years of debate in Congress over Reconstruction measures in the
late 1860s and early 1870s—the remarks of proponents and opponents of
civil rights legislation and the Fourteenth Amendment—Avins concluded
that neither party had believed the amendment to ban miscegenation measures. He discounted evidence to the contrary even in the debates. More
important, like Pittman, he declared that the Supreme Court had no authority to overturn such laws, which had, he said, "been upheld as constitutional by every appellate court" that had ever considered them, aside
from the 4–3 decision in California in 1948. He ignored the contrary appellate decisions during Reconstruction in Alabama and elsewhere.
Adopting and redirecting the language of segregationists, he rumbled that
any federal court decision that presumed to renovate the meaning of the
Fourteenth Amendment—by throwing out statutes previously considered
"subject to the state police power"—thereby "nullifies the basic value jus-
tifying the existence of a written constitution."[55]

On the other side, William D. Zabel published an article, "Interracial
Marriage and the Law," in *Atlantic Monthly* in late 1965. Zabel was a lawyer working in close cooperation with the ACLU's crusade against the anti-
miscegenation regime. His history was not faultless either, but he knew
about the 1872 case in which the Alabama Supreme Court had ruled a miscegenation law unconstitutional. Zabel, who agreed with the Alabama ruling, dismissed both Pittman and Avins in 1965: "No legal scholar of note
considers these laws constitutional."[56]

Zabel noted the inconsistencies and uncertainties associated with the
miscegenation laws of the seventeen states that retained them. A mixed-
race person might be white in Florida but black in Georgia, and several
states offered no legislative guidance as to who fell on which side of the
racial boundary. Regarding a recently elected member of Congress from
Hawaii—Patsy Takemoto Mink, a woman of Japanese ancestry—Zabel
noted that she and her Caucasian husband were not at liberty to live on the
south side of the Potomac River, for Virginia would not recognize their
marriage.

Regardless of such practical matters, insisted Zabel, "There are no laws more symbolic of the Negro's relegation to second-class citizenship. The fact that legislation cannot end prejudice does not mean that laws which foster it should continue to exist." Whatever might remain of racial feelings in a postmiscegenation world, Zabel declared it time for the U.S. Supreme Court to act. "The elaborate legal structure of segregation has virtually collapsed with the exception of the miscegenation laws," he said. "Whether or not the Supreme Court was wise to avoid this question in [the 1950s, as in the *Naim* case], it should now invalidate these laws." Thus he directly confronted people like Pittman who favored the traditional legal and social order and who insisted that the judiciary had no authority to intervene. But if southern courts were going to rule along the lines that Pittman and Avins thought they should and hoped they would, the question remained whether the nation's highest court would step in, as Zabel thought it should and hoped it would.

Let the Supreme Court Do It

In 1959, just days after the Lovings were convicted of interracial marriage in Virginia, Louisiana's supreme court ruled on the constitutionality of that state's allegiance to the antimiscegenation regime. Humming the old miscegenation melody, the court sang the usual words about the constitutionality of such action under the state's police power, the irrelevance of the Fourteenth Amendment, and the restricted role of the judicial system to interpret and apply a statute that only the legislature could repeal.[57]

In 1964 a local judge in Maryland passed on the opportunity to rule a miscegenation statute unconstitutional, and yet he avoided a showdown by redefining the racial identity of the prospective groom, who had a Caucasian grandmother. "Assuming that in general a Filipino is a member of the Malay race," the judge declared, "it is very clear that this Filipino is not."[58] The legislature repealed the statute three years later, but that was matter of a legislative majority, not a judicial override. The statute could, after all, be entirely constitutional and yet be taken off the state's books.

When the Supreme Court of Florida refused in 1963 to reconsider the constitutionality of that state's miscegenation measures, it used language that summed up the stance of southern states at the time. In that case, the convicted couple's lawyers had intimated that if they failed to get the right answer in Florida, they would carry the case to the nation's highest court. The Florida court responded that perhaps it was in fact "a mere way station on the route to" the U.S. Supreme Court and perhaps a different decision would be obtained there. But in the Florida court's view, the 1883 Supreme Court decision in *Pace* v. *Alabama* was still good law. "This Court," it said, "is obligated by the sound rule of stare decisis and the precedent of the well written decision" in *Pace*, which it quoted at length. If a new rule was to be applied and a new outcome achieved, "it must be enacted by legislative process," said the unanimous court, "or some other court must write it."[59]

In 1965, the year before the Virginia Supreme Court refused to reconsider Virginia's miscegenation law in the *Loving* case, the Oklahoma Supreme Court also made it clear that it would not change its position until forced to do so: "In view of this court's traditional practice of upholding its former decisions which involve questions of constitutional law, and in view of the fact that the great weight of authority holds such statutes constitutional, and the Supreme Court of the United States not having decided the question, we feel duty bound to again hold the statutes in question constitutional."[60]

One cannot conclude that had the lawyering been better, or the facts a bit different, the highest court in Virginia or Oklahoma or Florida—or in any other state in the South—would have ruled a miscegenation law unconstitutional. That was not going to happen. What was going to have to happen—and what did happen, as could be plausibly forecast by the mid-1960s—is that eventually the U.S. Supreme Court would act.

Any number of southern appellate judges no doubt understood that. Meanwhile, they would let inertia carry them, precedent guide them, and the local political culture shape their judicial behavior. What happened with regard to marriage is pretty much what had been happening in a host of other civil rights areas. Southern legislators had demonstrated that they felt far more comfortable shucking responsibility for change. If it had to come, let the federal government take the heat. Let an outside agency force the new regime. White constituents would be ever so much readier to forgive their state officeholders, legislative and judicial alike, if they went down in flames appearing all the while to have kept the good faith and fought the good fight. Surrender, if it had to come, was better accommodated in that fashion.

Southern courts did not simply persist in applying or interpreting laws that the legislature had lost interest in. In two cases in December 1958, the Mississippi Supreme Court interpreted the state's criminal statute of miscegenation in such a way as to result in overturning the convictions of a white woman and a black man, as well as a black woman and a white man. Charles W. Pickering, a law student at the University of Mississippi (and a future federal judge), in a note published some months later in the *Missis-*

sippi Law Journal, analyzed the rulings. Despite recent U.S. Supreme Court decisions "in the fields of education, transportation, and recreation," Pickering observed, the Court "will not invalidate the miscegenation statutes, for some time at least." "Therefore," he concluded, "if [the statute] is to serve the purpose that the legislature undoubtedly intended it to serve," it "should be amended," and he suggested how.[61]

At its next biennial session the Mississippi legislature, while retaining the description of the banned acts and the penalties for engaging in them, adopted Pickering's proposed language as to who was being targeted: "Persons who are prohibited from marrying by reason of race or blood and between whom marriage is declared to be unlawful and void, who shall cohabit, or live together as husband and white, or be guilty of a single act of adultery [*sic*] or fornication, upon conviction, shall be punished by imprisonment in the penitentiary for a term not exceeding ten years." This act was passed in February 1960, a year after the Lovings were exiled for their crime in Virginia.[62]

When the Florida case—*McLaughlin* v. *Florida* (1964)—reached the Supreme Court, the convictions were overturned. More than that, the nation's highest court rejected the ancient precedent in *Pace* v. *Alabama* and invalidated Florida's interracial cohabitation law. Justice Byron White, writing for a unanimous Court, observed, "*Pace* represents a limited view of the Equal Protection Clause which has not withstood analysis." Relying on decisions like *Brown* v. *Board of Education*, White went on to insist that "the central purpose of the Fourteenth Amendment was to eliminate racial discrimination emanating from official sources in the States," and "we deal here with a racial classification embodied in a criminal statute."[63]

The Court undid *Pace*, but it did not declare all miscegenation laws unconstitutional. The Florida statute regarding interracial cohabitation was unconstitutional, but Justice White said the Court had reached that conclusion "without expressing any views about the state's prohibition of interracial marriage." Potter Stewart and William O. Douglas used stronger language than did their colleagues. In view of the modern understanding of the equal protection clause, they wrote, "it is simply not possible for a state law to be valid under our Constitution which makes the criminality of an act depend on the race of the actor."[64]

The Lovings Take Their Case to the U.S. Supreme Court

The Lovings were reluctant parties to the law case that bears their name. This is not to say that someone had to convince them to bring the case, for they were committed to their marriage. Had they had their way, the question would never have been raised, so very rudely raised, back in July 1958. All they had ever wanted was to be left alone. Richard Loving, a private and taciturn man, explained their position in 1966, after the Virginia Supreme Court had rejected their position. "We have thought about other people," he told a reporter in Virginia, "but we are not doing it just because someone had to do it and we wanted to be the ones. . . . We are doing it for *us*—because we want to live here."[65] So they pressed on.

Bernard Cohen and Philip Hirschkop reflected, in their reasoning and their language, the close collaboration with William Zabel and others in the ACLU. In their jurisdictional statement to the U.S. Supreme Court, they pointed out why the case should be heard there: "The elaborate legal structure of segregation has been virtually obliterated with the exception of the miscegenation laws." They continued: "There are no laws more symbolic of the Negro's relegation to second-class citizenship. Whether or not this Court has been wise to avoid this issue in the past, the time has come to strike down these laws; they are legalized racial prejudice, unsupported by reason or morals, and should not exist in a good society."[66]

While the Court was considering whether to hear the case, Justice John Marshall Harlan's clerk wrote that "the miscegenation issue . . . was left open in *McLaughlin*, and appears ripe for review here." In fact, he went on, "I doubt whether this statute can stand."[67] On December 12, 1966, the court agreed to hear the case.

The time had come for Hirschkop, Cohen, and the ACLU to prepare a written argument to convince the Court to invalidate the Virginia law under which the Lovings had been indicted and convicted. Yet the power of miscegenation laws to affect interracial couples in the United States went far beyond the Virginia laws and far beyond the Lovings. And the ACLU wished to secure a ruling from the Court broad enough to address the wider issues and invalidate every state's miscegenation laws.

Hirschkop and Cohen played important roles in crafting the ACLU brief in *Loving*, but they were not alone. William D. Zabel, from his law office in New York City, wrote Arthur L. Berney at the Boston College Law School about his thoughts on how to proceed. The ACLU attorneys were in agreement that the Lovings' case should provide a vehicle for attacking all miscegenation laws. *McLaughlin* had produced only a narrow ruling, and Zabel warned, "We should not assume that the Court will try to avoid a narrow holding" in *Loving*. Zabel nonetheless argued against stressing the kind of sociological evidence that had been deployed in *Brown* v. *Board of Education*. In *Loving*, he explained, "there is no separate but equal problem. Two consenting, competent adults ought to have the right to marry regardless of race and there can be no separate but equal opportunity for them."[68]

The written arguments brought the two sides of the controversy into clear focus. One side emphasized how far the Fourteenth Amendment could reach, the other the limited intent of its framers. Where the ACLU emphasized the reasoning in *Brown* v. *Board of Education* and *McLaughlin* v. *Florida*, Virginia emphasized the doctrine in *Maynard* v. *Hill* that states had authority over the regulation of marriage. One side recounted the history of privacy cases from the 1920s into the 1960s: Supreme Court decisions that spoke in *Meyer* v. *Nebraska* (1923), for example, about "the right of the individual . . . to marry, establish a home and bring up children." The other side pointed instead to an unbroken string of federal cases in which statutes banning interracial marriage had been upheld, most recently in the 1940s in *Stevens* v. *United States*.[69]

The NAACP Legal Defense Fund—which was very much involved in the case when it reached the Supreme Court—bore in on the Virginia court's statement in *Naim* v. *Naim* that the 1924 law's purpose was to "preserve the racial integrity" of Virginia's citizens. Rebutting that position, the NAACP argued that "there is no rational or scientific basis upon which a statutory prohibition against marriage based on race or color alone can be justified as furthering a valid legislative purpose." Revealing an interest in the question that went beyond black-white marriages, the Japanese American Citizens League also submitted a brief as a friend of the court. Cohen and Hirschkop, in their brief, reviewed the history of Virginia's miscegenation laws from the seventeenth century to the twentieth and characterized those statutes as "relics of slavery" and at the same time "expressions of modern day racism."[70]

In oral argument on April 10, 1967, lawyers for Virginia did what they could to convince the Court that miscegenation laws should be left up to the states. Once again, a state mounted the old steed, the Tenth Amendment, to joust with its adversary, mounted on the Fourteenth; the Tenth Amendment, Virginia argued, and not the Fourteenth, ought to govern marriage. But while *Maynard* v. *Hill*, which declared marriage to be subject to state legislation, could be trotted back out for another fray, its twin from the 1880s, *Pace* v. *Alabama*, had died three years before in *McLaughlin* v. *Florida*, and so was no longer available to assist.[71]

The ACLU lawyers argued, of course, that Virginia's miscegenation laws could not pass constitutional muster. Philip Hirschkop focused on the equal protection clause, Bernard Cohen on the due process clause.

Hirschkop argued from the legislative history of the laws that their intent to secure the racial purity of the "white" race and their intent to demean and control black Virginians violated the Fourteenth Amendment. Cohen concentrated on the personal impact of the laws on the Lovings. He spoke of their "right" to marry, as he and they saw it, and their wish to live together in peace in Virginia. And he referred to their terror and humiliation at being dragged out of bed and off to jail for living as husband and wife.[72]

Cohen summarized some of the civil penalties (quite aside from the criminal penalties) that automatically attached to the couple under Virginia's laws. "The Lovings have the right to go to sleep at night," he declared, "knowing that should they not awake in the morning their children would have the right to inherit from them, under intestacy [in the absence of a will leaving them their parents' property]. They have the right to be secure in knowing that if they go to sleep and do not wake in the morning, that one of them, a survivor of them, has the right to social security benefits." The "injustices" that necessarily followed from the Virginia law, Cohen argued, "amount to a denial of due process," for those rights were being arbitrarily denied the Lovings.[73]

Cohen highlighted his argument by conveying to the Court the words of Richard Loving: "Mr. Cohen, tell the Court I love my wife, and it is just unfair that I can't live with her in Virginia."[74]

Loving v. Virginia

Two months later, on June 12, 1967, Chief Justice Earl Warren delivered the opinion of a unanimous Supreme Court. The Court rejected each of the state's arguments. The Virginia Supreme Court, in its decision the previous year, had incorporated the historical record, judicial precedents, and the legal logic of the state's brief. Making their way into the decision of the U.S. Supreme Court, by contrast, were those of the Lovings' attorneys, as well as the NAACP and the Japanese American Citizens League.

The Virginia court's decision in *Naim* v. *Naim* to the contrary, the chief justice wrote, the Tenth Amendment had to yield to the Fourteenth when it came to the claim of "exclusive state control" over the "regulation of marriage." As for the narrow construction of the Fourteenth Amendment, dependent as it was on the state's reading of the intent of the framers, the Court harked back to its statement in 1954 in *Brown* v. *Board of Education* that the historical record was "inconclusive." That Virginia's "miscegenation statutes punish equally both the white and the Negro participants in an interracial marriage" could no longer, said the Court, satisfy the standard of constitutionality.[75] The old rule of symmetry—holding otherwise, as in the Edmund Kinney case back in 1879—had been vanquished.

Warren gave the back of the hand to the state's contention that "these statutes should be upheld if there is any possible basis for concluding that they serve a rational purpose." The burden of proof rested on the state, for "the fact of equal application does not immunize the statute from the heavy burden of justification" required by the Fourteenth Amendment, particularly when racial classifications appeared in criminal statutes.[76] The doctrine voiced in *Maynard* v. *Hill* still held general sway, but the Fourteenth Amendment of the 1960s, unlike that of the 1880s, negated it when race entered the equation.

The chief justice declared that "we find the racial classifications in these statutes repugnant to the Fourteenth Amendment, even assuming an even-handed state purpose to protect the 'integrity' of all races." As Warren put it, "The clear and central purpose of the Fourteenth Amendment was to eliminate all official state sources of invidious racial discrimination in the States." Quoting from the *McLaughlin* case, he wrote: "Indeed, two members of this Court have already stated that they 'cannot conceive of a valid legislative purpose . . . which makes the color of a person's skin the test of whether his conduct is a criminal offense.'"[77]

Warren was sure of the Court's recent history in civil rights cases. "We have consistently denied the constitutionality of measures which restrict the rights of citizens on account of race. There can be no doubt that restricting the freedom to marry solely because of racial classifications violates the central meaning of the equal protection clause." As for the due process clause, the chief justice noted that "the freedom to marry has long been recognized as one of the vital personal rights essential to the orderly pursuit of happiness by free men."[78]

Connecting race with privacy, Chief Justice Warren explained: "To deny this fundamental freedom on so unsupportable a basis as the racial classifications embodied in these statutes, classifications so directly subversive of the principle of equality at the heart of the Fourteenth Amendment, is surely to deprive all the State's citizens of liberty without due process of law." Giving the Lovings and their lawyers everything they had asked for, the chief justice wrote that the Fourteenth Amendment "requires that the freedom of choice to marry not be restricted by invidious racial discriminations. Under our Constitution, the freedom to marry, or not marry, a person of another race resides with the individual and cannot be infringed by the State." Therefore, he concluded, "these convictions must be reversed."[79]

Free Now

A phone call brought the news. From their farm home in Bowling Green, southeast of Fredericksburg, Virginia, Mr. and Mrs. Loving drove north to Alexandria for a news conference at their lawyers' office. There he said, "We're just really overjoyed," and she, "I feel free now." A photographer snapped a picture, lawbooks in the background, of two happy people sitting close together, his arm around her neck. "My wife and I plan to go ahead and build a new house now," said Richard Loving, the construction worker, about the new home that Richard Loving, the husband and father, wanted his family to live in.[80]

The new house, in which the Lovings' three children grew up, symbolized the family's freedom to have a permanent dwelling where they could live in peace in their home state. As Mildred Loving later wrote, "The Supreme Court decision changed our life a lot. We moved our family into our community in Caroline County without fear of going to prison."[81]

Other families, too, shook free of the law of interracial marriage. In August 1967 Virginians were informed about "the first known partners to an interracial marriage in Virginia" since the *Loving* decision was handed down two months earlier. In a ceremony at Kingdom Hall Church, described as "a Negro Jehovah's Witnesses church" in Norfolk, a white woman, Leona Eve Boyd, married a black man, Romans Howard Johnson.[82] Thanks to the Lovings' persistence and the decision of the U.S. Supreme Court, the Johnsons had no need to leave the state to get married. Nor did they have to face the prospect of midnight arrest, felony conviction, or long-term exile for their marriage. A federal court decision had forced a change in public policy in Virginia, and the Johnsons' decision, like that of the Lovings, was now a private matter.

Not only could the Lovings and the Johnsons live in Virginia without fear of prosecution for their interracial marriages, but laws similar to Virginia's fell in fifteen other states as well. In much of the nation, King Color's power to govern who might marry whom had lived on in full force into the second half of the twentieth century. Everywhere in the South, in particular, miscegenation laws persisted into the 1960s. Only in 1967, in the area of marriage and family relations, did it become true—as Justice Stewart insisted in 1964 that it ought to be—that "the criminality of an act" could not "depend upon the race of the actor."[83]

By the time the case of *Loving* v. *Virginia* arrived at the Supreme Court, state action had already eliminated miscegenation laws everywhere outside the South. Maryland repealed its statute in early 1967, effective June 1. A few days later the Supreme Court handed down its ruling in *Loving*. As a consequence of that decision, couples with any combination of racial identities could legally marry and live together in any state in the nation. The law of race and slavery, dating in Virginia from the seventeenth century, had given way to the law of freedom.[84]

7

Power and Policy in an American State

Federal Courts, Political Rights, and Policy Outcomes

T HE DATE WAS TUESDAY, JUNE 16, 1964. PAGE 1 OF THE *RICHMOND Times-Dispatch* offered all kinds of evidence that the Virginia of U.S. Senator Harry F. Byrd Sr. found itself under assault. Among the front-page headlines that day, two reported on federal courts and segregated schools. "Negro Pupils Assigned to 3 White Schools Here," warned one. "Defiance to Court Order Hinted in Prince Edward," noted another. But the voice of Virginia's capital reserved much the largest type that day for a headline shouting "Court Orders State to Realign Districts." Three separate stories followed, each with a title in large print: "Population Ruled Key to Districting," "Decision Thought a Blow to Byrd," and "Virginia Officials Dismayed by Opinion."

Virginia had been caught up in what has been called the "reapportionment revolution."[1] Actually, the reapportionment revolution was only one significant part of a larger transformation of the American political system, akin to the changes associated, more than a century before, with Jacksonian Democracy. The Old Dominion, having introduced into the glossary of American political culture such terms as *state rights* and *massive resistance*, now faced the threat—or the promise, depending on which Virginians you asked—of major renovation. In the middle years of the 1960s, the Virginia of Byrd's worldview confronted the old polarities—state and federal, white and black—and a new one as well—rural and urban. And it faced these options from a defensive position greatly weakened in any number of ways.

The Byrd Organization had faced challenges before and had even lost some clashes, but through the late 1950s its power seemed overwhelming. The U.S. Supreme Court, though it could never have acted alone, played a central role in eroding that power. Virginia's passage through the 1960s era of political democratization left its political system very different from what it had been in the 1920s or even in the 1950s. Central as was the matter of apportionment, a significant related issue was the poll tax as a screen for voting in state and federal elections.

In these varied matters Virginia cut a path that in its details was its own. Yet by extension Virginia's experience offers a case study in southern history, certainly on the twentieth-century poll tax. Moreover, the South displayed a variant of national patterns, certainly regarding legislative apportionment. Thus the story of Virginia's encounter with the twentieth century—in fact the long saga of the period ever since the American Revolution—can offer insights about the ways Americans have contested over power and policy at all times and places. The rules of the game were perpetually important because the outcomes remained important. Each time a Virginian went to court to challenge the conventional practices regarding voter registration—or primary elections, or legislative apportionment—a citizen was seeking to use the law to reject the past, change the law, and thus modify the present to secure an alternative future.

Reconfiguring the Playing Field

How should the Virginia electorate be configured? Stated another way, who should be politically empowered? The core question in Virginia's constitutional convention of 1901–2—indeed, the central issue as far back as the Virginia convention of 1829–30—it remained a matter of much contention into the 1960s. It had been true in the 1830s, and it remained true in the 1960s, that such matters of political process as voting rights and legislative apportionment enhanced or diminished the likelihood that various items of substance—regarding such matters as taxes, schools, and roads—would be enacted in the Virginia General Assembly. The winners and losers in the game of legislative outputs depended on electoral inputs, and these depended on the rules that governed entry and participation.

The Virginia Constitution of 1902 was the handiwork of a convention that, as one of its prime supporters, Carter Glass of Lynchburg, a future U.S. senator, boldly declared, had one primary purpose: "Discrimination! Why that is exactly what we propose; that exactly, is why this Convention was elected—to discriminate to the very extremity of permissible action under the limitations of the Federal Constitution with the view to the elimination of every Negro who can be gotten rid of, legally, without materially impairing the strength of the white electorate." William A.

Anderson, who soon became the Virginia attorney general, exhorted that "an effective suffrage article" would be "a constitutional road to absolute Caucasian supremacy."[2]

Delegates to the 1901–2 convention could see, from a recent ruling by the U.S. Supreme Court, *Williams* v. *Mississippi*, that they had wide latitude in working up a means to reduce the electorate. As Delegate Alfred P. Thom of Norfolk put the matter, "We come here to sweep the field of expedients for the purpose of finding some constitutional method of ridding ourselves of [black enfranchisement] forever; and we have the approval of the Supreme Court of the United States in making that effort."[3]

Once the delegates had completed their work, they dared not risk it all by sending it to the pre-1902 electorate for ratification, so they declared it in effect. Doing so, they reneged on a promise made at the time elections for the convention were called. Poor white as well as black voters might show up at the polls to defeat this new constitution that provided for their own disfranchisement. Delegate John S. Barbour of Culpeper County framed the issue: "Shall we, after having spent several months here in earnest discussion of this instrument, go back and submit the Constitution which we shall adopt to the very electorate which the people have already declared incapable of properly exercising the powers of government?" Over the next ten years, a series of attacks on the legitimacy of the new constitution failed in state and federal courts.[4] The contest continued, but the core components—the basic rules of the political game in Virginia— remained in place into the 1960s.

Regarding the political changes in Virginia in the 1960s, one recent commentator has remarked: "The rules by which the political game was played in Virginia thus were being revised extensively at mid-decade— not by Virginians, but by federal courts and through federal enactments."[5] The statement is sound in that, had Virginia politics continued in its regular course, no such decisions could have been reached at that time. It is misleading, however, in that Virginians did, indeed, help cause these changes, did play roles in forcing changes in the way the game was to be played, whether concerning the poll tax or legislative apportionment. That is, some Virginians resorted to the courts in their efforts to obtain political decisions that, while desirable in many Virginians' eyes, were anathema to others and so could not have been otherwise secured.

In exploring Virginia's slow return to—or, at least, slow move toward—political democratization between 1902 and the 1960s, this essay emphasizes the transformed constitutional standing of such matters as the white Democratic primary, the poll tax, and legislative apportionment.

Where the other chapters in this book focus on substantive matters, this one emphasizes matters of process: not the political game itself over policy matters but the struggle to control the playing field and the rules, including the relative numbers of players on each side, and thus shape likely outcomes.

James O. West Goes to Court to Vote in a Democratic Primary

By 1902 black men had been voting—in some numbers, at some places and some times, at least—in Virginia and elsewhere in much of the South since Congressional Reconstruction began in 1867. The Fifteenth Amendment, ratified in 1870, declared, "The right of citizens of the United States to vote shall not be denied or abridged . . . by any State on account of race, color, or previous condition of servitude." And thus other criteria were employed, as surrogates for race, to prevent African Americans from voting.

The Virginia Constitution of 1902 offered up a collection of obstacles. One was payment of the previous three years' poll taxes. Another was a complex registration procedure. Such screens might, and did, prevent some white men from voting, too, though officials did not necessarily mourn this. Regardless, the Fifteenth Amendment, by forcing the use of surrogate criteria, continued to let through some black voters. In the 1920s, when the Virginia legislature was enacting a "racial integrity" measure stipulating that a single drop of African blood would classify a person as "colored" rather than "white," analogous efforts were made to bring racial purity to the election process.[6] In particular, an exclusionary policy was adopted to prevent black voters from participating in Democratic Party elections.

Here, too, federal policy offered guidelines that southern policymakers had to make their way past. As Virginia leaders well knew by the late 1920s, Texas lawmakers had mounted an effort to show the way, had been rebuffed, and had tried again. The "white Democratic primary" was an innovation that, in states where only Democratic candidates stood any chance of winning, was designed to exclude black voters from primary elections, the only elections that meant much. In *Nixon v. Herndon* the U.S. Supreme Court ruled in 1927 that the Texas legislature could not stipulate such an exclusion of black voters from that state's Democratic primaries. Texas had responded by granting the Democratic Party, a private organization, the authority to run the primary elections and, if it chose, to exclude black voters. The effect was the same. But was the procedure similarly unconstitutional? The U.S. Supreme Court eventually accepted this approach, at least for a time, but not until after the question had arisen in Virginia.[7]

In 1924 Virginia authorized the Democratic Party (or, rather, any party that garnered at least a quarter of the votes in a general election) to make the rules and run the primaries. The legislature, in effect, invited the parties to exclude black voters from participation in primaries. With certain exceptions, "all persons qualified to vote at the election for which the primary is held, and not disqualified by reasons of other requirements in the law of the party to which he belongs, may vote at the primary." At a state convention in Norfolk on June 11, 1924, the Democratic Party specified one condition in the "law of the party" by introducing a racial qualifier, "all white persons."[8]

Watching these developments were African Americans both in and outside the South. In Florida, Texas, and Virginia, actions were under way to challenge the latest efforts to disfranchise black voters. The National Association for the Advancement of Colored People assisted such efforts by contributing funds to offset some of the costs and by providing help in preparing the cases. NAACP leaders, including attorney Louis Marshall, had achieved victory in the Supreme Court in one Texas case and now worked to follow up that victory to ensure that it meant something at ballot boxes as well as in newspaper headlines.[9]

In March 1928 a large group of black Richmonders held a meeting and determined to go to court to obtain clearance to vote in Virginia primary elections. In early April, Democratic voters would be selecting the party's nominee for mayor of the city, and James O. West asked a local court to rule that he and others like him could vote, despite their racial identities, in that primary election. On March 30 Judge Beverly Crump denied the petition. He ruled that in Virginia the Democratic Party rules reflected actions taken by private individuals, unlike the Texas situation, where state law had directed that black voters be excluded. Because the state of Virginia had not acted to prevent West from voting, his Fourteenth and Fifteenth Amendment rights had not been violated, and the courts could not give him what he wanted.[10]

West and his colleagues proceeded to press their case. On April 3, 1928, two black men approached the election officials in the first precinct of Madison Ward in Richmond, Virginia. The Democratic primary was being held to select candidates for the forthcoming municipal elections, and the younger of the two men, James O. West, planned to vote. The more elderly man, J. R. Pollard, was his attorney. The election officials' refusal to permit West to vote—even though race was the only consideration that prevented his qualifying to vote—came as no surprise to either man. They and a host of other black Virginians well knew that the obstacles to voting in Virginia could be many, but both Pollard and West intended to succeed before long.[11]

In federal district court later that year, J. R. Pollard and a white lawyer, Alfred E. Cohen, faced off against Leon M. Bazile, state assistant attorney general. West sought $5,000 in damages from the election officials. Before Louis Marshall died that year, he wrote about the case that "what has been done in Virginia is only to pursue in a roundabout manner the same vicious method of holding a primary as was sought" in a more direct manner by the Texas legislature.[12]

West's attorneys pointed out that the city's public treasury, into which West had paid taxes, had financed the primary election from which he had been excluded. Noting that the winners in the primary had all gone on to victory in the general election, they argued that "the denial of the right of the plaintiff to vote in said primary election had the same effect upon the plaintiff's right to vote as though he had been denied a right to vote in said general elections for said offices."[13] And they argued that the Fourteenth and Fifteenth Amendments alike barred his being discriminated against on the basis of his race.

The defendants denied that West had any right to vote in the primary. While acknowledging that they had discriminated against West on the basis of his race, they denied that the Reconstruction amendments had any bearing on the issue at hand. The election judges were, they insisted, acting as private individuals, not agents of the state. A private organization, the Democratic Party, had established the rules governing the primary elections.[14] Would the federal court accept the distinction, or would it take Louis Marshall's approach that the difference was a sham and a nullity?

In June 1929 district judge Lawrence D. Groner observed, referring to the Supreme Court's ruling in *Nixon* v. *Herndon*, "Counsel for defendants admit, as of course they must, that a statute of a state which attempted to exclude negroes from voting in a Democratic primary would be in conflict with the Fourteenth Amendment." Only if defendants had been operating as private individuals might they act the way they had. Was this a private matter? Nobody said the Democratic Party had to hold primary elections. If the party chose to hold primaries "under its own rules and at its own expense," that would be one thing, but here, "in order to secure the greater safeguard and freedom of expense," the party had adopted "the legalized primary."[15]

Thus the central question in this case. "May a political party adopt the statutory method of naming its candidates for political office, and still preserve the absolute right to determine who shall participate in the election?" Here the federal judge had recourse to a decision by the Virginia Supreme Court in which Judge James Keith had observed that "the purpose of holding a primary election is to select a candidate to be voted for by a party organization at the ensuing general or special election." Thus "the primary when adopted by a political party becomes an inseparable part of the election machinery," and any feature of the primary was "an ineradicable constituent" of the outcome in the general election.[16]

In the Texas case the U.S. Supreme Court had faced a state law that shouted, "In no event shall a negro be eligible to participate in a Democratic party primary election held in the State of Texas." The Court had ruled the statute in conflict with the Fourteenth Amendment. As Judge Groner observed, "The statute of Virginia, unlike that of Texas," did not specifically exclude black voters, but it gave the parties "the right to do so. The result is the same." The legislature "may not indirectly, any more than it may indirectly," act to permit or achieve black exclusion.[17]

West had his victory. But he could not rest easily. The Democratic Party might abandon the primary, or it might seek to make it entirely a private affair, the way Texas soon did, as a means around the decision in West's case. Many black Virginians expected the case to go on to the Supreme Court. West's lawyer, Alfred E. Cohen, sent a letter to the editor of the *Richmond Planet*. He wrote that the Democratic Party in Virginia probably would appeal the decision, even to the Supreme Court, and if it did, that would "entail further costs and expenses in fighting the case. But the victory that has already been gained should be followed up and defended vigorously, so that Colored Democrats may be granted their rights as citizens." The decision, Cohen wrote, "is of far reaching importance not only to the Colored citizens in Virginia, but throughout the South."[18]

In fact, the decision held. The defendants took the case on to the fourth circuit court of appeals. On the major points in contention, the appeals court gave the Democratic Party no quarter. "We agree with the reasoning and conclusion set out in the [district court's] opinion," the appeals judges declared. "It is contended, by appellants, that the Legislature of Virginia may do indirectly that which it cannot do directly. With this contention, we cannot agree."[19]

Texas and the U.S. Supreme Court went back and forth across two decades as to what racial restrictions might be placed on prospective black voters in primary elections. Other states, too, waited into the 1940s to open the Democratic primary to voters regardless of racial identity. Virginia, by contrast, entered the 1930s with the racial barrier officially knocked down. Fossils of the past might come to light from time to time and place to place, but the right to exclude Virginia voters from a party primary because they were black had been taken away. One prop to black disfranchisement had fallen, but others remained in place. As the Norfolk *Ledger-Dispatch* observed, Virginia's "educational qualifications, poll-tax prepayment, registration and all other requirements prescribed by state law are still in effect."[20]

W. E. Davis Goes to Court to Register to Vote

A black attorney in tidewater Virginia, A. W. E. Bassette Jr., did what he could to tie the local court up with cases in which black residents of Hampton had tried to register to vote but were turned back. The local judge, Claude Vernon Spratley (who would soon be elevated to the Virginia Supreme Court), often proved receptive to Bassette's efforts. But not always.

On October 5, 1929, W. E. Davis approached Thomas C. Allen, the voting registrar. Producing receipts for payment of his poll tax for 1926, 1927, and 1928, he made it over the first hurdle, but that was not the only hurdle. Responding in his own handwriting to mandatory oral questions, Davis wrote in his application that he was forty-eight years old, a skilled laborer, and a native of North Carolina. He had lived in Hampton for twenty-six years and had never voted. Allen asked Davis a number of additional questions, found his answers unsatisfactory, and refused to register him.[21]

Rebuffed by the registrar, Davis became one of the many aspiring voters to seek Bassette's help in appealing to the Circuit Court of Elizabeth City County. Judge Spratley upheld the registrar, however, and Davis took his case to the state's highest court.[22]

As the *Richmond Planet*, the voice of black Richmond, reported, "for a long time" Bassette had found himself "compelled to appeal cases to Judge Spratley in order to have colored men and women placed upon the books as registered voters. In fact, much of the time of the Circuit Court has been taken in hearing cases of that character because the registrars were determined to evade the law and to embarrass colored applicants who came before them for registration." As the paper explained, "Lawyer Bassette has fought these cases with patience and persistence, has succeeded in placing a number of men and women on the books through the medium of the Circuit Court, but he finally decided that, with the adverse ruling of Judge Spratley in the Davis case, he would take the matter to the Supreme Court of this State so as to have it settled once and for all."[23]

The *Richmond Planet* highlighted the story in March 1930. The headline read, "Virginia Supreme Court Rules Favorably on Registration." The state's highest court had, indeed, agreed to hear the case. Virginians, black and white, would have to wait, however, to find out whether the court would rule favorably on matters of substance and not only of procedure. When the case came up, Bassette and another black attorney from tidewater, J. Thomas Newsome, represented Davis. They insisted that Virginia law imposed no requirement that prospective voters answer detailed questions about the political process, the state constitution, or anything else.[24]

The court overturned Davis's rejection as a voter. Writing for the court, Justice Louis S. Epes ruled that the registrar should have accepted Davis's answers as satisfying Virginia's laws, and the trial court should not have sustained the registrar's actions. The Virginia Supreme Court ordered Allen to register Davis as a voter on the basis of his original application.[25] Presumably registrars across the state took notice that their authority to impede registration among black voters was less far-reaching than they might have assumed in the past.

Showing that the court could have ruled another way, one justice, Henry W. Holt, dissented. He conceded that a prospective voter had no need to display a broad range of knowledge: "He may believe that the Polish corridor has to do with architecture and that the Rosetta stone was a crown jewel of Egypt, and yet be eligible." And yet, he observed, surely the registrar had authority to question the applicant regarding his qualifications to vote, and Justice Holt had grave doubts about those qualifications: "In this instant, we have a coached applicant, who repeated verbatim what he had been taught to write and who manifestly had no idea what it was all about."[26]

Nonetheless, another structural obstacle to black voter participation had fallen. Another court decision—this one by a state court—had ruled in a manner consistent with increased black voting. Voter registration might prove easier—the lawyer Bassette might be able to spend more of his time on other matters than getting black Virginians registered—and the white Democratic primary had been declared unconstitutional. The poll tax, however, remained.

Challenges to the Poll Tax

Poll taxes were a part of the fiscal scenery—in Virginia and across much of the nation—both before and after the Civil War. Yet the tax as a condition of voting put in its first appearance in post–Civil War Virginia in 1876, and six years later the Readjusters broke the linkage again. The poll tax remained on the books, but paying it was no longer a requirement for voting. Under the Constitution of 1902, however, Virginia voters had to prove they had paid a poll tax for each of the three years preceding the election in which they wished to participate. The tax each year was $1.50, and penalties and interest on overdue taxes could raise the total three-year amount due—payable before one could register to vote—to about $5.[27]

People in various states attacked the poll tax, sometimes with success. Before World War II three southern states—North Carolina in 1920, Louisiana in 1934, and Florida in 1937—dropped the poll tax as a requirement for voting.[28] Dissenters from the dominant political groups took the lead in challenging the means through which they had been marginalized. In partisan terms, Republicans challenged Democrats, or dissenting Democrats challenged the group in power. In racial terms, black southerners challenged white southerners.

During and soon after World War II, Virginians went to federal court to bring four different challenges to the poll tax. Each challenge entered a judicial environment in which a major precedent stood in the way of successful litigation, for, in a case that came from Georgia—*Breedlove* v. *Suttles*—the Supreme Court had ruled in 1937 in favor of the permissibility of a poll tax as a condition of voting. A white man named Breedlove had demanded that he be registered to vote even though he had not paid the Georgia poll tax. Rebuffed, he took his case to the Supreme Court. His argument relied on the Fourteenth Amendment's equal protection clause and privileges and immunities clause.

A unanimous Supreme Court rejected the argument. Regarding the privileges and immunities clause, Justice Pierce Butler wrote: "Privilege of voting is not derived from the United States, but is conferred by the State and, save as restrained by the Fifteenth and Nineteenth Amendments and other provisions of the Federal Constitution, the State may condition suffrage as it deems appropriate."[29] The poll tax had withstood a challenge as to its constitutionality as a condition for voting. Given the express imprimatur of the nation's highest court, it would surely be difficult to mount a successful challenge.

Yet challenges emerged. Millions of people from across the nation had a profound interest in curtailing the inordinate power of a few senior members of Congress—elected by unrepresentative electorates in the poll-tax states—to thwart progressive federal legislation on a wide range of issues. The first bill to end the poll tax in federal elections was introduced in Congress in 1939. Beginning in 1942, such bills were passed almost every year by the U.S. House of Representatives, but they always died in the Senate. There, cloture votes failed to cut off filibusters by diehard southern advocates of the poll tax, who were fearful that if the federal government could intervene on that front, it might take other action as well to support voting rights.[30]

So it was that whatever the odds of success, efforts were sometimes directed to the courts. As for the Virginia poll tax, it was challenged repeatedly in the federal courts in the 1940s, in each case by a would-be candidate for Congress—not a candidate supported by the Byrd Organization—who saw himself put at an enormous disadvantage by the poll-tax requirement for voting.

The Virginia Poll Tax in the Federal Courts: The 1940s

Henry L. Saunders wanted to run for Congress from Virginia—from the state-at-large, not any one congressional district—in 1944. Secretary of the Commonwealth Ralph E. Wilkins consulted with the Virginia attorney general, Abram Penn Staples, who advised that "no such office as member of the House of Representatives from the State at large existed, and no election was being held for that position." Wilkins therefore refused to certify Saunders as a candidate-at-large, a refusal that could have come as no surprise, since elections to Congress were routinely held in Virginia on a district basis.[31] But that was the point Saunders was trying to make.

Saunders claimed that the poll tax was unconstitutional in that it prevented the free exercise of the franchise. It denied a majority of potential voters in Virginia—60 percent, according to Saunders—their right to participate in congressional elections. And thus, he concluded, pending a suspension of the poll tax as a condition for the vote, the U.S. Constitution required that Virginia's members of the House of Representatives be elected at large. Saunders relied on the Fourteenth Amendment for his position. Even if Section 1's language about "equal protection" could not help him, as the decision in *Breedlove* held, Section 2 should. That is, if the Virginia poll tax acted to reduce the electorate by 60 percent in elections for presidential electors and members of Congress, then Congress had the duty to reduce the number of Virginia's representatives from nine to no more than four.[32]

Saunders sued Wilkins for $20,000, equal to the salary for the two years of a term in Congress. He took his case to federal district court, which ruled against him by adopting the state's motion to dismiss on the grounds that apportionment was a political question. Congress had apportioned Virginia nine seats, and the state legislature had divided the state into nine districts. Saunders had been denied no right that he could secure in the courts.[33]

He took his case to the fourth circuit court of appeals, which upheld the lower court. The appeals court viewed it as "manifest" that Saunders had as his "underlying purpose . . . to bring about the abolition of the Virginia poll tax law." It guessed that he had not made "a direct attack upon its constitutionality" because he could not hope to pierce the defenses that *Breedlove* and other decisions supplied the state. It characterized Saunders's contention as holding that "even if the Virginia poll tax law does not offend the first section of the Fourteenth Amendment," it nonetheless had to satisfy the terms of the second section. But the court termed his question as "political, rather than judicial, and it is difficult to perceive in what ways the courts can remedy the defect." Congress had displayed no inclination to act to enforce the second section, and the judicial branch had no means to carry out the responsibilities of the legislative branch.[34]

Saunders took his case to the U.S. Supreme Court, which denied certiorari in June 1946. Observers might have detected some straws in the wind, however, for the American Civil Liberties Union filed a brief as friend of the court in support of his petition for review by the high court, and among the court's nine members, Justice William O. Douglas wanted to grant the petition and review the case.[35]

In 1946 Sidney H. Kelsey brought another case. Kelsey was an attorney in Norfolk and the Republican Party's nominee for Congress from Virginia's Second District. He took the position that the Virginia poll tax, as a condition for voting, violated the Fifteenth Amendment. And he sued twenty officials, among them Attorney General Staples, Governor William M. Tuck, and the treasurers and commissioners of the counties and cities in the Second District.[36]

The Virginia attorney general filed a motion to dismiss the case on the grounds that the poll tax was a revenue measure—and thus the statute demanding it was constitutional—and that Kelsey should seek relief in the state courts. Judge Sterling Hutcheson sustained Staples's motion for dismissal. The judge said he failed to see how he could rule the poll tax discriminatory. And he pointed Kelsey to the state courts to pursue his challenge to it. None of the defendants had appeared in court for the hearing.[37] None could have been surprised to hear later of Hutcheson's ruling.

Unlike Saunders, Kelsey let the matter die there. In a statement after the hearing, he told reporters:, "Naturally, I am disappointed. I would like to carry this case on to the Supreme Court, if necessary, but I do not feel that I have the time nor the money to do so personally at this moment."[38]

In the Eighth District, Lawrence H. Michael—the treasurer of Arlington County and another Republican candidate for Congress—also brought suit before Judge Hutcheson in 1946. The state asked for dismissal on grounds that the court lacked authority to throw out the poll tax and that the suit, if successful, would prevent the collection of state revenue. In a hearing on that motion, Michael's attorney, John Locke Green, took a lengthy tour of Virginia political history to make his case. Congress had enacted a law in 1870, he pointed out, that established conditions for the readmission of Virginia to the Union and the seating of its congressmen. A major condition warned Virginia against subsequently depriving "any citizen or class of citizens of the right to vote." In contravention of that federal law, Green argued, the Virginia constitutional convention of 1901–2 had established a collection of measures designed to deprive large numbers of Virginians, particularly black Virginians, of the right to vote. Central among them was the poll tax.[39]

Judge Hutcheson, seeing the central question to be "the validity of the payment of the poll tax as a prerequisite of the right to vote," relied on *Breedlove* and dismissed the case. Six months later, in April 1947, the fourth circuit court of appeals upheld the decision. Judges John Johnston Parker, Morris A. Soper, and Armistead M. Dobie observed that the complaint, if properly presented, looked compelling and would have to be considered, but it was not properly presented. Michael had brought the case in federal court, rather than beginning in state court; he had brought it against tax officials, rather than election officials; and the election for which he sought a remedy had already been held. The federal appeals court could do nothing for him.[40]

Henry L. Saunders, Sidney H. Kelsey, and Lawrence H. Michael were all in the federal courts in 1946. All failed. At the end of the decade, the Virginia poll tax still stood tall.

Jessie Butler Goes to Court to Challenge the Poll Tax

In 1950 someone challenged the poll tax who was not white, not male, and not a candidate for Congress. Jessie Butler, a fifty-five-year-old black woman living in Arlington, attempted to register on December 19, 1949, so she could vote in the November 1950 elections, but she was turned back. Mary A. Thompson, central register at Arlington, refused to register her until she had paid her poll tax.[41]

Jessie Butler took the matter to federal court. In addition to asking $5,000 damages from Mary Thompson, whom Butler accused of refusing to register her to vote, she sought a court order that she be permitted to register and vote in all elections. Thus she named as other defendants Levin Nock Davis, secretary of the State Board of Elections; two other members of that board; and three judges of the Woodlawn election precinct in Arlington.[42]

John Locke Green represented Butler. He argued, as he had in the Michael case back in 1946, that—the *Breedlove* decision to the contrary—the 1870 act of Congress, together with the Fifteenth Amendment, permitted a reconsideration of the constitutionality of the 1901–2 state convention and its deformed progeny, the Virginia poll tax. The Virginia Constitution of 1869, which required no payment of a poll tax before voting, should still govern Virginia elections.[43]

In July 1950 district judge Albert V. Bryan dismissed the case. It raised, he said, "no substantial Constitutional or Federal question." After all, he noted, the U.S. Supreme Court had upheld the constitutionality of the poll tax in the *Breedlove* decision in 1937, and more recently, in the *Saunders* decision in 1945, the fourth circuit court of appeals had rejected such arguments as Butler's attorneys mounted.[44]

That October the fourth circuit court of appeals heard Butler's case. Less sure than was Judge Bryan that Butler's complaint raised "no substantial Constitutional or Federal question," this court ruled that "substantial constitutional questions were unquestionably involved," and it directed that her case be heard by a three-judge district panel.[45]

The three members of the panel were district judge Bryan, who had dismissed the case in the first place; circuit court judge Dobie, of Charlottesville; and district judge Hutcheson. In the one-day hearing in January 1951, Virginia attorney general J. Lindsay Almond asked for a dismissal, but the court went ahead and heard the case. Among the witnesses that day, Mary Thompson testified that she had told Jessie Butler—and others in the group that accompanied Butler when she tried to register—that she "would be happy to register them" if they were current in their poll-tax obligations.[46]

In February 1951 Judge Dobie spoke for a unanimous court in dismissing Butler's case after all. He cited *Breedlove* as well as *Saunders* in rejecting each of Butler's contentions. Butler had contended that the tax, even if fair on its face, was administered in a manner that discriminated against black Virginians, but the court professed to be mystified by this line of attack: "There is not a shred of evidence in the record of this case showing either that any Negro so applying has been refused assessment or that any white person, duly assessable, has been permitted to vote without the payment of taxes." Butler had been assessed for her poll taxes in each of the previous ten years but had paid none. The registrar, in refusing to register her until she had paid her taxes, had told her how to comply with the regulations and had been ready to register her as soon as she met the qualification. "How, then, can this plaintiff maintain that she personally has been discriminated against by virtue of her race?"[47]

Butler's case then went to the Supreme Court. But that court showed no inclination to reconsider the matter. In a per curiam decision in May 1951, it affirmed the decision of the district court, although Justice William O. Douglas dissented.[48]

Two members of the Virginia House of Delegates called for a limited constitutional convention in 1950 for the purpose of repealing the poll tax as a requirement for voting. Other members of the legislature preferred an open convention that might introduce various changes to the state constitution. What such legislators shared was a sense of "grave danger" that federal action would eliminate the poll tax as a prerequisite in presidential and congressional elections. Keep the poll tax, they argued, but uncouple it from voting rights. Replace it with a literacy test, they said, and thereby "settle the suffrage problem and forestall Federal interference in Virginia elections."[49] Despite such calls, nothing happened to affect the Virginia poll tax across the 1950s; Congress passed no such act or constitutional amendment, and the state took no action on the poll tax either.

Although Virginia retained the poll tax, other southern states dropped it. Georgia did so in 1945, followed by South Carolina in 1951 and Tennessee in 1953. Only five of the eleven states of the former Confederacy—Alabama, Arkansas, Mississippi, and Texas, along with Virginia—still kept the tax to restrict the electorate.

Challenges to the Poll Tax in the 1960s

In the 1960s a second set of four challenges to the Virginia poll tax arose. Again, litigation was brought both by white Republican political figures and by black Virginians. But the new challenges took place in a very different context. First of all, the Supreme Court had opened up questions of voting rights in a series of cases, notably those challenging malapportioned state legislatures. Perhaps, some people mused, it would prove receptive, too, to challenges to the poll tax. Second, the Twenty-fourth Amendment, ratified in early 1964, banned the requirement that any taxes be paid as a condition of voting in federal elections. Thus the new challenges had as their targets either new laws passed in Virginia to address the implications of that amendment or the laws that retained the poll tax as a condition of voting in state and local elections. And third, for various reasons, many Virginians were coming out against the poll tax, which might then—sooner or later—fall as a consequence of action by the legislature rather than the judiciary.

In late 1963, expecting that the Twenty-fourth Amendment would likely soon be ratified—and knowing that the Virginia Democratic Party was making plans for a special session of the state legislature to take action to retain the poll tax in state elections—newspaper editorials from across the state commented on the poll tax. Those comments expressed concern with such matters as the well-being of the Democratic Party, the relationship between electoral integrity and the poll-tax requirement, and the administrative problems that would prove inescapable if eligibility for voting in federal elections differed from that in state elections.

The *Petersburg Progress-Index* favored keeping what was left of the poll tax. Recognizing that its retention would be "denounced routinely and in parrot style as an evil effort to keep people from voting," that paper nonetheless saw it as "the best hope of preserving some sort of electoral order." By contrast, the *Staunton Leader* worried that a dual system of voter requirements would "have more disadvantages than advantages, causing difficult electoral complications and damaging the Democratic organization's popular prestige." Indeed, it feared, retaining the poll tax in state elections "would encourage the new militancy of the Republican party in Virginia as nothing else has done." The *Roanoke World-News* opposed retention of the tax in part because it would necessitate "two separate registration systems." More than that, it said, the poll tax should simply no longer "be connected with the right to vote. . . . It is outmoded, outdated, anachronistic and wholly indefensible. It ought to be abolished entirely." [50]

Falling midway between the extremes that the Roanoke paper in southwestern Virginia and the Petersburg paper in the Southside represented, the *Charlottesville Daily Progress* nonetheless objected to retention. It expressed "skepticism" that the poll tax deserved credit for fraud-free elections: "Experience in Southwest Virginia and in other states" demonstrated that the tax could not supply "sure protection against fraud"; rather, it could "even be used as an instrument for fraud." And "in any case, if it isn't necessary for the preservation of the integrity of our federal elections, why should it be necessary in state elections?" "Our objection is not to the poll tax or even to the using of it as a voter-eligibility requirement," the Charlottesville paper observed. In fact, "it should be retained and strengthened as a source of revenue." But should it be retained as a condition of voting? Only "if it could thus be applied in all elections." [51]

Lars Forssenius and Horace Henderson

The Twenty-fourth Amendment was proposed in August 1962. As it moved swiftly toward ratification (completed in January 1964, no thanks to Virginia), Governor Albertis Sydney Harrison Jr.—who hailed from Brunswick County in the Southside—called a special session of the Virginia General Assembly to prepare for that eventuality. In November 1963 the special session passed two laws to address the imminent change. Payment of the poll tax would continue, as before, to be required for voting in state and local elections, but something new, certificates of residence, were established as an optional way to qualify for voting in federal elections. A Virginian could qualify for federal as well as state elections by staying current with poll-tax payments. To gain exemption for federal elections, however, one had to fill out a certificate of residence and turn it in at least six months before the election—the same lead time that the poll tax required.[52]

A veteran Republican expressed disgust with the Organization's latest ploy to restrict the electorate: "It's time we quit letting the anti-organization Democrats and the NAACP fight our legal battles against the Byrd machine," he said. Republicans went into federal court to challenge Virginia's response to the poll-tax amendment. Horace E. Henderson, state GOP chairman, filed suit in Fairfax County, and Lars Forssenius, state vice-chairman of the Young Republicans, filed suit in Roanoke County.[53]

Time was short for pursuing any kind of court action. The laws were passed in November, and the amendment was ratified in January 1964. With presidential and congressional elections coming in November 1964, the certificates of residence had to be filed by early May that year, less than six months after the new law was passed.

A three-judge federal district court was convened to address the two suits' challenge to the new state laws' constitutionality. The state argued that the matter should go first to the state courts. With only two months left before the May deadline, however, and only eight before the elections themselves, the district court refused to defer to the state courts and declared, instead, that the statutes violated the new amendment.[54]

The state appealed the district court rulings to the U.S. Supreme Court. Oral argument took place the first two days of March, and on April 27—days before the deadline for registering under the new law—the Supreme Court handed down its ruling. First, said the Court, the district court had been right not to abstain. The Virginia statutes were sufficiently clear as to require no interpretation by the state courts. As to the merits of the matter, wrote Chief Justice Earl Warren for a unanimous

Court, "We hold that [the new legislation] is repugnant to the Twenty-fourth Amendment and affirm the decision of the District Court on that basis."[55]

The Supreme Court took two approaches to its conclusion. For one, it pointed out that the new law "unquestionably erects a real obstacle to voting in federal elections for those who assert their constitutional exemption from the poll tax." Moreover, it imposed a new requirement "solely upon those who refuse to surrender their constitutional right to vote in federal elections without paying a poll tax." Not only did the Twenty-fourth Amendment abolish the poll tax; it "was also designed to absolve all requirements impairing the right to vote in federal elections by reason of failure to pay the poll tax."[56]

In a complementary approach, the chief justice drew on the historical record to buttress the Court's decision. "The Virginia poll tax," he observed, "was born of a desire to disenfranchise the Negro." He quoted at length Delegate Carter Glass's declaration at the 1901 convention that began: "Discrimination! Why, that is precisely what we propose." In fact, Warren went on to say, Glass's "statement was characteristic of the entire debate on the suffrage issue; the only real controversy [in the convention] was whether the provisions eventually adopted were sufficient to accomplish the disenfranchisement of the Negro."[57]

The days of black disfranchisement might not be entirely over, Chief Justice Warren suggested, but the poll tax should die. Under the substitute system Virginia had enacted, voters who wished to bypass the poll tax had to register again every year they wished to vote. "In addition, the certificate must be filed six months before the election, thus perpetuating one of the disenfranchising characteristics of the poll tax which the Twenty-fourth Amendment was designed to eliminate." The Court was unprepared to compromise on this matter: "For federal elections, the poll tax is abolished absolutely as a prerequisite to voting, and no equivalent . . . may be imposed. Any material requirement imposed upon the federal voter solely because of his refusal to waive the constitutional immunity subverts the effectiveness of the Twenty-fourth Amendment and must fall under its ban."[58]

Evelyn Butts and Annie Harper: The Supreme Court and the Poll Tax, 1966

The Twenty-fourth Amendment was ratified in time, and the Supreme Court acted in time, to eliminate the poll tax as a factor in Virginia in the presidential and congressional elections in 1964. At the same time that

Virginia's response to the Twenty-fourth Amendment was in the courts, other Virginians were challenging the continued use of the poll tax in state elections. A persistent obstacle to black political power in twentieth-century Virginia, the poll tax was under assault from every direction: in federal elections and state elections, by white Republicans and black Democrats.

Evelyn Butts, long a civil rights activist in Norfolk, challenged the constitutionality of the Virginia law that required her to pay a poll tax as a condition of voting in state and local elections. Having lived all her life as a black Virginian in the poll-tax, Jim-Crow South, she had seen great changes in her lifetime, but her own fight was far from over. In November 1963 she filed a class-action suit in federal district court seeking a declaratory judgment that the tax was unconstitutional and a permanent injunction against its enforcement. In Northern Virginia, Annie Harper did the same.[59] Although previous efforts of this sort had proved unavailing, Evelyn Butts and Annie Harper went to court anticipating victory.

Justice Douglas had waited a very long time for the opportunity that came his way in 1966. Not only did a majority of the Court finally agree with him that the question should be reopened, but Chief Justice Earl Warren assigned him the task of writing the majority opinion. In some respects, though, the opinion Douglas wrote in 1966 in *Harper* v. *Virginia* was quite different from the one he might have liked to write back in 1951 in Jessie Butler's case. Much had happened, in the courts and outside them, in the intervening decade and a half. Many of the decisions that he relied on as authority in 1966 had not existed when Butler's case came to the court. Douglas was even able to cite two cases decided in the preceding few weeks, when three-judge federal district courts struck down the poll-tax requirement for voting in state elections in Alabama and Texas.[60]

Justice Douglas relied on the equal protection clause to overturn the Virginia poll tax. He had no quarrel, he said, with the result in *Breedlove* as regarded the legitimacy of a poll tax in general, but only "so long as it is not made a condition to the exercise of the franchise." The majority in *Harper*, unlike that in *Butler* fifteen years earlier, put the burden of proof on the state, not on the plaintiff. "We conclude," wrote Justice Douglas, "that a State violates the Equal Protection Clause of the Fourteenth Amendment whenever it makes the affluence of the voter or payment of any fee an electoral standard." Indeed, he declared, "the right to vote is too precious, too fundamental to be so burdened or conditioned."[61]

The *Harper* decision was by no means unanimous. The state's arguments sounded more convincing to three members of the Court, and they dissented. Together they wrote two opinions, each of which argued that the Court should not intervene in this matter and that the original decision, the one in *Breedlove*, ought to be left undisturbed.

Justice Potter Stewart joined Justice John Marshall Harlan in one dissenting opinion. Harlan noted that because few states retained a poll-tax requirement for voting in state elections, little of substance remained at issue. "The final demise of state poll taxes, already totally proscribed by the Twenty-fourth Amendment with respect to federal elections and abolished by the States themselves in all but four States with respect to State elections, is perhaps in itself not of great moment." That the end was "administered by this Court," however, violated his sense of "the proper role of this tribunal under our scheme of government." It would have been far better for the remaining states to be left to their own devices, regardless of whether they acted to put the poll tax away.[62]

Justice Harlan was writing no blank check to cover the poll tax. He acknowledged that if evidence was conclusive that a state employed the poll tax as a proxy for denying the vote on the basis of race, the Fifteenth Amendment would come into play and such a tax could properly "be struck down by this Court." Indeed, the *Butts* case raised such questions. But the majority opinion had not addressed the Fifteenth Amendment, and "the record here" did not strike Harlan as "sufficient to invalidate this $1.50 tax whether under the Fourteenth or Fifteenth Amendment."[63]

Harlan acknowledged that Douglas had deployed "captivating phrases" in his opinion. But, argued Harlan, "they are wholly inadequate to satisfy the standard governing adjudication of the equal protection issue: Is there a rational basis for Virginia's poll tax as a voting qualification?" Harlan was certain the answer was yes. As far as constitutional challenges went, Harlan had no patience with the complaint that taxpaying qualifications were, as he put it, "not in accord with current egalitarian notions of how a modern democracy should be organized." If so, then legislatures should act to accommodate such changes in public opinion. It was not a constitutional question that the Court should address as it had.[64]

"It is all wrong, in my view," Harlan explained, "for the Court to adopt the political doctrines popularly accepted at a particular moment of our history and to declare all others to be irrational and invidious, barring them from the range of choice by reasonably minded people acting through the political process." Whatever the Court majority would choose to rule in these cases, Justice Harlan insisted, the equal protection clause did not "rigidly impose upon America an ideology of unrestrained egalitarianism." He would have affirmed the district court decision, left *Breedlove* intact, and left Harper and Butts without a vote as long as Virginia chose to leave the poll-tax requirement in place and they did not meet that requirement.[65]

Justice Black, too, parted company with Justice Douglas in these cases. A leading advocate of an expansive interpretation of the First Amendment, he nonetheless rejected its relevance to the poll tax and voting as political expression. Whatever the case with free speech, he wrote, "there is no comparable specific constitutional provision absolutely barring the States from abridging the right to vote."[66]

Black made it clear that he joined the Court majority in "disliking the policy of the poll tax," but "this is not in my judgment a justifiable reason for holding this poll tax law unconstitutional." He failed to see the relevance of the equal protection clause to any of the poll-tax cases he had seen. Back in 1937, he recalled, only "a few weeks after I took my seat as a member of this Court," he had participated in the unanimous ruling in *Breedlove*. Later, he wrote, "I joined the Court's judgment" in the *Butler* case. "Since the *Breedlove* and *Butler* cases were decided the Federal Constitution has not been amended in the only way it could constitutionally have been," he contended. "The Equal Protection Clause itself is the product of the people's desire to use their constitutional power to amend the Constitution to meet new problems."[67]

"The amendatory power which the Court exercises today" truly troubled him, Black said, for it seemed to constitute "an attack not only on the great value of our Constitution itself but also on the concept of a written constitution which is to survive through the years as originally written unless changed through the amendment process which the Framers wisely provided." The Court should not act in the way that the majority was taking it; an alternative approach, easier to accomplish than a constitutional amendment, could be taken in Congress. "I have no doubt at all that Congress has the power [under Section 5, the enforcement section, of the Fourteenth Amendment] to pass legislation to abolish the poll tax in order to protect the citizens of this country if it believes that the poll tax is being used as a device to deny voters equal protection of the laws."[68]

Neither Justice Black nor Justice Douglas had changed his mind about how to rule on the poll tax. Douglas had been ready to listen to challenges to its constitutionality since the 1940s. Black had seen no legitimate path to invalidating it at any time in his nearly three decades on the Court. But Black had represented a majority on the Court in 1937 and again in the cases that arose a decade or so later. Douglas spoke for a Court majority in 1966.

Jessie Butler, Annie Harper, and Evelyn Butts had all taken on the Virginia poll tax. The courts were not prepared to give Jessie Butler a favorable hearing. The story of Annie Harper and Evelyn Butts had a different ending. In 1966 the last vestiges of the poll-tax South vanished.

Butts celebrated her victory in the courts by registering to vote—and continued her celebration by urging other black residents of Norfolk to register, too.[69] In the congressional elections of 1966, no poll tax could have prevented Virginians from voting anyway, thanks to the Twenty-fourth Amendment. Beginning in Virginia's off-cycle year, 1967, the poll tax could no longer restrict voting in state or local elections, either. And the *Harper* decision, like the poll-tax amendment, applied to Americans everywhere.

The Reapportionment Revolution

The poll-tax revolution was only one face of the transformation of Virginia politics in the 1960s. The reapportionment revolution was another. Important as the story of court-mandated legislative reapportionment in Virginia in the 1960s would appear to be, it is not well known. For one thing, the Virginia case—though highlighted in the state's newspapers that Tuesday in June 1964—was one of six cases that the U.S. Supreme Court decided regarding reapportionment the previous day. The name of the lead case, *Reynolds* v. *Sims*, is the one by which we tend to know all six. Nonetheless, in *Davis* v. *Mann*, the U.S. Supreme Court directed Virginia to make significant changes in the tilt of the playing field of politics there.[70]

Rumblings beneath the surface—and on the surface, too—had suggested for some time that substantial changes were in store for Virginia politics. The 1960 census had demonstrated so much population growth in Fairfax County in the north, and in the Norfolk area in the east, that the 1962 legislature had balked at making any reapportionment at all. Called into special session to do their constitutional duty, legislators had made such minimal changes as to jolt some aggrieved citizens into litigation. Hence the case that the Court decided in June 1964.

Meantime, other straws in the wind promised a new Virginia. The Twenty-fourth Amendment to the U.S. Constitution swept away the poll tax as an impediment to participation in federal elections in America.[71] In the presidential election later that year, the state's electoral votes went to Lyndon B. Johnson instead of Barry Goldwater—probably as a direct consequence of that amendment, and in any case despite the best efforts of white voters in the Southside, Virginia's share of the Deep South. For the only time in the second half of the twentieth century, Virginia—one of the former "Solid South" of traditionally Democratic states—returned briefly in 1964 to the Democratic fold.[72]

According to the 1960 U.S. census, rural residents enjoyed much greater effectiveness than did urban people in gaining representation in the Virginia state legislature. On average, each member of the House of Delegates represented 40,000 people, yet individual delegates in fact served constituencies that ranged in size from a rural district with 20,000 people all the way up to Fairfax County with 143,000 for each of its two delegates. The Virginia Senate, too, was malapportioned. In both houses it took many more urban residents than it did rural residents to elect one legislator.[73]

The Virginia legislature's passage of the 1962 reapportionment measure offered the cities of Northern Virginia and the tidewater only half a loaf—not even half a loaf. To smooth out disparities in representation would have required that Norfolk get one additional delegate and one additional senator and that Northern Virginia pick up seven more delegates and two more senators. Transferring only three delegates and one senator from rural to urban districts, the act failed to satisfy urban leaders. Several state representatives from Northern Virginia—C. Harrison Mann Jr. and Kathryn H. Stone (both of Arlington) and John C. Webb (of Fairfax County)—laid the groundwork for a challenge in the courts.[74]

The U.S. Supreme Court's decision in *Baker* v. *Carr* spurred these three people, together with a state senator, John A. K. Donovan (of Fairfax County), to file suit in federal district court. Basing their case on the equal protection clause of Section 1 of the Fourteenth Amendment, they challenged the constitutionality of the new apportionment scheme. They emphasized, as one direct result of Virginia's malapportionment, the "inequitable distribution" to their constituencies of state tax revenues. Urban taxpayers did not get their share of state spending. Clearly, votes by urban residents had much less purchasing power in the electoral marketplace than did rural votes. Urban voters each had a right, they claimed, denied under the state's apportionment law, to cast a vote as effective as that of a rural resident.[75]

When the petitioners from Northern Virginia (joined by voters in Norfolk) proved successful—on a split decision, 2–1, at the district level —the state appealed to the Supreme Court. *Mann* v. *Davis* became *Davis* v. *Mann*. At the high court it was grouped together with cases from New York, Maryland, Delaware, Colorado, and Alabama, and its history came to be submerged in that of the Alabama case, *Reynolds* v. *Sims*.[76]

Virginia officials remained at least cautiously optimistic, secure in the knowledge that, in fact, Virginia's legislature was among the less invidiously discriminatory among the American states of the early 1960s. But Virginia's malapportionment proved too great. The Court ruled 8–1 against Alabama's apportionment law. It did the same to Virginia's. In a separate ruling on the Virginia case that relied on the reasoning in *Reynolds* v. *Sims*, Chief Justice Warren required that the state restructure its legislative districts—in both the House of Delegates and the Senate—on the basis of one-person, one-vote.[77] Urban Virginia—Northern Virginia and the Chesapeake area—had its victory.

It may be worth pointing out that Virginia's political reformers of an earlier time—the 1830s and 1840s—would have been astonished to hear that their 1960s counterparts adopted a rallying cry to the effect of "one person, one vote." Across the South in the years between the "Compromise of 1787" and emancipation, full population—the equivalent of "five-fifths," or even more than the three-fifths employed in the federal ratio under slavery—had supplied a favorite formula for those who wished to see blackbelt whites dominate state government. Moreover, ever since Virginia's 1901–2 disfranchising convention, the Southside had consisted of a collection of rotten boroughs, with few voters but great power. Small numbers of white voters, living in counties with large—and largely nonvoting—black populations, had political clout far beyond their own numbers.[78]

Now, however, the cry for "one person, one vote" served the interests of the voters of the cities, not the voters of the blackbelt. For one thing, Virginia's population continued to undergo a long-term process of whitening. The censuses of 1870 and 1880, after West Virginia had gone its separate way, found Virginia's population to be more than 40 percent black. During the 1960s, by contrast, for the first time in two-and-a-half centuries, that figure slipped below 20 percent.[79] The major struggle, in the minds of many white Virginians, no longer hinged on race, nor did it any longer consist of a clash between rural east and rural west. Now it was time for the voters of the cities to grab their share of power in the state legislature. And that share had become very substantial.

Governor Godwin's Virginia: State, Region, Nation

In November 1965 a renovated electorate chose a new governor and a reapportioned legislature. In his inaugural speech in January 1966, Governor Mills E. Godwin Jr. sought to close the books on Massive Resistance, Virginia's response to *Brown* v. *Board of Education*. "For a dozen years," he said about schools and segregation, "we have wrestled with a question that tore at the foundations" of Virginia's society. "Now the major decisions have been made. If they do not please us all, they are realities with which we all must live."

And he called upon legislators for ambitious policy initiatives. "Virginia is of the South," the new governor assured his constituents. "But the South is also of the nation." So Virginia "is of the nation, and it is by the nation's standards that we are now called upon to judge her. As we do, we will be prompted to still greater effort." Two centuries earlier, he recalled, the Virginia Founders had worked mightily to build the state and the nation, and now it was a new generation's turn to build on what they had done. "Their example," he urged, "reminds us to be practical dreamers, who know that whatever we build, . . . we must begin from where we are. How then shall we build? Our people [in the recent election campaign] have told us how. They have told us of their dreams, of the schools and colleges and highways and hospitals they envision across Virginia." And he would be offering Virginia citizens and their representatives "a positive plan of action . . . , first in the field of education, then in highways and in other areas of opportunity and of need, for we must move Virginia forward everywhere."[80]

Power, Policy, and the Sales Tax Legislature

Reapportionment—along with its companion changes in Virginia's political system—had a striking, immediate impact on public policy in Virginia. At its first session, in 1966, the newly reapportioned legislature adopted several major proposals that had made no appreciable headway in the past.

That year a statewide general sales tax was adopted, the proceeds designated for public education and other functions of a progressive state. A tax of 2 percent on auto sales, earmarked for highway costs, received approval as well. Virginia pulled together its medley of minor efforts into a statewide system of community colleges. Governor Godwin, who presided over the tremendous expansion of educational institutions that his leadership and the legislature's actions brought about, dedicated new buildings in 1969 at Virginia Western Community College in Roanoke. There he spoke of the man in Appomattox who had told him, "Governor, if it hadn't been for the community college system, my daughter would never have had a chance to go to college."[81] That year, too, Virginia Commonwealth University, erected upon some fragments that had long existed in Richmond, began operations.

Not since the 1920s had the state embarked on such an expanded effort to promote education and transportation. Thus the first fruits of reapportionment proved impressive indeed. Legislators gave evidence of their awareness that, in the Old Dominion's new-look electoral and legislative environment, "pay as you go" might permit, even require, much more paying as you went. Voters wanted to see more money spent on schools and roads, and they were willing to pay the taxes that would supply that money. With greater power to target the increased spending, urban voters proved more willing to pay higher taxes.

Redistricting had another major immediate dimension and consequence in 1966. In February 1964, just four months before *Davis* v. *Mann*, the U.S. Supreme Court had handed down a decision in a case that came from Georgia, *Wesberry* v. *Sanders*, in which it declared malapportioned congressional districts unconstitutional. The Court had spoken, but Virginia's power elite offered a rebuttal. In the U.S. House of Representatives, Virginia congressmen William M. Tuck and Howard W. Smith successfully promoted a bill that would have stripped the federal courts of jurisdiction in apportionment cases. When the U.S. Senate rejected the bill, however, the Virginia legislature had to comply with the Court's decision.[82]

As a result, the Eighth District, the home base of Congressman Smith, picked up large numbers of voters from Fairfax County. Running in the Democratic primary for reelection in 1966, Smith, the chairman of the House Rules Committee, the bane of liberal legislation in Congress for a generation, went down to a narrow defeat, his first and only electoral setback during fifty-eight years of public life.[83] The Eighth District was no longer the same; Congress, too, would reflect that change. Congressman Smith had sought to kill reapportionment. Reapportionment had, instead, ended Smith's career in Congress.

Toward a New Politics in the Old Dominion

Participants in the "reapportionment revolution" of the 1960s—litigants and judges alike—spoke of "people." So did analysts at the time, and since then historians and political scientists have done the same. As a rule, they have asked how many people resided in a given district. They have not asked how many people voted in that district. Advocates of "one person, one vote" representation—from Delegate/litigant Harrison Mann to Chief Justice Earl Warren—assumed that representation should be a function of population, that legislative districts should have equivalent numbers of residents. As the Court said in *Reynolds* v. *Sims*, "Legislators represent people, not trees or acres." The decision next stated, "Legislators are elected by voters, not farms or cities or economic interests."[84]

The assumption—that the noun *people* carried much the same meaning as *voters*—has seemed to make so much sense precisely because a wave of enfranchisement was building at the same time. The two phenomena came closely enough together in time as to merge in observers' assessments of the reapportionment revolution.

The right to vote, like the right to have that vote count for something, is central to the operations of representative democracy. Tens of thousands of men in western Virginia had known the distinction between the two facets of the political system when, back in the constitutional convention of 1829–30 and again in 1850–51, they had pushed for changes in both. Nonlandholding white men should have the right to vote, went one argument for change. Just as important—more important, to the minds of western Virginia proponents, and eastern Virginia opponents, of change in state politics and policy—was the question of legislative apportionment.[85] The question was: Which section—or which class—should rule? After the end of slavery, the question was often couched in racial terms: Which race should rule?

By the 1960s the question took a new form. What should be the relative power of rural Virginia and urban Virginia? Should the white voters of the cities and suburbs be permitted the say they thought they deserved, or would the white voters of the countryside continue to dominate? Both kinds of voting rights—the right to vote and the right to have that vote count for something—were major issues and had major consequences in the politics of Virginia in the 1960s.

Virginia's political system thus underwent a partial transformation between 1964 and 1966. Changes in the U.S. Constitution—through formal amendment and judicial interpretation—eliminated the poll tax as a barrier to voting in either federal or state elections. The enfranchisement of large numbers of new voters, in combination with the reapportionment of seats in the Virginia Senate and the House of Delegates, not to mention the redistricting of Virginia's congressional seats, created a very different political environment and therefore a very different policy environment. Among the first results in state policy was a large rise in taxation for, and funding of, education and transportation.

Power and Policy, 1816–1966

If basic questions remained the same across the century and a half between 1816 and 1966, very much had changed. By 1816 Virginia had inaugurated both a Literary Fund and a Board of Public Works. A hundred and fifty years later, the 1966 legislative session embarked on significant new initiatives to promote educational opportunities and transportation facilities. In between those two dates, Virginians contested each other not only over the substantive issues of education and transportation but also over such matters as voting rights and legislative apportionment, matters of process that would affect the struggle over substance.

The Literary Fund, to take one example, lived on through the generations, but the world turned as it did so. In the beginning the fund was meant to assist white youngsters from poor families to obtain elementary schooling. When the University of Virginia opened its doors in 1825, it absorbed much of the Literary Fund, and it provided advanced schooling for very small numbers of elite white men. What remained of the Literary Fund did what it could to foster its original objectives. Meanwhile, from 1831 into the 1860s, the state maintained a law against schools for black Virginians, regardless of whether they were free or enslaved.

Emancipation led to a lifting on the ban against black education, but it led, too, to a racially segregated system of schools. By 1900 the state was supporting higher education for white men, white women, and black men and women. It did so in three separate sets of institutions, very different as to funding, facilities, and curricular opportunities. By the 1920s the state was providing greatly increased funding for public elementary and secondary education, though the children of white families in eastern Virginia received far greater support than did black Virginians or western whites. By 1970 most public institutions of higher education in the Virginia had opened their doors to students whatever their race or gender, and by the time Virginia Military Institute—as a result of a lawsuit in federal court—admitted women in 1997, every one of them had.[86]

The changes in education mirrored changes in voting and in a host of other dimensions of public and private life in the Old Dominion. Throughout the years Virginians struggled over who would control the political game, just as they struggled over what policy outputs would emerge from the political system.

8

From Harry Byrd to Douglas Wilder

Gender, Race, and Judgeships

JAMES W. WILDER AND AGNES W. JOHNSON WERE THE PARENTS OF thirteen children. They were slaves in Virginia when they married in 1857 and when their older children were born but had long since gained their freedom when their youngest child, Robert Judson Wilder, was born in Richmond in 1886. Robert Wilder and his wife, Beulah, had ten children, the next youngest of them born in 1931, also in Richmond, and named after poet Paul Lawrence Dunbar and abolitionist Frederick Douglass. Lawrence Douglas Wilder graduated from Virginia Union University in 1951, served in the Korean War, where he was awarded a Bronze Star, and earned a law degree in 1959 from Howard University, where one of his friends and classmates was Henry Marsh.[1] Soon he began a law practice, and then he went into politics.

Harry Flood Byrd was a generation older than Doug Wilder, and his world was white Virginia. His paternal grandfather, William Byrd, was a lawyer in Texas when the Civil War began, served in the Confederate army, and then after the war was over moved into his father's house in Winchester, Virginia, together with his wife, Jennie, and a young son, Richard Evelyn Byrd. Richard Byrd went on to marry Eleanor Bolling Flood—whose father had served in the Civil War with Robert E. Lee and then retired to his plantation in Appomattox County—in 1886, and Harry was born the next year. Richard Byrd continued to practice law, but he went to Richmond as a member of the House of Delegates for four terms beginning in 1906, and during the 1908, 1910, and 1912 sessions he served as House speaker.[2]

Harry F. Byrd was elected to the Virginia Senate in 1915 and again in 1919 and 1923. Among his colleagues in the Senate was another newcomer elected in 1915, A. Willis Robertson, with whom Byrd went on to have a durable political relationship. By 1922 Byrd had become chairman of the state Democratic Party. In the 1924 session, Byrd's last as a senator, the General Assembly passed Virginia's Racial Integrity Act and also a law providing for "the sexual sterilization of inmates of State institutions in certain cases." Other provisions enacted that year—each touching on topics in this book—related to the convict workforce on the state highway system, a gasoline tax to pay for highway construction, payment of the poll tax as a prerequisite for voting, the employment of state employees on Sundays, and the four state colleges for training white women as teachers. Yet another bill, one that celebrated Virginia's seventeenth-century past, designated the part of the state highway system extending from Newport News to Richmond the "Pocahontas Trail."[3]

In 1925 Byrd gained election to the Virginia governorship. A reform governor, although he remained committed to low state taxes and low state spending, Byrd pushed energetically for a number of changes, including streamlining state administration. Among various constitutional amendments he pushed through, one reduced the list of officials chosen through statewide election to the governor, lieutenant governor, and attorney general (Douglas Wilder would later fill two of those three offices); another one designated the members of the state supreme court "justices" rather than "judges" and gave the former "president" a new title, "chief justice."[4]

Limited by the Virginia constitution to a single term as governor, Byrd secured appointment to the U.S. Senate when Senator Claude Swanson was named to President Franklin D. Roosevelt's cabinet, so Senator Byrd took office in 1933 at the same time President Roosevelt did. Byrd gained election to a full term in 1934 and then reelection every six years through 1964. A. Willis Robertson went to Washington at the same time Byrd did; he gained election to Congress in 1932 (two years after Howard W. Smith did) and served there until he himself entered the Senate in 1946. Texas congressman Sam Rayburn once said of Byrd, "He runs Virginia," but Rayburn said it in a context of Byrd's tremendous power in the U.S. Senate over a long career, safe from challenge in a state with a one-party system and a small electorate. From his perch in the Senate, Byrd opposed all measures that might undermine his power at home, including bills to put an end to the poll tax in federal elections. He cosponsored (with Strom Thurmond) the "Southern Manifesto" in reaction to the 1954 and 1955 rulings in *Brown* v. *Board of Education*, and he opposed the Civil Rights Act of 1964 and the Voting Rights Act of 1965.[5] Meanwhile, his son Harry F. Byrd Jr. gained election in 1947 to the Virginia Senate, where he served all through the tumultuous 1950s and into the 1960s.

In 1965 Harry F. Byrd Sr. retired from the U.S. Senate after thirty-two years, and the governor appointed Harry F. Byrd Jr. to succeed him. In the Democratic primary of 1966, in an election to complete the elder Byrd's six-year term, the younger Byrd faced a strong challenge from a liberal opponent, Northern Virginia's Armistead Boothe, an old critic of the Byrd Organization who had been first elected to the Virginia legislature the same year Byrd Jr. was. Boothe denigrated his foe as "not a chip, or even a splinter, off the old block and . . . hardly a feather off the old Byrd." Boothe did not prevail, but Harry F. Byrd Jr. barely survived the Democratic primary that year, the same primary that ended Congressman Howard W. Smith's career and that resulted, too, in the defeat of Senator A. Willis Robertson by a very narrow margin.[6]

New Rules, New Results

Reapportionment itself had no direct impact on statewide elections, such as those for U.S. senator or state governor, but in combination with the end of the poll tax it had tremendous effect in Virginia politics. The poll-tax amendment operated alone to supply Lyndon Johnson's margin of victory over Barry Goldwater in the 1964 presidential election and to end the career of Senator Robertson. Reapportionment goes far to explain the sales-tax legislature of 1966. To bring Congressman Smith's career to an end required both the poll-tax amendment and congressional redistricting.[7]

The Byrd Organization, so relatively unchallenged for decades, had appeared securely in control of the Virginia political system even through the years of Massive Resistance in the 1950s. But the 1960s brought massive change to Virginia politics. Like the issue of school desegregation, legislative apportionment and voting rights took the direction they did, and with the timing they did, as a direct consequence of rulings by the federal courts—at the behest of some Virginians who challenged the dominance and the policies of other Virginians.

In 1936 southern writer Margaret Mitchell became famous when she published a historical novel she called *Gone with the Wind*. It focused on the transformation that in the 1860s had swept aside traditional landmarks in southern society and politics and inaugurated new patterns. Three decades after her book appeared, a newer "Old South"—that of Harry F. Byrd Sr. and his colleagues and supporters—fell subject to renewed efforts to renovate southern society and politics. In the 1960s, unlike the 1860s, the men who brought change to Virginia wore black robes, not blue uniforms. In both periods federal power proved a potent ally of some political groups in the South against other southerners.

Completing a Process Begun in 1954

Neither side in Virginia surrendered easily in the war over Jim Crow. By some point in the 1960s, however, *Brown* v. *Board of Education* was, in fact, being implemented, and official efforts to restrict the electorate, especially in terms of race, had been turned back. In two cases from Virginia, moreover, the U.S. Supreme Court ruled in 1963 against courtroom segregation and in 1967 against bans on interracial marriage. The long siege against Jim Crow across the 1940s, the sustained assault in the 1950s, and then the widespread mop-up efforts of the 1960s had proved successful on a great many fronts.

Reporting on the Supreme Court's 1967 decision on interracial marriage, the *New York Times* noted the case's larger significance: "In writing the opinion that struck down the last group of segregation laws to remain standing—those requiring separation of the races in marriage—Chief Justice Warren completed the process that he set in motion with his opinion in 1954 that declared segregation in public schools to be unconstitutional."[8]

As black Virginians knew, of course, "the process" had been "set in motion" long before 1954. They had helped to set that process in motion. They knew, too, that courtroom victories left much yet to be accomplished. In that sense, the process had by no means been "completed."

Hill, Tucker, and Marsh: Electoral Politics

After the 1960s the courts would remain important in civil rights strategy but would no longer supply the only, or perhaps even the primary, arena in which to seek change. Oliver Hill had led the way in late 1940s, a pioneer in politics at a time when black Virginians' electoral prospects seemed bleak but, as he demonstrated with his election to the Richmond City Council in 1948, no longer quite out of the question. The absolute drought in black electoral success in Virginia—lasting for fifty years, from the 1890s to after World War II—had come to an end. And by the late 1960s, black Virginians had been elected to both houses of the state legislature.

The law firm of Hill, Tucker, and Marsh—the successor to the firm of Hill, Martin, and Robinson—still operates in Richmond. One of the three original members of the firm, Martin A. Martin, died in 1963.[9] Another, Spottswood W. Robinson III, served beginning in 1964 as a federal judge, on the District Court for the District of Columbia from 1964 to 1966 and then on the Court of Appeals for the District of Columbia.[10] Oliver Hill's old friend Sam Tucker joined the firm in 1961. Two much younger men, Henry W. Marsh III and his brother Harold Marsh, joined at about the same time as Tucker did.

Henry Marsh's "baptism by fire" as a young civil rights attorney, as he later remembered it, came in the dozens of court cases that, well into the 1960s, sought implementation of *Brown* v. *Board of Education.* Then he "drifted," he said, into politics. In the mid-1960s Marsh determined that much of the work in the courts had perhaps already been accomplished. He recognized how slow the "legal process" could be, and by that time the "political arena" had opened to black Virginians, for the mid-1960s brought the Voting Rights Act of 1965, as well as an end in 1966 to the poll tax in state as well as federal elections. Elected to the Richmond City Council in 1966, he subsequently served for five years (1977–82) as the city's first black mayor.[11]

Some of the elder lawyers—the civil rights generation—also sought, even gained, elective office in the new political order. As a resident of Emporia in the Southside, Tucker ran for a seat in Congress in 1964, 1966, and 1968, but he was unable to topple Watkins M. Abbitt, a warhorse of the old regime who opposed such initiatives as the Civil Rights Act of 1964.[12]

In 1983 Richmond resident Roland D. "Duke" Ealey won a special election to complete a term in the House of Delegates after the incumbent died. Three decades earlier he had run for a seat but had lost. Now he won and became one of four black members in the House of Delegates. At sixty-eight, he was not young. "But age is no barrier," he said, or at least "like race and sex should not be barriers anymore. I am against discrimination in all its ugly faces. And I don't feel I am too old." Ealey continued to serve in the legislature until his own death in 1992.[13]

Douglas Wilder

L. Douglas Wilder—who was born in 1931, in between the end of Harry Byrd's term as governor and his appointment to the U.S. Senate— won a seat in the Virginia Senate in 1969. Voters in Richmond elected him the first black member of the Virginia Senate in the twentieth century, and he gained reelection in 1973, 1977, and 1981. In 1985, when he won election to the lieutenant governorship, he became the first successful black candidate in a statewide election for any legislative or executive post in any southern state since the 1870s. Four years later he won the Virginia governorship, a position he filled from 1990 to 1994 as the first African American ever elected governor of any state.[14]

At the beginning of "Negro History Week" in February 1970, a few weeks into his first term, Wilder rose to make his first speech to the Senate. On that occasion he decried the continued use of "Carry Me Back to Old Virginny," with the line "that's where this ole darkie's heart am longed to go," as the state song. Beginning in 1975, he pushed for adoption of a day honoring Martin Luther King, although, in a Virginia compromise, when the bill obtained both legislative passage and a governor's signature in 1984, King had to share billing with Confederate heroes Stonewall Jackson and Robert E. Lee in the new Lee-Jackson-King Day.[15]

On election day in 1989, a majority of white voters supported Wilder's white opponent, but, by the slenderest of margins, Wilder won the office of governor of Virginia. In a state with a population less than 20 percent black, he had to convince a good many white voters to come his way, since he had to have more white supporters than black ones. At the same time, therefore, that this election displayed the continuing importance of race in Virginia politics, and by extension in American politics, it also revealed the declining significance of race. The combination made for a new politics in the Old Dominion.[16]

At the time Samuel Tucker died in 1990, Henry Marsh said of him that he "believed in the law and he tried to make the law work the way it was supposed to work."[17] Memorial services were held in all three of Tucker's hometowns: Alexandria, Emporia, and Richmond. Virginia governor Wilder wrote Tucker's widow, Julia Spaulding Tucker, that he would always remember Tucker and the "grin on his face," a grin that seemed to reveal Tucker's "confidence in his arguments and [in] the fairness and legitimacy of his cause." Moreover, said Robert Sykes, who had grown up in the Youth Council NAACP, "If there hadn't been an S. W. Tucker, there would not have been a Henry Marsh [a black mayor of Richmond], and there definitely would not have been an L. Douglas Wilder [a black governor of Virginia]."[18] At the law offices of Hill, Tucker, and Marsh, a large portrait of him continued in the years ahead to gaze down on all who entered the office lobby, as though Tucker himself, ebullient and committed as ever, were still monitoring progress on the racial front in Virginia.

In 1992, during Wilder's term in the governor's mansion, Virginia voters elected a black congressman, Robert C. "Bobby" Scott, only the second African American—and the first in a century—to represent any Virginia district in the House of Representatives.[19] Into the twenty-first century, Scott kept running successfully for reelection.

Judges—Not Necessarily White or Male

As Samuel Tucker said in the 1980s, a few years before he died, "The job's not over." Yet he also said, about "the judiciary being the cutting edge," that such an approach—the path of civil rights litigation that he and his colleagues had pursued in the 1940s and after—"had about played out."[20] Nonetheless, appointments to judgeships were important, both substantively and symbolically. That was true for gender as well as race. Changes in the makeup of the judiciary would be one measure of how much had changed during the twentieth century.

Through the 1970s all appointees to the Virginia Supreme Court and to federal judgeships in Virginia were white men. In the 1970s and 1980s, however, in Virginia as throughout America, growing numbers of white women, black women, and black men had been entering the legal profession and, moreover, accumulating the experience and credentials that might make them plausible candidates for appointment to judgeships. Already by 1980 the proportion of Virginia attorneys who were both white and male had dropped to 85 percent (see table 1). From the Virginia lawyers not in that 85 percent would come a number of strong candidates for promotion to state and federal judgeships in the 1980s.[21] By 1990 the proportion of lawyers in Virginia who were both white and male had dropped below 75 percent. And, year by year, that proportion continued to decline.

As late as the mid-1970s, very few black judges and very few female judges had ever sat on the federal courts or on any state's highest court. Even at the end of the 1970s, change had only begun, and all such judgeships in Virginia were still held by white men.[22] Changes in the racial and gender makeup of the Virginia courts would signal that tremendous changes had taken place across the twentieth century. One might expect such changes to take place in the circuit courts—in Virginia, the highest courts just below the courts of statewide jurisdiction—sooner than in higher courts.

The fraternity of Howard University law graduates from the 1930s, as part of their continuing efforts to "change the world" and end racial inequality, pushed for the selection of black judges. In 1974, when a vacancy opened for a circuit court judge in Richmond—yet another white man, A. Christian Compton, had been elevated to the Virginia Supreme Court—a delegation of black lawyers including Oliver Hill and Roland Ealey successfully lobbied Governor Mills E. Godwin Jr. to appoint James E. Sheffield, a 1963 graduate of Howard Law School. The new judge, the first African American to become circuit court judge in Virginia, observed, "I

TABLE 3. Appointees to the Virginia Supreme Court, 1983–2003

Year	Retiring justice	Replacement justice
1983	W. Carrington Thompson	John Charles Thomas
1988	Richard H. Poff	Elizabeth B. Lacy
1989	John Charles Thomas	Leroy Rountree Hassell Sr.
1991	Charles S. Russell	Barbara Milano Keenan
1995	Henry Whiting	Lawrence L. Koontz Jr.
1997	Roscoe B. Stephenson Jr.	Cynthia D. Kinser
2000	A. Christian Compton	Donald W. Lemons
2003	Harry Lee Carrico	G. Steven Agee

regret that men like Sam Tucker, Oliver Hill and Roland Ealey didn't come before me." Having made the breakthrough, he added, "I look forward to the day when a black can be appointed to a judgeship without fanfare."[23]

Eight years later, in 1982, Barbara M. Keenan became the first woman judge of a circuit court in Virginia. Keenan, a 1974 graduate of the George Washington University Law School in Washington, D.C., had served as assistant commonwealth's attorney in Fairfax County and then, beginning in 1980, as a judge in a local court. Just shy of her thirty-second birthday at the time of her appointment in 1882 to the Fairfax County Circuit Court, she declared as she took on her new role, "As a woman, I will be particularly conscious of my responsibility to do the best possible job I can, not only because the job itself demands it but also so that other women will be encouraged to apply and be accepted on the bench in Virginia." Judge James E. Sheffield, back in 1974, had expressed such concerns regarding race—as a role model for black youngsters and as a test case in the eyes of white Virginians.[24]

In 1983 Democratic governor Charles S. Robb had an opportunity to make an interim appointment to the Virginia Supreme Court. He named John Charles Thomas, a black 1975 graduate of the University of Virginia Law School (table 3). From Hill came a statement that he was "elated": "Something we've been dreaming about for fifty years has finally come to pass." The General Assembly, as it had with Judge Sheffield, subsequently approved the interim appointment by electing Justice Thomas to a full term. An interviewer observed to Oliver Hill, "You started out in the practice when blacks could not go to [law school at] the University of Virginia, and now you have a [black] Virginia Supreme Court justice who attended" that school.[25]

The following year, 1984, the legislature acted on its own initiative. In hopes of lifting some of the workload from the Virginia Supreme Court, the Virginia General Assembly created a new court of statewide jurisdiction, called the court of appeals. The NAACP and the Old Dominion Bar Association hoped to get two black judges selected among the ten charter members. One of their choices, Jacqueline G. Epps, a black woman lawyer, was not selected. Nevertheless, the legislature chose a black law graduate of the University of Virginia (class of 1970), James W. Benton Jr.— an attorney in Richmond at the firm of Hill, Tucker, and Marsh—and a white woman, circuit court judge Barbara Keenan.[26]

Another breakthrough came in March 1985, when Governor Robb named Elizabeth B. Lacy the first woman on Virginia's three-member State Corporation Commission. Lacy, forty years old at the time, was serving as one of four deputy attorneys general, having been appointed by Gerald L. Baliles in 1982 when he took office as state attorney general. She was the first woman to hold that position in Virginia. As a writer for the *Washington Post* described it, "To get to the SCC hearing room, Lacy must walk past the stern-faced photographs of 27 commissioners who have served since the inception of the agency, an unintended gallery of male clothing styles since 1902 and a reminder of the chain Lacy is breaking."[27]

Also in 1985—the same year Douglas Wilder was elected Virginia's lieutenant governor—Mary Sue Terry won election as state attorney general.[28] Only a late surge by Donald S. Beyer Jr. in the race for lieutenant governor, giving the Democrats a sweep of the three positions, prevented an outcome in which none of the three posts went to a white man.

In late 1988, when Justice Richard Harding Poff announced his retirement from the Virginia Supreme Court, Democratic governor Gerald L. Baliles had an opportunity to make an interim appointment. Politicians and journalists alike spoke of the probability that Baliles would appoint a woman, though they were uncertain whether he would pick Elizabeth Lacy of the State Corporation Commission or Barbara Keenan of the court of appeals. Baliles chose Lacy, and the legislature subsequently ratified the appointment by electing her to a full twelve-year term.[29] By 1988 not only did women attend law school, earn law degrees, and practice in all the courts. One woman sat on the Virginia Supreme Court, another sat on the court of appeals, and yet another represented the state in suits before those courts.

In late 1989 Justice John Charles Thomas stepped down, and Governor Baliles made another interim appointment. Among his possible choices was Judge Keenan of the court of appeals, whom he had bypassed when he selected Justice Lacy, so that he would be replacing a black man with a white woman. Another was Judge Benton, also of the court of appeals, in which case one black man would replace another. A third possibility was Jacqueline Epps, the black woman lawyer who, after being pushed for a seat on the court of appeals in 1984, had assisted Wilder in his election as lieutenant governor in 1985.[30] Baliles chose none of these but instead named Leroy Rountree Hassell Sr., a black man who had earned his undergraduate degree at the University of Virginia (1977) and his law degree at Harvard (1980).[31]

Both male and female justices took seats on the Virginia Supreme Court in the 1990s. When a vacancy arose in 1991, the legislature turned to Judge Keenan of the court of appeals. That meant that two white women, together with one black man, were serving with four white male justices.[32] Replacing a white man in 1995 was another white man, Lawrence L. Koontz Jr., who had served on the court of appeals since its establishment. In 1997 a divided legislature could not agree on a replacement, and Republican governor George Allen appointed Cynthia D. Kinser, a Republican and a 1977 graduate of the University of Virginia Law School.[33] Beginning in 1997, then, one black man, three white women, and three white men sat on the Virginia Supreme Court.

For the court's first two centuries—until 1983—every member of it had been a white man. By 1997 white men held a minority of seats on Virginia's highest court. Subsequent changes in 2000 and 2003—both times, a white man replaced a white man—left the racial and gender makeup of the court unchanged. At the dawn of the twenty-first century, the roster of justices on the court captured the transformation in the rules of race and gender that had taken place in the previous generation.

Moreover, when Harry Lee Carrico stepped down in 2003 after forty-two years on the Virginia Supreme Court and twenty-two as its chief justice, Justice Hassell was chosen by his colleagues as the new chief justice. Beginning in 2003, an African American presided over the state's highest court.[34]

In the 1980s gender, like race, became a manifest consideration. Race and sex alike had always been important; the fact that by the 1980s and 1990s judges might be black or female meant that such considerations, now negotiable rather than prohibitive, had become less controlling, not more so, though perhaps they remained more important than party, philosophy, or geography. The race and gender of Virginia's judges had been certain in the past. By the 1990s they had generally become matters of routine contention.

If this was largely true in Virginia, it was also largely true elsewhere—across the South and throughout the nation. In New Hampshire, Governor Jeanne Shaheen named Linda Dalianis to the state supreme court in early 2000. As the *New York Times* reported the news, "The state's first female governor swore in its first female Supreme Court justice today [April 26], leaving South Dakota as the only state yet to name a woman to its highest court."[35]

Federal Judges: Black or Female

Even as gender, like race, lost its power to screen out candidates for membership on Virginia's state courts, each retained, for a time, its vitality with regard to the federal judiciary. Again, race proved the barrier that fell before gender.

Until the presidency of Jimmy Carter, who made one of the hallmarks of his four years in office the elevation of minority and female judges to the U.S. district courts, no black judge had ever sat on a federal court in any former Confederate state. Carter nominated James E. Sheffield, Virginia's first black circuit court judge, to the U.S. District Court for the Eastern District of Virginia, but the nominee lost out when Senator Harry F. Byrd Jr. put up a strenuous fight. Oliver Hill said at the time, "Byrd has decided to follow his daddy and be the last bastion of massive resistance." When Carter's term in the White House ended in 1981, only Mississippi and Virginia still had only white federal judges. In October 1986, during Ronald Reagan's second term as president, black nominee James Randolph Spencer (a federal prosecutor who had graduated from Harvard Law School in 1974) gained confirmation and became a judge of the U.S. District Court for the Eastern District of Virginia. Three years later, in November 1989, Rebecca Beach Smith (who graduated first in her law class at the College of William and Mary in 1979) became Virginia's first female federal judge when she joined the same court.[36]

Increasingly, it would not be a lily-white judiciary that ruled on civil rights matters or, indeed, any other cases. Yet efforts to appoint a black appellate judge in the 1990s ran into a roadblock similar to the one the first black nominee to federal district court in Virginia had encountered back in the 1970s. At the end of the 1990s, the fourth circuit court of appeals, which meets in Richmond, Virginia, remained the nation's only circuit court never to have had a black judge. There had long been a vacancy, and President Bill Clinton had made three efforts to appoint a black judge to that bench, but Senate Republicans—especially Jesse Helms of North Carolina—blocked every effort. In December 2000—in the closing weeks of his term in office—Clinton made a recess appointment, and Roger L.

Gregory, a black lawyer in Richmond, took a seat on the fourth circuit court. The next summer Judge Gregory was confirmed.[37]

In desegregating a court by means of a recess appointment, Clinton followed in the footsteps of President Harry S. Truman, who in 1949 appointed William H. Hastie the first black judge on the federal bench, and President John F. Kennedy, who appointed Thurgood Marshall to a federal appeals court. The Senate subsequently confirmed both appointments. With a recess appointment Judge Gregory would have had a place on the bench for nearly a year even if the Senate had not, in the end, confirmed him as well.

From the 1890s to the 1990s

Judgeships in Virginia in the 1990s depicted the transformation of Virginia at the same time that they displayed the transformation of the legal profession. Black men and white women sat in judgment in the highest positions in the state judiciary and even on the federal bench. It continued to be true, as it was when Belva Lockwood went before the Virginia Supreme Court of Appeals, that like the issues to be considered by the court, the judges on the court mirrored society, politics, and culture in Virginia. Yet consider how these had changed across one hundred years.

Not until the 1920s might a woman, even if white, gain admission to the Virginia bar and represent clients in the courts, nor could she earn a degree from any law school in Virginia. Before 1950, no black Virginian, even if male, could gain admittance to any public law school in the state. By 1990, by contrast, a black male graduate of the University of Virginia Law School had served on the state's highest court, and the federal district judges in Virginia included a white woman and a black man. By 1997, the number of white men among the seven members of the state supreme court had dropped to three. By 2003, the court's most senior members were a white woman and a black man, and the black man was the chief justice.

Epilogue

Neither Blue Laws nor Black Laws

IN 1889 A MIXED-RACE AMERICAN WRITER, CHARLES W. CHESNUTT, took aim at laws that restricted people's opportunities and behavior on the basis of their racial identities. Such laws were very real at the time he wrote, but he hoped for a time when they would be no more: "Some day they will, perhaps, become mere curiosities of jurisprudence; the 'black laws' will be bracketed with the 'blue laws,' and will be at best but landmarks by which to measure the progress of the nation."[1]

At the time Chesnutt wrote, black laws governed the South with particular force, though—as with laws governing interracial marriage—they could be found elsewhere as well. The particulars of the first post–Civil War black codes had been modified by then, but some features lived on and new ones soon took shape. The South's post-1860s racial restrictions reached their high point in the half century after Chesnutt wrote. After another half century, however, they had—one after another—been declared unenforceable, and neither the "black laws" nor the "blue laws" remained in force in Virginia. There, as elsewhere across the South, *Loving* v. *Virginia* ended the last of the black laws in 1967. As for the blue laws, they had lost more and more of their force after the mid-twentieth century, and by 1988 a state supreme court ruling had largely put an end to them in Virginia.

The southernness of southern history was receding by the late 1960s. By then, state-mandated segregation had officially died across America in housing and transportation, major targets during the 1940s, as well as in education, the major target of the 1950s, and even in marriage. Virginia had always looked a lot like other southern states. By the 1970s or the 1990s, to a far more substantial degree than before, Virginia also looked like states outside the region.

Law and Liberty

Belva Lockwood is hardly the only American to have been driven to bewilderment, fury, despair—or elation—over the turns the law has taken. The couple who yearned to live in Virginia as Mr. and Mrs. Loving spring to mind. And then there were Oliver Hill, Spottswood Robinson, and Samuel Tucker, who celebrated their victory in *Brown* v. *Board of Education* and then found themselves, for years, trying to get the decision implemented and to avoid being disbarred for their efforts.

Doug Carr wanted only to be let alone, as he said, to run his business, without the law intervening, used as a weapon by his competitors. The Lovings wanted only to be let alone to raise their family. And white policymakers and school board members wanted to be let alone to run the schools on their own terms.

The law could cut in many directions. Regardless, it supplied a key idiom in which conflict was negotiated, as the courts often provided the venue. The law mediates conflict, and it mirrors change, permits change, causes change, and legitimates change. In chapter after chapter in this book, at least some participants in the process of changing the law have spoken the language of constitutionality. Their discourse is what, perhaps more than anything else, has distinguished the process of change and accommodation in American law and society, power and policy.

I have detailed a collection of test cases, initiated by people whose postures, when they engaged in the behavior that brought them into court, ranged from deliberate to inadvertent. Some knowingly challenged the law in order to secure a hearing in the courts, while others had merely meant to go about their business and did not necessarily know that their behavior would be construed as illegal. Among these people were Pete Proffitt contesting the road laws, Doug Carr the Sunday closing laws, Annie Harper the poll tax, Mildred Loving the law against interracial marriage, and Ford Johnson the segregation of a courtroom. Direct action— or inaction—led to some of these court decisions, as when Ford Johnson declined to sit, as directed by the judge, in the "colored" section of a Richmond courtroom, or when Pete Proffitt refused to show up, as directed according to law, to work on the roads in Louisa County.

Judicial reinterpretation of the state and federal constitutions has appeared as the agent of change in many cases, but judges could act only when cases came before them requiring some sort of decision. And then they had to act in ways that seemed to them to fit the constitution to the statutes and the statutes to the facts of the case before them.

Judges at every level found themselves having to make law. Local judges had to decide whether Sunday movies came under the ban of the blue laws or whether showing movies could fit, for example, under the exemption of business activities that were "necessary." State judges came to the conclusion that the labor tax violated the state constitution's provisions limiting poll taxes, and they also eventually concluded that the blue laws discriminated against businesses that had been prosecuted for operating on Sundays. Federal judges entered the so-called political thicket to address questions of whether voters' rights were violated by various apportionment schemes related to seats in the U.S. House of Representatives, the Virginia Senate, and the Virginia House of Delegates, and whether would-be voters' rights were violated by a poll tax that impeded their participation in state elections.

State and federal judges, each in their own way, came to judgments about what was required by way of equal opportunity in segregated education, whether in terms of teachers' salaries, pupils' transportation, school facilities, high school curricula, or racial segregation itself. In decisions that were handed down between the 1940s and the 1960s, federal judges determined that the formula "separate but equal" has no constitutional place in transportation, education, courtrooms, or marriage, and in so doing, the courts had to overturn earlier decisions that had gone the other way. The Virginia Supreme Court, which almost always found pro-segregation decisions by local courts "plainly right," could not be counted on to promote equality within segregation and certainly did not often act to dismantle segregation. On the racial front, those major tasks fell to federal judges.

State Judges, Federal Courts, and the Law of the Land

Although it might be thought that federal judges have brought change, and state judges have resisted it, the Virginia story has sometimes taken a different turn. The Virginia high court interpreted the state constitution in the 1890s to throw out the traditional system of road labor and in the 1980s to throw out the traditional restrictions on Sunday commerce. Each of those decisions flew in the face of centuries of tradition not only in Virginia but across America and much of the world. In each instance the Virginia Supreme Court took a position that the U.S. Supreme Court was not yet prepared to take and, over the years to come, never did take. Stepping in where the U.S. Supreme Court refused to get involved, moreover, the Virginia Supreme Court in the 1890s determined that the traditional exclusion of women from the legal profession should come to an end in Virginia (though the same court soon proved just as assertive in reversing that particular decision).

Yet those examples of initiative by the state supreme court point up something about the areas in which a southern state court would—and would not—take the lead. None of those three cases had any semblance of controversy over race. On racial matters the Virginia courts resisted change that would breathe greater life into the Fourteenth Amendment.

On racial matters, if any court was going to break with recent precedent and expand the definition of black freedom, it was going to be a federal court, whether the case began in state court and then was appealed from the Virginia Supreme Court to the U.S. Supreme Court or began in federal district court. Sometimes the civil rights victory, if it came at all, came early on, at the federal district level. Sometimes—as with racially discriminatory teachers' salaries—the proponents of civil rights lost in district court but prevailed in the fourth circuit court of appeals. Sometimes victory came only when the case reached the U.S. Supreme Court, and, as regards the poll tax, not necessarily the first or second time it got that far.

The treatments in some chapters of this book—on Sunday closing or women lawyers—could have been based on materials from any state, inside or outside the South. Other chapters, by contrast—"The Siege against Segregation" or "To Sit or Not to Sit"—could not have been framed in terms of the history of any state outside the South. The salience of racial matters—the intractability, the power and stubbornness, of racial proscriptions under the law—largely defines the South in the realm of American legal history. The law governed white behavior some, and black behavior a great deal, even as it reflected the central concerns over racial identity, black opportunity, and white privilege that were long the hallmarks of society, economics, and politics just about everywhere across the South.

State, Region, Nation: Citizens and the Law

Some changes in the law in Virginia during the twentieth century came about through intrastate politics. Other changes resulted from federal-state relations. Through conflict over a wide range of matters—Sunday closing laws, for example—Virginians collectively wrought changes in the laws that govern their lives and in the ways that, as individuals, they live their lives. Those decisions were made within the state. In matters relating to racial identity and white privilege, Virginians contested the issues as well, but the outcomes—their shape, in degree; their timing, for certain—were more often a result of decisions handed down by federal judges. On the racial front, some Virginians pushed for change, other Virginians resisted change, and decisions by federal judges altered the outcome. Both sets of changes—those that were centered on race and those that were not—took place in a southern setting, but the racial dimension gave the process in Virginia its peculiarly southern texture.

Virginians struggled to give voice to their wishes and dreams, and they often worked out their differences through the legal system. That was true in constitutional conventions and legislative sessions. It was true when they went to state court over whether the Virginia constitution permitted the labor tax on the public roads or legal restrictions under the Sunday closing laws. And it was true when they jousted in the federal courts over whether the U.S. Constitution permitted segregation in public education at any and every level, over poll taxes as a prerequisite to voting at all or racial tests as to whether one could vote in a primary election, or over racial restrictions on who could marry whom and who could sit where in a courtroom.

Along the way, people outside Virginia had a say in what happened inside the state—not in the sense that they introduced changes that no large group of Virginians wanted, but, rather, in the very different sense that they helped shape the outcome of struggles that Virginians themselves contested. In the 1860s men in gray uniforms contested men in blue uniforms. At the same time, people in western Virginia broke free from the rest of the state, and black Virginians did what they could to shape the outcome of the Civil War and the struggle over slavery. In the twentieth century the state attorney general tried to convince federal judges that state laws should be permitted to regulate public behavior—and even private behavior—of various sorts that had come under challenge by at least one group of Virginians or another. Moreover, the nation's people spoke through their elected representatives in Congress and even on occasion, as on women voters and on poll taxes, through the process of formal amendment to the U.S. Constitution.

Conflict, Law, and Change: Virginia in the Years Ahead

In the twenty-first century Virginians will, no doubt, continue to deploy the instruments of law to mediate conflict over policy and to impel— or impede—changes in society. They will continue to argue over whether, under the state or federal constitution, a given policy is permitted or prohibited. They will, moreover, continue to seek to shape the political universe in whatever ways seem most likely to facilitate securing their party or policy preferences. The legislative reapportionment that took place after the 2000 census revealed one more example, as a Republican-controlled legislature redistricted a number of leading Democratic legislators out of office.

Fossils of the past and harbingers of the future alike appeared in news headlines in the first years of the twenty-first century. Public policy questions might change their tenor, but citizens and the legislators who represent them in Richmond, together with the judges who hear their cases in court, continue to face decisions they must make. And regardless of the normative answers to these questions, questions regarding Virginia's typicality persist: Which objective phenomena reveal Virginia as retaining considerable southernness, and which ones place Virginia within national norms?

As the century turned, among the questions about social policy and its consequences were these: What kinds of laws should there be regarding abortion? Should the state continue to refuse to recognize same-sex marriages? Should it put additional barriers in the way of adoption by a lesbian couple or the availability of marital benefits to a same-sex couple?[2] Is it all right that—a half century after *Brown* v. *Board of Education*—formerly all-black schools like Virginia State continue to enroll student bodies that are well above 90 percent African American, and that formerly nonblack schools like Virginia Tech continued to enroll student bodies that are well above 90 percent non–African American?[3]

Some important questions were connected to the criminal justice system: Should Virginia retain a rule that gives people convicted of crimes no more than twenty-one days to come up with additional evidence that might exonerate them? Should people convicted of felonies be denied the right to vote, not only while they are in prison—even inmates can vote in Maine and Vermont—but also after they have paid the penalty for their infractions? Virginia is among the nation's leaders in the use of the death penalty: Why is that?[4]

Questions arose, too, regarding electoral politics and the process of choosing representatives. Should state legislators continue to carve up the state and map the districts in which they run for reelection, or should such matters be put in the hands of a bipartisan commission?[5] How was it that in the 2001 state elections, Virginia voters elected Democrats to the governorship and lieutenant governorship yet, by approximately two-to-one margins, sent Republican majorities to both houses of the state legislature? How true was it that Virginia voters had reverted to earlier norms of pay-

ing low taxes for limited public services? Regarding the community colleges, in particular, how high should tuition go—how much should access
be a public good, and how much private?

On matters like these, Virginians will contest among themselves. They
will employ the law to work out their policy differences, whether change
or continuity appears to be dominant on one question or another. On
most matters of substance they might start with the General Assembly, but
if unhappy about what the legislature does, they might, as circumstances
advise, appeal to the state courts, the federal courts, or Congress. And, in
these procedural ways, they will act much as citizens in other states do on
matters of substance—though the policy outcomes will sometimes differ,
as Virginia continues to chart a course that in some respects makes it look
like a southern state and in other matters reveals little if any regional dis-
tinctiveness among the states of the Union. The people of Virginia, like
their counterparts across America, will continue to use whatever legal
tools are at their disposal to shape the political playing field, deflect policies that they oppose, and foster policies that they welcome.

Notes

Abbreviations

ANB	John A. Garraty and Mark C. Carnes, eds., *American National Biography*, 24 vols. (New York, 1999)
CDP	*Charlottesville Daily Progress*
CRLDP	Civil Rights Lawyers Documentary Project, Richmond
Debates, 1901–2	*Report of the Proceedings and Debates of the Constitutional Convention, State of Virginia, Held in the City of Richmond, June 12, 1901, to June 26, 1902*, 2 vols. (Richmond, 1906)
DVB	John T. Kneebone et al., eds., *Dictionary of Virginia Biography* (Richmond, 1998–)
JHR	*Journal of the House of Representatives*
JNE	*Journal of Negro Education*
JS	*Journal of the Senate*
JSH	*Journal of Southern History*
Landmark Briefs	Philip B. Kurland and Gerhard Casper, eds., *Landmark Briefs and Arguments of the Supreme Court of the United States: Constitutional Law* (Arlington, Va., 1975–)
NA	National Archives, Washington, D.C.
NJG	*Norfolk Journal and Guide*
NYT	*New York Times*
PW	Peter Wallenstein
RAA	*Richmond Afro American*
RD	*Richmond Dispatch*
RNL	*Richmond News Leader*
RT	*Roanoke Times*
RTD	*Richmond Times-Dispatch*
RTWN	*Roanoke Times and World-News*
Thorpe, *Constitutions*	Francis Newton Thorpe, comp., *The Federal and State Constitutions*, 7 vols. (Washington, D.C., 1909)
UVA Lib.	Albert and Shirley Small Special Collections Library, University of Virginia, Charlottesville
VMHB	*Virginia Magazine of History and Biography*

VRHC   Valentine Richmond History Center, Richmond
VSCOB   Virginia Supreme Court Order Book (microfilm, Library
                of Virginia)
VSSJ   *Virginia Social Science Journal*
WP   *Washington Post*

Introduction: Amending the South, Amending America

1. Richard B. Bernstein with Jerome Agel, *Amending America: If We Love the Constitution So Much, Why Do We Keep Trying to Change It?* (New York, 1993); see also Sanford Levinson, ed., *Responding to Imperfection: The Theory and Practice of Constitutional Amendment* (Princeton, N.J., 1995), and David E. Kyvig, *Explicit and Authentic Acts: Amending the U.S. Constitution, 1776–1995* (Lawrence, Kans., 1996).

2. PW, *From Slave South to New South: Public Policy in Nineteenth-Century Georgia* (Chapel Hill, N.C., 1987), 26–38, 63–68; Douglas R. Egerton, *Charles Fenton Mercer and the Trial of National Conservatism* (Jackson, Miss., 1989), 100–105, 116–28; George B. Tindall, *The Emergence of the New South, 1913–1945* (Baton Rouge, La., 1967), chap. 8; William A. Link, *A Hard Country and a Lonely Place: Schooling, Reform, and Society in Rural Virginia, 1870–1920* (Chapel Hill, N.C., 1986).

3. Louis P. Masur, *1831: Year of Eclipse* (New York, 2001), 9–62; William A. Link, *Roots of Secession: Slavery and Politics in Antebellum Virginia* (Chapel Hill, N.C., 2003); see also Woody Holton, *Forced Founders: Indians, Debtors, Slaves, and the Making of the American Revolution* (Chapel Hill, N.C., 1999).

4. Julian A. C. Chandler, *Representation in Virginia* (Baltimore, 1896); Craig Simpson, "Political Compromise and the Protection of Slavery: Henry A. Wise and the Virginia Constitutional Convention of 1850–1851," *VMHB* 83 (Oct. 1975): 387–405; Alison Goodyear Freehling, *Drift toward Dissolution: The Virginia Slavery Debate of 1831–1832* (Baton Rouge, La., 1982); William W. Freehling, *The Road to Disunion*, vol. 1, *Secessionists at Bay, 1776–1854* (New York, 1990), chaps. 9–10; Daniel W. Crofts, *Old Southampton: Politics and Society in a Virginia County, 1834–1869* (Charlottesville, Va., 1992); William G. Shade, *Democratizing the Old Dominion: Virginia and the Second Party System, 1824–1861* (Charlottesville, Va., 1996).

5. Richard Lowe, *Republicans and Reconstruction in Virginia, 1856–70* (Charlottesville, Va., 1991); Ervin L. Jordan Jr., *Black Confederates and Afro-Yankees in Civil War Virginia* (Charlottesville, Va., 1995).

6. Lowe, *Republicans and Reconstruction*, 46–48; Alrutheus Ambush Taylor, *The Negro in the Reconstruction of Virginia* (Washington, D.C., 1926), 8–28; Eric Foner, *Reconstruction: America's Unfinished Revolution, 1863–1877* (New York, 1988), 199–201.

7. PW, *Virginia Tech, Land-Grant University, 1872–1997: History of a School, a State, a Nation* (Blacksburg, Va., 1997), 7–52; Edgar Toppin, *Loyal Sons and Daughters: Virginia State University, 1882–1992* (Norfolk, Va., 1992), 13–21.

8. Jack P. Maddex Jr., *The Virginia Conservatives, 1867–1879: A Study in Reconstruction Politics* (Chapel Hill, N.C., 1970); James Tice Moore, *Two Paths to the New South: The Virginia Debt Controversy, 1870–1883* (Lexington, Ky., 1974); Jane Dailey, *Before Jim Crow: The Politics of Race in Postemancipation Virginia* (Chapel Hill, N.C., 2000).

9. PW, *Virginia Tech*, 53–61; Luther Porter Jackson, *Negro Office-Holders in Virginia, 1865–1895* (Norfolk, Va., 1945); Michael B. Chesson, "Richmond's Black Coun-

cilmen," in *Southern Black Leaders of the Reconstruction Era*, ed. Howard N. Rabinowitz (Urbana, Ill., 1982), 191–222; William Cheek and Aimee Lee Cheek, "John Mercer Langston: Principle and Politics," in *Black Leaders of the Nineteenth Century*, ed. Leon Litwack and August Meier (Urbana, Ill., 1988), 102–26; Lawrence L. Hartzell, "The Exploration of Freedom in Black Petersburg, Virginia, 1865–1902," in *At the Edge of the South: Life in Nineteenth-Century Virginia*, ed. Edward L. Ayers and John C. Willis (Charlottesville, Va., 1991), 134–56.

10. PW, *Virginia Tech*, 59–64, 98–102; Toppin, *Loyal Sons and Daughters*, 77–83.

11. PW, "Cartograms and the Mapping of Virginia History, 1790–1990," *VSSJ* 28 (1993): 90–110.

12. Andrew Buni, *The Negro in Virginia Politics, 1902–1965* (Charlottesville, Va., 1967), 15–33; Raymond H. Pulley, *Old Virginia Restored: An Interpretation of the Progressive Impulse, 1870–1930* (Charlottesville, Va., 1968); Allen W. Moger, *Virginia: Bourbonism to Byrd, 1870–1925* (Charlottesville, Va., 1968), chap. 9; J. Morgan Kousser, *The Shaping of Southern Politics: Suffrage Restriction and the Establishment of the One-Party South, 1880–1910* (New Haven, 1974); Wythe Holt, *Virginia's Constitutional Convention of 1901–1902* (New York, 1990); Michael Perman, *Struggle for Mastery: Disfranchisement in the South, 1888–1908* (Chapel Hill, N.C., 2001), chap. 10; Ann Field Alexander, *Race Man: The Rise and Fall of the "Fighting Editor," John Mitchell Jr.* (Charlottesville, Va., 2002), 107–16.

13. Quoted in John Douglas Smith, "Managing White Supremacy: Politics and Culture in Virginia, 1919–1939" (Ph.D. diss., Univ. of Virginia, 1998), 179, printed in part in J. Douglas Smith, *Managing White Supremacy: Race, Politics, and Citizenship in Jim Crow Virginia* (Chapel Hill, N.C., 2002), 131.

14. William C. Pendleton, *Political History of Appalachian Virginia* (Dayton, Va., 1927), 459; see Kousser, *Shaping of Southern Politics*, 264 (quotation), 297.

15. Louis R. Harlan, *Separate and Unequal: Public School Campaigns and Racism in the Southern Seaboard States, 1901–1915* (Chapel Hill, N.C., 1958), chap. 5.

16. Pulley, *Old Virginia Restored*, 85.

17. Suzanne Lebsock, "Woman Suffrage and White Supremacy: A Virginia Case Study," in *Taking off the White Gloves: Southern Women and Women Historians*, ed. Michele Gillespie and Catherine Clinton (Columbia, Mo., 1998), 28–42; see also Marjorie Spruill Wheeler, *New Women of the New South: The Leaders of the Woman Suffrage Movement in the Southern States* (New York, 1993).

18. Buni, *Negro in Virginia Politics*, chaps. 3–13; J. Harvie Wilkinson III, *Harry Byrd and the Changing Face of Virginia Politics, 1945–1966* (Charlottesville, Va., 1968); Bruce J. Dierenfield, *Keeper of the Rules: Congressman Howard W. Smith of Virginia* (Charlottesville, Va., 1987); Ronald L. Heinemann, *Harry Byrd of Virginia* (Charlottesville, Va., 1996).

19. Thomas R. Morris, *The Virginia Supreme Court: An Institutional and Political Analysis* (Charlottesville, Va., 1975), 17–20.

20. Ibid., 20–24.

21. Ibid., xi, 64–65.

1. The Case of the Laborer from Louisa

An early version of this chapter appeared as "The Case of the Laborer from Louisa: Three Central Virginians and the Origins of the Virginia Highway System," *Magazine of Albemarle County History* 49 (1991): 18–47. I wish to thank Melinda B. Frierson, executive director of the Albemarle County Historical Society at that time, for inviting me to prepare and give that paper in October 1990 as part of the society's fiftieth-anniversary lecture series. The Virginia Foundation for the Humanities and Public Policy provided me a fellowship in the summer of 1989 at the Virginia Center for the Humanities, where I worked on this project, and also helped fund the society's lecture series. E. Terry Long, a librarian at the Virginia State Law Library, Richmond, supplied me a copy of what there is of the Proffitt record file. A special thanks to Louise Proffitt Spencer, who, after I identified her and tracked her down in Charlottesville, altered some of my preliminary impressions about her father's case, gave me a photo of him, and attended my Albemarle County talk. Photographs of L. J. Haley, R. T. W. Duke Jr., and William F. Proffitt appear in PW, "Laborer from Louisa," 18, 23, 28.

1. Claudia Anderson Chisholm, ed., "The Reverend L. J. Haley's Diary," *Louisa County Historical Magazine* 4–13 (June 1972–summer 1981). The diaries cover a period from 1871 through 1916.

2. James J. Flink, *America Adopts the Automobile, 1895–1910* (Cambridge, Mass., 1970), 19, 25; Bruce E. Seely, *Building the American Highway System: Engineers as Policy Makers* (Philadelphia, 1987), 11–16.

3. Lyon Gardiner Tyler, ed., *Encyclopedia of Virginia Biography*, 3 vols. (New York, 1915), 3:346 (see 3:115–16 for a sketch of R. T. W. Duke Sr.); U.S. Census, Population Schedules, Albemarle County, 1900, NA. The diary entries—all from 1892, 1906, or 1917—are drawn from Richard Thomas Walker Duke Jr., Annual Diaries, Duke Papers, UVA Lib.

4. Charles W. Turner, *Chessie's Road* (Richmond, 1956), 132–33.

5. For transportation changes in general and road improvements in particular in the Charlottesville area, see John Hammond Moore, *Albemarle: Jefferson's County, 1727–1976* (Charlottesville, Va., 1976), chaps. 13–14, esp. 245.

6. PW, *From Slave South to New South*, chap. 18.

7. I have drawn from the Supervisors' Journals, vols. 1 (1870–89) and 2 (1889–1905), in the Louisa County Courthouse, Louisa, Va.

8. *Acts* (1891–92), 686–96 (ch. 417).

9. Phone conversation with Louise Proffitt Spencer, 26 Sept. 1990.

10. *Proffit[t]* v. *Anderson*, Petition for Habeas Corpus, 5 Nov. 1892, Virginia State Law Library, Richmond. Though the court case spells the name with only one *t*, letters from the family patriarch are signed "W. W. Proffitt."

11. Claudia Anderson Chisholm and Ellen Gray Little, *Old Home Places of Louisa* (Louisa, Va., 1979), 115; U.S. Census, Population Schedules, Albemarle County, 1900, NA; *Chataigne's Virginia Gazeteer and Classified Business Directory*, 1884–85 (the section on Louisa County), in *Louisa County Historical Magazine* 7 (winter 1975): 61, 65.

12. Letters to Bibb cited in this and subsequent paragraphs can be found in the William E. Bibb Papers, UVA Lib.

13. VSCOB 30 (1892–95): 128, 243, 420–23. The court's per curiam opinion appears in *Virginia Decisions: A Collection of Virginia Cases Not Officially Reported*, 2 vols. (Charlottesville, Va., 1902), 1:908–11, and in 20 S.E. 887. Margaret Virginia Nelson, in *A Study of Judicial Review in Virginia, 1789–1928* (New York, 1947), fails to mention the case; as she states (24), she made no use of *Virginia Decisions*, and it does not appear in *Virginia Reports*.

14. R. R. Fauntleroy was a young attorney, barely older than the plaintiff. He also

was a son of Judge Thomas T. Fauntleroy of the Virginia Supreme Court of Appeals, one of the three judges who sided with Proffitt.

15. "Road Law Invalid," *RD*, 2 Feb. 1894, 4.

16. *In re Dassler*, 35 Kan. 678 (1886).

17. *Dennis* v. *Simon*, 51 Ohio 233 (1894); *Leedy* v. *Town of Bourbon*, 12 Ind. App. 486 (1895); *State* v. *Rayburn*, 2 Okla. Cr. 413 (1909). For other such cases, see *Johnston* v. *The Mayor*, 62 Ga. 645 (1879); *Town of Tipton* v. *Norman*, 72 Mo. 380 (1880); and *City of Faribault* v. *Misener*, 20 Minn. 396 (1874).

18. *State* v. *Wheeler*, 141 N.C. 589 (1906). For a similar case, see *Short* v. *State*, 80 Md. 392 (1895).

19. *State* v. *Sharp*, 125 N.C. 628, 634 (1899); *State* v. *Holloman*, 139 N.C. 641, 647 (1905). Another decision mentioned the system's history in France, where it was known as the *corvée*, "a grievance which contributed powerfully to their revolution of a century ago, since which time the roads have been worked by taxation" (*State* v. *Covington*, 125 N.C. 641, 644 [1899]).

20. *Butler* v. *Perry, Sheriff of Columbia County, Florida*, 67 Fla. 405 (1914).

21. *Butler* v. *Perry*, 240 U.S. 328, 331, 333 (1916).

22. Ibid., 330, 333.

23. *Hassett* v. *Walls*, 9 Nev. 387 (1874).

24. Virginia Constitutional Convention (1867–68), *Debates and Proceedings*, vol. 1 (Richmond, 1868), 32, 734–44, 746, 748–50 (a projected volume 2 was never published); "The Virginia Convention," *RD*, 3 Feb. 1868, 2.

25. *JHD* (1893–94), 46–48.

26. *JHD* (1895–96), 30–31. O'Ferrall made no mention of the issue in his autobiographical account of his years as governor: Charles T. O'Ferrall, *Forty Years of Active Service* (New York, 1904), 228–49.

27. *JHD* (1893–94), 48–81, 641; *JHD* (1895–96), 197; *JS* (1893–94), 581–82.

28. "Now for Good Roads," *RD*, 19 Oct. 1894, 1, 3. Susie Chilton Palmer, "The Development of Virginia Highways" (M.A. thesis, Univ. of Virginia, 1930), mentions (12) the October 1894 convention in Richmond but not the Supreme Court of Appeals and its February decision. Subsequent writers relied upon Palmer's version, and thus they, too, missed the *Proffitt* case: Moger, *Virginia*, 258–62; Andrew Lewis Shifflett, "'Good Roads' in Virginia, 1916–1923" (M.A. thesis, East Carolina Univ., 1971), 1–4. But both trace the early twentieth-century developments, Shifflett in much the greater detail.

29. Constitution of 1869, art. 10, sec. 15, and Constitution of 1902, art. 13, sec. 185, in Thorpe, *Constitutions* 7:3895, 3953; *Debates, 1901–2* 2:2889–92.

30. *JHD* (1906), 452–53, 601; *Acts* (1906), 71–78 (chs. 73–74); Moger, *Virginia*, 258–62; William E. Larsen, *Montague of Virginia: The Making of a Southern Progressive* (Baton Rouge, La., 1965), 170–81; Henry C. Ferrell Jr., *Claude A. Swanson of Virginia: A Political Biography* (Lexington, Ky., 1985), 75–76; Fred Helsabeck, "Convict Labor Systems in Virginia (1858–1907)" (M.A. thesis, George Peabody College for Teachers, 1932), 137–45; Shifflett, "Good Roads," 2–16; Paul W. Keve, *The History of Corrections in Virginia* (Charlottesville, Va., 1986), 118–25.

31. Census figures for Louisa County in 1890 show 9,805 blacks (57.7%) and 7,192 whites (42.3%); see U.S. Census Office, *Twelfth Census of the United States: 1900*, vol. 1, *Population* (Washington, D.C.), 561. Regarding the lack of paved roads where black Virginians lived, see Smith, *Managing White Supremacy*, 50.

32. Eugene M. Scheel, *Culpeper: A Virginia County's History through 1920* (Culpeper, Va., 1982), 235–37.

33. Steven G. Meeks, in collaboration with Ray Page McCauley, *Crozet: A Pictorial History* (Crozet, Va., 1983), 53.

34. PW, "Laborer from Louisa," 40.

35. Frederic L. Paxson, "The Highway Movement, 1916–1935," *American Historical Review* 51 (Jan. 1946): 236–53; Shifflett, "Good Roads," 6–7, 19–27; Ferrell, *Swanson*, 109–10; Guy B. Hathorn, "The Political Career of C. Bascom Slemp" (Ph.D. diss., Duke Univ., 1950), 122–29.

36. *CDP*, 26 Jan., 12 July 1917, 24 Sept. 1924.

37. *CDP*, 17, 20 Jan. 1917.

38. *CDP*, 13 Sept. 1924.

39. For federal policy during the second half of the twentieth century, see Mark H. Rose, *Interstate: Express Highway Politics, 1939–1989*, rev. ed. (Knoxville, Tenn., 1990), and Tom Lewis, *Divided Highways: Building the Interstate Highways, Transforming American Life* (New York, 1997).

40. Seely, *Building the American Highway System*, 9–65 passim; PW, *From Slave South to New South*, 205–7; Alex Lichtenstein, *Twice the Work of Free Labor: The Political Economy of Convict Labor in the New South* (London, 1996), chap. 7. For the transformation in the South's roads during the period on which this essay focuses, see Howard Lawrence Preston, *Dirt Roads to Dixie: Accessibility and Modernization in the South, 1885–1935* (Knoxville, Tenn., 1991), and Robert E. Ireland, *Entering the Auto Age: The Early Automobile in North Carolina, 1900–1930* (Raleigh, N.C., 1990). Perhaps the fullest treatment of the transformation in any American state is Michael R. Fein, "Public Works: The Politics of Highway Construction in New York State, 1890–1956" (Ph.D. diss., Brandeis Univ., 2003).

41. John Chynoweth Burnham, "The Gasoline Tax and the Automobile Revolution," *Mississippi Valley Historical Review* 48 (Dec. 1961): 435–59; Frank McVey Winston, "The Highway Policy of the State of Virginia" (M.A. thesis, Univ. of Virginia, 1943), 64–69. In October 1990, with a "deficit-reduction" package, the federal government broke the linkage that from the beginning had allocated the federal gasoline tax to highway improvements. With the 1990 measure the federal gas tax jumped from $.09 to $.14 per gallon (Republicans had proposed $.19), with the increment intended for absorption into general funds.

42. *CDP*, 24 Sept. 1924.

43. Albert W. Coates Jr., ed., *The Most Convenient Wayes: A Story of Roads in Virginia* (n.p., 1972), 21.

44. For photographs that evoke the changes of the years from the 1880s through the 1920s and after, see Moore, *Albemarle*, 247, 280, 291, 298; Coates, *Most Convenient Wayes*, 9–20; and A. Lawrence Kocher and Howard Dearstyne, *Shadows in Silver: A Record of Virginia, 1850–1900, in Contemporary Photographs Taken by George and Huestis Cook* (New York, 1954), 13, 177–79, 209.

2. Necessity, Charity, and a Sabbath

Portions of this chapter were previously published as "'Works of Necessity and Charity Only Excepted': The Courts and the Sunday Closing Laws in 20th Century Virginia," *VSSJ* 29 (1994): 15–30, and "Never on Sunday: Blue Laws and Roanoke, Virginia," *Virginia Cavalcade* 43 (winter 1994): 132–43.

1. "Sunday Baseball Test Case Made at Portsmouth," *RTD*, 18 May 1925, 1; *Crook v. Commonwealth*, 147 Va. 593, 595–96 (1927), and Record 306, case file (a printed version of this material and other such case files is available at the Virginia Supreme Court Library and at various law libraries in Virginia).

2. PW, "Sunday Sports," in *Religion and American Law: An Encyclopedia*, ed. Paul Finkelman (New York, 2000), 493–95; John A. Lucas, "The Unholy Experiment: Professional Baseball's Struggle against Pennsylvania Sunday Blue Laws, 1926–1943," *Pennsylvania History* 38 (1971): 163–75; Steven A. Riess, "Professional Sunday Baseball: A Study in Social Reform, 1892–1934," *Maryland Historian* 4 (1973): 95–108.

3. *Levering* v. *Park Commissioners*, 134 Md. 48 (1919).

4. *Acts* (1908), 259, ch. 180, sec. 3799 (subsequently amended), quoted in *Pirkey Bros.* v. *Commonwealth*, 134 Va. 713, 716 (1922); the 1656 act is in David N. Laband and Deborah Hendry Heinbuch, *Blue Laws: The History, Economics, and Politics of Sunday-Closing Laws* (Lexington, Mass., 1987), 20, a work that draws on William Addison Blakely, *American State Papers Bearing on Sunday Legislation* (1890; rept. New York, 1970). See also Stephen K. Schutte, "Sunday Closing Laws," in Finkelman, *Religion and American Law*, 479–87, and John Wigley, *The Rise and Fall of the Victorian Sunday* (Manchester, Eng., 1980), chap. 1.

5. Laband and Heinbuch, *Blue Laws*, 28–30, 32, 36–37.

6. John G. West Jr., "Sunday Mails," in Finkelman, *Religion and American Law*, 487–89; Bertram Wyatt-Brown, "Prelude to Abolitionism: Sabbatarian Politics and the Rise of the Second Party System," *Journal of American History* 58 (Sept. 1971): 316–41; Richard R. John, *Spreading the News: The American Postal System from Franklin to Morse* (Cambridge, Mass., 1995), chap. 5; Alexis McCrossen, *Holy Day, Holiday: The American Sunday* (Ithaca, N.Y., 2000), 22–26.

7. McCrossen, *Holy Day, Holiday*, 71–77; see also Gaines Foster, *Moral Reconstruction: Christian Lobbyists and the Federal Legislation of Morality, 1865–1920* (Chapel Hill, N.C., 2002), chap. 5.

8. McCrossen, *Holy Day, Holiday*, 162–63 n. 1 (listing a number of dissertations); Andrew King, "Sunday Regulations in the Nineteenth Century," in Finkelman, *Religion and American Law*, 489–93; John Thomas Jable, "Sport, Amusements, and Pennsylvania Blue Laws, 1682–1973" (Ph.D. diss., Pennsylvania State Univ., 1975); Forrest L. Marion, "The Gentlemen Sabbatarians: The Sabbath Movement in the Upper South, 1826–1836" (Ph.D. diss., Univ. of Tennessee, 1998), and his "'All That Is Pure in Religion and Valuable in Society': Presbyterians, the Virginia Society, and the Sabbath, 1830–1836," *VMHB* 109:2 (2001): 187–218. Regarding the West Coast states during the second half of the nineteenth century, see Vernon Lestrud, "Early Theatrical 'Blue Laws' on the Pacific Coast," *Rendezvous* 4 (1969): 15–24; Arnold Roth, "Sunday 'Blue Laws' and the California Supreme Court," *Southern California Quarterly* 55 (1973): 43–47; and Joseph B. Marks and Lisa J. Sanders, "The Blue Laws Debate: A Sacramento Shopkeeper's Story," *Western States Jewish History* 25 (1993): 211–24. Regarding other parts of the nation, see Harold E. Cox, "'Daily except Sunday': Blue Laws and the Operation of Philadelphia Horsecars," *Business History Review* 39 (1965): 228–42, and J. E. Ericson and James H. McCrocklin, "From Religion to Commerce: The Evolution and Enforcement of Blue Laws in Texas," *Southwestern Social Science Quarterly* 45 (1964):

50–58. Regarding the nation's neighbor to the north, see Sharon Patricia Meen, "The Battle for the Sabbath: The Sabbatarian Lobby in Canada, 1890–1912" (Ph.D. diss., Univ. of British Columbia, 1979), and J. F. Paul Laverdure, "Canada on Sunday: The Decline of the Sabbath, 1900–1950" (Ph.D. diss., Univ. of Toronto, 1990).

9. *Pirkey Bros.* v. *Commonwealth*, 716. For two cases regarding railroad freight cars in the 1890s, see PW, "Works of Necessity and Charity," 16–17.

10. *Pirkey Bros.* v. *Commonwealth*, 717, 722.

11. Ibid., 725–26; *Soon Hing* v. *Crowley*, 113 U.S. 703, 710 (1885).

12. *Pirkey Bros.* v. *Commonwealth*, 730.

13. Ibid., 726.

14. Ibid., 730–31.

15. Petition for Writ of Error, 17–38, case file, *Lakeside Inn Corporation* v. *Commonwealth*.

16. *Lakeside Inn Corporation* v. *Commonwealth*, 134 Va. 696, 702, 704 (1922).

17. Ibid., 706.

18. Ibid., 705–6.

19. Ibid., 701. See also George Hart, "Lakeside's First 60 Years," *Roanoker* 7 (Aug. 1980): 24ff., and George Orwig, "Days of Lakeside Come to an End," *RTWN*, 19 Oct. 1986, A1.

20. *Crook* v. *Commonwealth*, 147 Va. 593, 599 (1927).

21. Ibid., 601, 603.

22. Ibid., 605.

23. Ibid., 606, 608.

24. "The Sunday Decision," *RNL*, 21 Jan. 1927, 8.

25. *Acts* (1916), 751, and (1932), 596 (ch. 328, sec. 4570).

26. George Prince Arnold, "Change in Sunday Blue Law Is Forecast by Candidate," *RTD*, 20 July 1935, 1, 18.

27. "Norfolk Teams Arrested for Blue Law Test," *RTD*, 30 April 1934, 1, 13.

28. "Norfolk Teams Arrested for Blue Law Test," *RTD*, 30 April 1934, 1; David Lidman, "Mooers Interested in Tars 'Test' Case," ibid., 13; David Lidman, "Police Arrest 27 Colts and Rivals after Sunday Tilt," *RTD*, 7 May 1934, 1.

29. Lidman, "Police Arrest 27," 12.

30. Ibid., 1.

31. PW, "Never on Sunday," 136, 138–39. Richardson ran a theater for white moviegoers. A few blocks away Alfred R. Hunter was arrested, also in spring 1935, when he opened a black movie house on a Sunday.

32. *Williams* v. *Commonwealth*, 179 Va. 741 (1942).

33. Ibid., 745, 748.

34. Ibid., 750.

35. Ibid., 750–51.

36. *Francisco* v. *Commonwealth*, 180 Va. 371, 374 (1942).

37. Ibid., 379.

38. Ibid., 380.

39. Ibid., 380–81. See also Forrest L. Marion, "Blue Laws, Knoxville, and the Second World War," *Journal of East Tennessee History* 68 (1996): 41–62.

40. *Acts* (1954), 127–28 (ch. 131).

41. File Record 2940, *Pettit* v. *City of Roanoke*, Virginia Supreme Court. The record misspells Petitt's name.

42. Petition, 11, ibid.

43. Ibid., 18–19.

44. Ibid., 15–16.

45. Brief on Behalf of the City of Roanoke, ibid., 5, 8–9.

46. *Pettit v. City of Roanoke*, 183 Va. 816, 817 (1945). The court noted, too, that the city should properly have prosecuted the owners and then, after securing a conviction, required them, as the statute provided, to give bond not to violate the law yet again.

47. Phone conversation with Bernice S. Petitt, 18 Aug. 1990.

48. *Rich v. Commonwealth*, 198 Va. 445, 446 (1956).

49. Ibid., 447–48.

50. Ibid., 446.

51. Ibid., 452–53.

52. Ibid., 452.

53. Ibid.

54. *Mandell v. Haddon*, 202 Va. 979 (1961).

55. Ibid., 989–90.

56. Ibid., 992; *McGowan v. Maryland*, 366 U.S. 420 (1961). A concurring opinion by Justice Felix Frankfurter (ibid., 459–560) supplies a lengthy analysis of the history of Sunday closing laws in the United States; appendix 2 to that opinion (ibid., 553–59) gives a tabular summary of all fifty states' Sunday closing laws in effect at that time. See also *Braunfield v. Brown*, 366 U.S. 599 (1961), and *Arlan's Department Store of Louisville v. Kentucky*, 371 U.S. 218 (1962). For brief treatments of the larger topic, see Schutte, "Sunday Closing Laws," and Lucas A. Powe Jr., *The Warren Court and American Politics* (Cambridge, Mass., 2000), 183–85. For longer examinations, see Neil J. Diloff, "Never on Sunday: The Blue Laws Controversy," *Maryland Law Review* 39 (1980): 679–714; Barbara J. Redman, "Sabbatarian Accommodation in the Supreme Court," *Journal of Church and State* 33 (1991): 495–523; and Alan Raucher, "Sunday Business and the Decline of Sunday Closing Laws: An Historical Overview," *Journal of Church and State* 36 (1994): 13–33.

57. *Acts* (1974), 509–12 (ch. 330; quotation from sec. 15.1–29.5).

58. Ibid. (sec. 18.1–363.1).

59. *Bonnie BeLo Enterprises v. Commonwealth*, 217 Va. 84, 87 (1976).

60. *Malibu Auto Parts v. Commonwealth*, 218 Va. 467, 470 (1977).

61. Mike Hudson, "Blue-Law Charges Filed by Roanoke against Merchant," *RTWN*, 1 June 1987, B1-B2.

62. Ibid.; Mike Hudson, "Merchant Vows Sunday Blue Law Fight," *RTWN*, 2 June 1987, B3; Richard Lovegrove, "Sunday-Closing Law Charges against Merchant Dismissed," *RTWN*, 30 June 1987, B1; see also Ben Beagle, "Obsession: Man's Blue Law Fight Not Open-and-Shut Case," *RTWN*, 9 Sept. 1987, B2.

63. Mike Hudson and Ben Beagle, "County May Recognize Blue-Law Decision," *RTWN*, 9 Oct. 1987, A1, A7.

64. *RTWN*, 1 Nov. 1987, A7, A12.

65. Caroline E. Mayer, "Retailers to Challenge Va. Blue Law," *WP*, 5 March 1985, D9; Jan Greene, "Retail Group to Appeal Virginia Blue Law Ruling," *Daily News Record*, 23 Aug. 1985.

66. Appellants' Reply Brief, *Benderson v. Sciortino*, ii.

67. Ibid., 21; *Benderson Development Co. v. Paul A. Sciortino*, 236 Va. 136, 139, 144 (1988).

68. *Benderson* v. *Sciortino*, 139.

69. Ibid., 146 (quoting *McGowan* v. *Maryland*, 425), 147.

70. Ibid., 141 (quoting *Mandell* v. *Haddon*, 990), 148–49.

71. Ibid., 144–46.

72. Ibid., 150–51.

73. Sharon Waxman, "France Reconsiders Sunday Sales Ban," *WP*, 13 Oct. 1993, C3; Brent Bowers, "Ballot Battles over Taxes, Blue Laws Rally Small-Business Owners," *Wall Street Journal*, 26 Oct. 1993, B1.

74. *Estate of Thornton* v. *Caldor*, 472 U.S. 703 (1985).

75. Laband and Heinbuch, *Blue Laws*, 41–42, 162–63; see also Paul Finkelman and Stephen E. Gottlieb, eds., *Toward a Usable Past: Liberty under State Constitutions* (Athens, Ga., 1991).

76. *Williams* v. *Commonwealth*, 750.

77. "Movies on Sunday Are Legalized by Verdict of Jury," *RT*, 18 July 1935, 4.

78. Bill Cochran, "Opponents of Sunday Hunting Carry the Day," *RT*, 5 April 1998, C11.

79. Phone conversation with Bernice S. Petitt, 20 May 1991.

3. These New and Strange Beings

An earlier version of this chapter was published as "'These New and Strange Beings': Women in the Legal Profession in Virginia, 1890–1990," *VMHB* 101 (April 1993): 193–226. For funds and access to sources that contributed to this project, I wish to thank the Virginia Historical Society for a Mellon Fellowship during the summer of 1991, the American Historical Association for a Littleton-Griswold Research Grant in American Legal History in 1991, and the Virginia Foundation for the Humanities and Public Policy for a fellowship at the Virginia Center for the Humanities in the summer of 1992. My thanks, too, to April D. Haynes and Robert A. Wells, undergraduate research assistants at Virginia Tech; the anonymous readers for the *VMHB*; and my able copyeditor there, Sara Bearss. Photographs of Belva Lockwood, Rebecca Lovenstein, Elizabeth Tompkins, Marian Poe, and Martha Conway appear in PW, "Strange Beings," 197, 204, 210, 211, 213.

1. On gender and access to the legal profession in America, the best surveys are Cynthia Fuchs Epstein, *Women in Law* (Garden City, N.Y., 1983); Karen Berger Morello, *The Invisible Bar: The Woman Lawyer in America from 1638 to the Present* (New York, 1986); Virginia G. Drachman, *Sisters in Law: Women Lawyers in Modern American History* (Cambridge, Mass., 1998); and—on Virginia—Sandra Gross Schneider, "Women's Entry into the Legal Profession in Virginia," *Virginia Bar News* 34 (April 1986): 11–14, 44–48. Other notable works are Ronald Chester, *Unequal Access: Women Lawyers in a Changing America* (South Hadley, Mass., 1985), on Chicago, Boston, and Washington, D.C., in the 1920s and 1930s; Emily Couric, ed., *Women Lawyers: Perspectives on Success* (New York, 1984), a collection of first-person accounts; Barbara J. Harris, *Beyond Her Sphere: Women and the Professions in American History* (Westport, Conn., 1978), a survey through four centuries; and Judith Hope, *Pinstripes and Pearls: The Women of the Harvard Law Class of '64 Who Forged an Old Girl Network and Paved the Way for Future Generations* (New York, 2003). On race, the best works are Geraldine R. Segal, *Blacks in the Law: Philadelphia and the Nation* (Philadelphia, 1983); J. Clay Smith Jr., *Emancipation: The Making of the Black Lawyer, 1844–1944* (Philadelphia, 1993);

and—on Virginia—Gerald Bruce Lee, Veryl Victoria Miles, and G. Nelson Smith III, "The Black Lawyer in Virginia: Reflections upon a Journey, 1938–1988," *Virginia Lawyer* 37 (Oct. 1988): 28–36 and (Dec. 1988): 32–33. Related studies are Mari J. Matsuda, ed., *Called from Within: Early Women Lawyers of Hawai'i* (Honolulu, 1992), and Gloria Moldow, *Women Doctors in Gilded-Age Washington: Race, Gender, and Professionalization* (Urbana, Ill., 1987).

2. Elizabeth Cady Stanton, Susan B. Anthony, and Matilda Joslyn Gage, eds., *History of Woman Suffrage*, 6 vols. (1881–1922; rept. New York, 1969), 1:70–71.

3. Ibid., 71–73.

4. Smith, *Emancipation*, 93–99, 152, 391–92.

5. Josephine F. Pacheco, "Margaret Douglass," in *Three Who Dared: Prudence Crandall, Margaret Douglass, Myrtilla Miner—Champions of Antebellum Black Education*, ed. Philip S. Foner and Josephine F. Pacheco (Westport, Conn., 1984), 55–95.

6. Cheek and Cheek, "John Mercer Langston."

7. Smith, *Emancipation*, 209–17, 611–13. Pioneer black lawyers in the South included Robert Brown Elliott and Jonathan Jasper Wright (both admitted in 1868) in South Carolina. Not until 1929 did Louis L. Redding become the first black lawyer in Delaware, a laggard state on race even more than on gender.

8. Ibid., 225. As with the first female lawyer in Virginia (see note 44 below), a number of black lawyers have been identified as first; see PW, "Strange Beings," 194 n. 4.

9. Smith, *Emancipation*, 225–37; Luther Porter Jackson, *Negro Office-Holders in Virginia, 1865–1895* (Norfolk, Va., 1945), 36; Walter Dyson, *Howard University, the Capstone of Negro Education: A History, 1867–1940* (Washington, D.C., 1941), 233; Thomas Calhoun Walker, *The Honey-Pod Tree* (New York, 1958); Maxwell Bloomfield, *American Lawyers in a Changing Society, 1776–1876* (Cambridge, Mass., 1976), 328–31.

10. PW, *Virginia Tech*, 59; Toppin, *Loyal Sons and Daughters*, 13–21.

11. Jackson, *Negro Office-Holders in Virginia*, 16–17, 20 (photograph of Fields, 11).

12. Smith, *Emancipation*, 227–37, 262–67; PW, "Joseph Thomas Newsome," *ANB* 16:355–56; Michael E. Hucles, "Andrew William Ernest Bassette," *DVB* 1:388–89; Leah Pollard Jones Johnson, "I Remember Papa: Joseph R. Pollard, Esquire, 'The Black Socrates,'" *Richmond Literary and Historical Quarterly* 4 (summer 1981): 45–47.

13. W. Hamilton Bryson, ed., *Legal Education in Virginia, 1779–1979: A Biographical Approach* (Charlottesville, Va., 1982), 53–54. See also Robert M. Goldman, "Peter James Henry," "George William Lewis," "Cyrenius August McKenzie," and "Josiah Curtis Robertson," ibid., 281–84, 340–42, 390–92, 549–51.

14. Smith, *Emancipation*, 231–32, 237.

15. U.S. Census Bureau, Tenth Census, 1880, Manuscript Population Schedules, Henrico County, Va., NA.

16. Lelia J. Robinson, "Women Lawyers in the United States," *Green Bag* 2 (Jan. 1890): 11–12; William Hall Cato, "The Development of Higher Education for Women in Virginia" (Ph.D. diss., Univ. of Virginia, 1941), 341–42; "Letter from Mrs. Smith," *RD*, 14 Jan. 1890, 2; "No Female Lawyers," *RD*, 23 Jan. 1890, 1; "Female Lawyers, *RD*, 31 Jan. 1890, 2 (quotation).

17. U.S. Census Bureau, Twelfth Census, 1900, Manuscript Population Schedules, Goochland County, Va., NA. That the census schedules for 1890 no longer exist prevents confirmation of whether Annie Smith is the female Virginian who was identified as a lawyer.

18. Robinson, "Women Lawyers," 10–32; Morello, *Invisible Bar*, 10–38.

19. *In re Bradwell*, 55 Ill. 535 (1869); *Slaughter-House Cases*, 83 U.S. (16 Wall) 36 (1873); *Bradwell v. Illinois*, 83 U.S. 130 (1873); Jane M. Friedman, *America's First Woman Lawyer: The Biography of Myra Bradwell* (Buffalo, 1993); Joan Hoff, *Law, Gender, and Injustice: A Legal History of U.S. Women* (New York, 1991), 164–70; Sandra F. VanBurkleo, *"Belonging to the World": Women's Rights and American Constitutional Culture* (New York, 2001), 155–59.

20. Rosamond M. Scott, *The Women of Virginia: A Retrospect* (Richmond, 1893), quoted in James S. Wamsley and Anne M. Cooper, *Idols, Victims, Pioneers: Virginia's Women from 1607* ([Richmond], 1976), 216.

21. Louis Filler, "Belva Ann Bennett McNall Lockwood," in *Notable American Women, 1607–1950: A Biographical Dictionary*, ed. Edward T. James, Janet Wilson James, and Paul S. Boyer, 3 vols. (Cambridge, Mass., 1971), 2:413–14. For the Canadian counterparts to the pioneers in the United States, see Constance Backhouse, *Petticoats and Prejudice: Women and Law in Nineteenth-Century Canada* (Toronto, 1991), 293–326. In 1897 Clara Brett Martin, admitted to the bar in Ontario, became the first woman to break into the legal profession in the British Commonwealth.

22. Filler, "Lockwood," 414–15. Lockwood's account, "My Efforts to Become a Lawyer," *Lippincotts Monthly Magazine* 87 (Feb. 1888): 215–29, is reprinted in *Women in the American Economy: A Documentary History, 1675 to 1929*, ed. W. Elliot Brownlee and Mary M. Brownlee (New Haven, 1976), 297–307 (quotations at 302, 304).

23. *Boyd's Directory of the District of Columbia* (1880), 438; ibid. (1894), 657.

24. Madeleine B. Stern, *We the Women: Career Firsts of Nineteenth-Century America* (New York, 1963), 205–34, supplies a full narrative of Lockwood's life and career.

25. Friedman, *America's First Woman Lawyer*, chaps. 1, 7–10; Barbara Sicherman and Carol Hurd Green, eds., *Notable American Women, the Modern Period: A Biographical Dictionary* (Cambridge, Mass., 1980), 11–13, 55–56, 60–61, 454–56, 544–45. See also Morello, *Hidden Bar*, 108–13; VanBurkleo, *"Belonging to the World,"* 155–63; and PW, "Strange Beings," 198 n. 10.

26. "Governor Harris Signs Woman Lawyer Bill," *Atlanta Constitution*, 20 Aug. 1916, B1; *Ex parte Hale*, 145 Ga. 350 (1916); Georgia, *Acts* (1916), 76 (no. 471). See also "Woman at the Bar" (editorial), *Atlanta Constitution*, 17 Aug. 1916, 8.

27. They found, too, that the right to vote did not necessarily bring jury duty: J. Stanley Lemons, *The Woman Citizen: Social Feminism in the 1920s* (Urbana, Ill., 1973), 68–73; Linda K. Kerber, *No Constitutional Right to Be Ladies: Women and the Obligations of Citizenship* (New York, 1998), chap. 4; Alan Rogers, "'Finish the Fight': The Struggle for Women's Jury Service in Massachusetts, 1920–1994," *Massachusetts Historical Review* 2 (2000): 27–54.

28. Morello, *Invisible Bar*, 37–38; Robinson, "Women Lawyers," 12. Not until after the turn of the century did any woman again become a lawyer in North Carolina.

29. *Code of Virginia* (1887), secs. 3191–93; *Acts* (1891–92), 209 (ch. 122).

30. "Mrs. Lockwood Sat Upon," *RD*, 27 May 1894, 9, gives an account of the U.S. Supreme Court's decision *Ex parte Lockwood*, 154 U.S. 116 (1894).

31. "Victory for Mrs. Belva Lockwood," *NYT*, 16 June 1894, 1; "Belva Lockwood Will Practice," *NYT*, 2 Oct. 1894, 4. Lockwood's story to this point has been sketched elsewhere. Suzanne Lebsock, *Virginia Women, 1600–1945: "A Share of Honour"* (Richmond, 1987), 100, draws on a brief account by Valarie Edinger, "An 1894 Portia," under "Virginia Women in Vanguard in 100-Year Effort for Equal Suffrage," *RTD*, 22 Oct. 1950, Richmond "centennial" section, 22. W. Asbury Christian supplied an ear-

lier account in *Richmond: Her Past and Present* (1912; rept. Spartanburg, S.C., 1973), 439. Schneider ("Women's Entry," 12–13, 47) draws on (but goes beyond) the accounts in Christian and the 1950 Richmond paper. For other versions and contexts, see Joseph Gordon Hylton Jr., "The Virginia Lawyer from Reconstruction to the Great Depression" (Ph.D. diss., Harvard Univ., 1986), 28–29, 57–58 n. 42; Albie Sachs and Joan Hoff Wilson, *Sexism and the Law: A Study of Male Beliefs and Legal Bias in Britain and the United States* (New York, 1979), 105–6; and Hoff, *Law, Gender, and Injustice,* 183–84.

32. See Introduction, above, for an account of the Readjusters as well as an account of the Virginia Supreme Court.

33. VSCOB 30 (1892–95): 706; "Mrs. Lockwood's Motion Denied," *RD,* 26 April 1895, 5. Christian, *Richmond,* 439, reports simply that having received her license in October 1894, "Mrs. Lockwood, however, did not have many cases in the Virginia courts." None of the sources cited in note 31 above indicates the 1895 conclusion to Lockwood's experience in Virginia.

34. Edward C. Burks in *Virginia Law Register* 1 (June 1895): 151. Burks also declared that Lockwood had failed to qualify in 1894 in that she was not present when the court ruled in her favor.

35. *Acts* (1895–96), 49–50 (ch. 41).

36. *Matter of Charles Taylor,* 48 Md. 28, 33 (1877); Maryland, *Laws* (1876), ch. 264, and (1888), ch. 204. For detailed accounts, see David Skillen Bogen, "The Transformation of the Fourteenth Amendment: Reflections from the Admission of Maryland's First Black Lawyers," *Maryland Law Review* 44 (1985): 939–1046 (see esp. 939–41, 1029–46), and his "The First Integration of the University of Maryland School of Law," *Maryland Historical Magazine* 84 (spring 1989): 39–49. See also Smith, *Emancipation,* 143–45. Bogen, "Transformation," rebuts the statement by Richard L. Abel in *American Lawyers* (New York, 1989), 108, that "the Reconstruction amendments ended de jure exclusion" of African Americans from the profession.

37. *In re Etta H. Maddox,* 93 Md. 727, 736 (1901); "Bars Woman Lawyer," *Baltimore Sun,* 22 Nov. 1901, 10; Maryland, *Laws* (1902), 566 (ch. 399); Mary Katherine Scheeler, "Etta Haynie Maddox, 1860–1933: Pioneer Lawyer and Suffragist," in *Notable Maryland Women,* ed. Winifred G. Helmes (Cambridge, Md., 1977), 225–29. The Maryland court harked back as well to its own action in Charles Taylor's case.

38. On this distinction in roles, see PW, "Strange Beings," 203 n. 21.

39. *Virginia Law Register* 7 (Jan. 1902): 645–46 and (April 1902): 867. Before 1898 the Maryland statute had explicitly restricted the profession to men, and the 1898 law dropped the exclusionary language. As the observer from Virginia noted, "The entire opinion reads as if the court were saying sotto voce, 'We don't want you at our bar, and we shall not allow you to practise until the legislature says that we must.'"

40. *JS* (1918), 484.

41. *Acts* (1920), 66 (ch. 77), and (1922), 654 (ch. 389).

42. Philip A. Bruce, *History of the University of Virginia, 1819–1919: The Lengthened Shadow of One Man,* 5 vols. (New York, 1920–22), 5:86–103; John Ritchie, *The First Hundred Years: A Short History of the School of Law of the University of Virginia for the Period 1826–1926* (Charlottesville, Va., 1978), 96–99; "Admit Women to University," *CDP,* 13 Jan. 1920. It has been said that the school "was one of the leaders in the admission of women to study law" (Ritchie, *First Hundred Years,* 96), and indeed it preceded various schools, including Harvard. Nevertheless another scholar (Abel, *American Lawyers,* 90) has pointed out that though only 41 of 137 law schools in the nation

admitted women for the year 1915–16, by the year that the University of Virginia acted only 7 of 129 continued to exclude all women. Thus the University of Virginia acted toward the end of a brief period when most schools became less restrictive in their policies on gender. For more detail, see Epstein, *Women in Law*, 49–51, and Morello, *Invisible Bar*, 39–107.

43. VSCOB 38 (1917–22): 415, 476, 571; Morello, *Invisible Bar*, 36–38; Hoff, *Law, Gender, and Injustice*, 164; VanBurkleo, *"Belonging to the World,"* 162; PW, "Strange Beings," 205–6 n. 26.

44. "Mrs. Lovenstein First Woman to Argue in Supreme Court," *RTD*, 8 Jan. 1925, 3. Yet another candidate—aside from Belva Lockwood and Rebecca Lovenstein or Carrie Gregory—has been named Virginia's first woman lawyer: Laura Vayle Snell was said to be "the first woman to be admitted to the Virginia Bar," in 1923 ("Woman Attorney, Miss Snell, Dies," *RTD*, 27 April 1963, 4).

45. "Mrs. Lovenstein First"; *Mazer* v. *Commonwealth*, 142 Va. 649 (1925). Lovenstein and Lovenstein won the case.

46. William M. Lile, Department of Law, Univ. of Virginia, Annual Reports to President (1920–21), 69–70, UVA Lib.

47. Ibid. (1921–22), 75; ibid. (1922–23), 1–2; ibid. (1923–24), 4.

48. Reuben E. Alley, *History of the University of Richmond, 1830–1971* (Charlottesville, Va., 1977), 170–71; Susan H. Godson et al., *The College of William and Mary: A History*, 2 vols. (Williamsburg, Va., 1993), 2:506–11, 568–73; PW, "Strange Beings," 209 n. 33.

49. Maud Tucker Drane and Walter Harding Drane, eds., *Private Journals of William Minor Lile*, 2 vols. (n.p., 1987–88), 2:140 (19 June 1923).

50. "Careers for Women: Law Profession," *RTD*, 2 Oct. 1936, 19; Eudora R. Richardson, "Elizabeth Tompkins, Richmond Attorney, First Woman to Graduate from Law School at University," *RNL*, 14 Jan. 1937, 24; "Area Attorney, Hit by Car, Dies," *RTD*, 26 June 1981, B1–B2; "Lawyer, 83, Struck, Killed," *RNL*, 26 June 1981, 18.

51. Schneider, "Women's Entry," 13–14, 44, 48.

52. Constitution of 1902, art. 9, sec. 140, in Thorpe, *Constitutions* 7:3934.

53. PW, "L. Marian Poe," *ANB* 17:611–12; Okianer Christian Dark and Allen R. Moye, "L. Marian Poe: A Model of Public Service," *Virginia Lawyer* 38 (Mar. 1990): 32–35; "Atty. L. Marian Poe Says 'Keep Busy' to Succeed," *NJG*, 17 Sept. 1955, 9; VSCOB 39 (1922–26): 585, 40 (1927–31): 4; Smith, *Emancipation*, 201, 344. At the Newsome House in Newport News, Va., 13 Sept. 1991, Lillian W. Lovett introduced me to helpful materials on Poe, and Philip S. Walker shared with me his recollections of her; and community people cleared her nearby gravesite, which enabled me to clarify her family history. See also J. Clay Smith Jr., ed., *Rebels in Law: Voices in History of Black Women Lawyers* (Ann Arbor, Mich., 1998).

54. Interview with Roland D. Ealey, Richmond, 22 March 1991; Mary Y. Zimmermann, ed., *75 Year History of National Association of Women Lawyers, 1899–1974* (n.p., 1975), 160, 303, 350; Smith, *Emancipation*, 581.

55. "Lady Lawyers," *NJG*, 16 Feb. 1929; "Norfolk Has Woman Practicing Lawyer" (letter to the editor), *NJG*, 23 Feb. 1929; VSCOB 40 (1927–31): 9, 226; "52 Lawyers Are [Black] Women," *RAA*, 19 July 1941, 17. To undo the gaffe, Bertha Douglass was invited to come to the meeting and be the one who introduced Marian Poe. Douglass, too, represented Virginia at meetings of the National Association of Women Lawyers, twice in the early 1940s (Zimmermann, *75 Year History*, 92, 99).

56. "Lady Lawyers," *Ebony* 2 (Aug. 1947): 18–21; Morello, *Invisible Bar*, 143–72.

57. "The Lawyer," *RTD*, 31 Aug. 1980, H1, H13; Richard Lee Morton, *Virginia Lives: The Old Dominion Who's Who* (Hopkinsville, Ky., 1964), 203–4.

58. *Code of Virginia* (1950), art. 54.1–3900.

59. For figures on race for each state in 1970 and 1980, see Segal, *Blacks in the Law*, 276–77. For aggregate annual enrollment figures by gender in the nation's law schools, see Epstein, *Women in the Law*, 53; Abel, *American Lawyers*, 285. For Virginia's figures on gender, see James N. Woodson, "'Lady Lawyers' Make Haste Slowly," *RTD*, 26 Jan. 1969, F1.

60. This proved a grudging kind of change, a clear example of what has been dubbed a change "from exclusion to tokenism" (Sachs and Wilson, *Sexism and the Law*, 95); the fact that a school admitted one black student by no means meant that a second student, equally qualified, would be admitted too. The stories of Gregory Swanson and Edward Travis are told briefly in Virginius Dabney, *Mr. Jefferson's University: A History* (Charlottesville, Va., 1981), 379–80, and Godson et al., *College of William and Mary* 2:767, and with much more detail and analysis in Anthony Blaine Deel, "Virginia's Minimal Resistance: The Desegregation of Public Graduate and Professional Education, 1935–1955" (M.A. thesis, Virginia Polytechnic Institute and State Univ., 1990), 92–146.

61. PW, "Strange Beings," 214 n. 45.

62. Woodson, "'Lady Lawyers' Make Haste Slowly." The combined total number of female law students at the three schools was 58 out of 1,272 (4.6%): the University of Virginia with 42 of about 700 (6.0%); the College of William and Mary with 9 of 196 (4.6%); and the University of Richmond with 7 of 189 (3.7%).

63. Schneider, "Women's Entry," 14.

64. Woodson, "'Lady Lawyers' Make Haste Slowly." On women law professors, see Epstein, *Women in Law*, 219–36.

65. Thomas A. Silvestri, "Women Lawyers Are No Longer Oddity in State," *RTD*, 20 Oct. 1985, K14-K15.

66. For more on the Vietnam War, see Epstein, *Women in Law*, 52–54, who makes a similar observation about the Korean War, except that the figures snapped back in that case to the *status quo ante bellum*; see also PW, "Strange Beings," 215 n. 50.

67. For more on Title VII (1964) and Title IX (1972), see Epstein, *Women in Law*, 94–95; Carl M. Brauer, "Women Activists, Southern Conservatives, and the Prohibition of Sex Discrimination in Title VII of the 1964 Civil Rights Act," *JSH* 49 (Feb. 1983): 37–56; and PW, "Strange Beings," 216 n. 51.

68. Maria Carillo, "Female Lawyers' Ranks Growing . . . Slowly," *RTD*, 29 July 1985, B1.

69. Alumni Association of the University of Virginia, *Alumni Directory* (Charlottesville, Va., 1990), 886–904.

70. Quoted in Carillo, "Female Lawyers' Ranks Growing."

71. On a sudden shift at this time in career objectives among college women, see William H. Chafe, *Women and Equality: Changing Patterns in American Culture* (New York, 1977), 139–40. For a graph displaying the surge in numbers of women earning degrees not only in law but in other professions as well in the 1970s, see Steven D. McLaughlin et al., *The Changing Lives of American Women* (Chapel Hill, N.C., 1988), 38.

72. *Review of Legal Education in the United* States (fall 1990), 58–60; *Official Guide to ABA-Approved Law Schools*, 2003 ed. (New York, 2002), 282, 570, 742, 758, 796. Af-

rican Americans and Asian Americans combined for 6.1% of all J.D. degrees awarded in 2001 at the University of Richmond, 8.7% at George Mason, 7.5% at Washington and Lee, 12.5% at the University of Virginia, and 16.6% at William and Mary; and growing numbers of Hispanic students were earning law degrees at those schools as well. In the academic year 2001–2, female enrollments ranged from 41.9% at George Mason and at William and Mary up to 47.2% at the University of Richmond. Two newer law schools, the Regent and Appalachian programs, are not included here, but there, too, the female percentages were in the 40s in 2001–2.

   73. *ABA Approved Law Schools* (1997), 451; Abel, *American Lawyers*, 89, 285.

4. The Siege against Segregation

I am grateful for the time I was able to spend with Oliver Hill and Roland Ealey in Richmond. Many thanks as well to Lillian Lovett in Newport News for introducing me to her cousin in Richmond, Julia Tucker, Samuel Tucker's widow, who in turn introduced me to Tucker's sister, Elsie Tucker Thomas, in Alexandria, who added even more to the story. And it was Raymond J. Jirran of Thomas Nelson Community College who first put me in touch with Lillian Lovett. Special thanks, too, to William A. Elwood, who was associate dean of the Graduate School of Arts and Sciences, University of Virginia, when he made various materials available to me, and to Teresa Roane of the VRHC, who made available to me interview materials with Oliver Hill and Henry Marsh. I presented portions of this chapter in two conference papers: "'I Went to Law School to Fight Segregation': Oliver W. Hill and the Siege in Virginia against Jim Crow," at the annual meeting of the Southern Historical Association, in Atlanta, 6 Nov. 1992, and "Seizing the 'Equal' in 'Separate but Equal': The NAACP and the Public Schools—Virginia in the 1940s," at the annual meeting of the American Society for Legal History, Richmond, 18 Oct. 1996.

   1. PW, "Samuel Wilbert Tucker," *ANB* 21:904–5; interview with Elsie Tucker Thomas in Alexandria, 9 March 1994; Smith, *Managing White Supremacy*, 285. Regarding the segregation of public transport in Virginia and resistance to it, see August Meier and Elliott Rudwick, "Negro Boycotts of Segregated Streetcars in Virginia, 1904–1907," *VMHB* 81 (Oct. 1973): 479–87, and Alexander, *Race Man*, 131–42.
   2. The literature on the early history of post–Civil War segregation begins with C. Vann Woodward, *The Strange Career of Jim Crow* (1955; 3d rev. ed., New York, 1974), and continues with such works as Charles E. Wynes, *Race Relations in Virginia, 1870–1902* (Charlottesville, Va., 1961), and, especially, Howard N. Rabinowitz, *Race Relations in the Urban South, 1865–1890* (New York, 1978). Woodward focuses on transportation—passenger railroads—and gives little or no consideration to legally mandated racial segregation in such matters as education and marriage.
   3. Constitution of 1902, art. 9, sec. 140, in Thorpe, *Constitutions* 7:3934; Harlan, *Separate and Unequal*, chap. 5; Moger, *Virginia*, 255–58.
   4. Genna Rae McNeil, *Groundwork: Charles Hamilton Houston and the Struggle for Civil Rights* (Philadelphia, 1983), chaps. 6–7; Charles H. Houston, "The Need for Negro Lawyers," *JNE* 4 (Jan. 1935): 49–52; PW, "Higher Education and the Civil Rights Movement: Desegregating the University of North Carolina," in *Warm Ashes: Issues in Southern History at the Dawn of the Twenty-first Century*, ed. Winfred B. Moore Jr., Kyle S. Sinisi, and David H. White Jr. (Columbia, S.C., 2003), 280–300.

5. August Meier and Elliott Rudwick, "Attorneys Black and White: A Case Study of Race Relations within the NAACP," *Journal of American History* 62 (March 1976): 913–46 (focusing on the quarter century after the founding of the NAACP in 1909).

6. *City of Richmond* v. *Deans*, 37 F.2d 712 (1930); Smith, *Managing White Supremacy*, 204–18.

7. Previous treatments of the crucial roles played by black lawyers include Paul Finkelman, "Not Only the Judges' Robes Were Black: African-American Lawyers as Social Engineers," *Stanford Law Review* 47 (Nov. 1994): 161–209; Jack Greenberg, *Crusaders in the Courts: How a Dedicated Band of Lawyers Fought for the Civil Rights Revolution* (New York, 1994), on white as well as black civil rights lawyers in the 1950s and 1960s; and Darlene Clark Hine, "Black Lawyers and the Twentieth-Century Struggle for Constitutional Change," in *African Americans and the Living Constitution*, ed. John Hope Franklin and Genna Rae McNeil (Washington, D.C., 1995), 33–55.

8. Regarding their preparing for, taking, and passing the bar exam, see the video-taped interview of William A. Elwood with Oliver W. Hill and S. W. Tucker (CRLDP, Oct. 1987; Elwood supplied me with a transcript), 26–29. Regarding Hill's child-hood, his years at Howard, and passing the bar, see Oliver W. Hill Sr., *The Big Bang—Brown v. Board of Education, and Beyond: The Autobiography of Oliver W. Hill, Sr.*, ed. Jonathan K. Stubbs (Winter Park, Fla., 2000), 1–89.

9. Notes of an interview by Richard Kluger with Oliver W. Hill, Richmond, 4 April 1971, in the *Brown* v. *Board of Education* Collection, Sterling Memorial Library, Yale Univ., New Haven; Richard Kluger, *Simple Justice: The History of Brown versus Board of Education and Black America's Struggle for Equality* (New York, 1976), 471 (re-phrased from the original to "I went to law school so I could go out and fight segrega-tion"); videotaped VRHC interview with Samuel Tucker; interview with Roland D. Ealey, Richmond, 22 March 1991.

10. A number of sketches of Oliver Hill's earlier life and later career exist, among them Shelley Rolfe, "Integration: Still a Long Way to Go," *RTD*, 30 March 1969, B1; Carol O'Connor Wolf, "Oliver Hill: A Life of Change," *Style Weekly* 4 (11 Feb. 1986): 38–43; Mike Hudson, "Hill v. Board of Education," *Southern Exposure* 17 (spring 1989): 30–33; Steve Clark, "Hill Never Thought His Role in History Would Be a Movie Role," *RNL*, 13 April 1991; and Hill, *Big Bang*.

11. Hill, *Big Bang*, 90–100; videotaped interview by A. Leon Higginbotham Jr. with Oliver W. Hill (CRLDP, 25 May 1985; Elwood supplied me with a transcript), 8–10. That interview has been published in part, but without this section (or some other passages cited later in this essay), in A. Leon Higginbotham Jr., "Conversations with Civil Rights Crusaders [Oliver Hill and Samuel Tucker]," *Virginia Lawyer* 37 (Feb. 1989): 11–16, 37–41.

12. Mrs. Hill is listed in the Washington, D.C., city directories until the late 1940s. For long stretches of time, there were many weekend visits, to and from Roanoke, then Richmond, and then, after World War II, Richmond again. Oliver Hill speaks about her living in Washington in his interview with Elwood (transcript, 24).

13. Higginbotham's interview with Hill, 10; PW, "Leon Andrew Ransom," *ANB* 18:154–55.

14. Higginbotham's interview with Hill, 10, 20.

15. "Richmonder Elected Va. Bar Group Head," *RAA*, 25 April 1942, 20. In an earlier incarnation the ODBA was organized in the 1920s ("Colored Lawyers Form

New Bar Association," *RTD*, 25 Aug. 1925, 2). See the Old Dominion Bar Association Collection, 1940s–1980s, Virginia Black History Archives, Virginia Commonwealth Univ., Richmond.

16. Elwood's interview with Hill, 8, 10.

17. Ibid., 13–14.

18. Videotaped interview with Oliver W. Hill (Richmond Community Interviews, 1985, Richmond, VRHC, my transcription), 10–11.

19. Ibid., 11; Gilbert Ware, *William Hastie: Grace under Pressure* (New York, 1984), 171–72.

20. "Captain Slade Is Named to Pa. Section," *NJG*, 15 Aug. 1936, 18; "Negro Officers Take Charge of CCC Camp Here," *Gettysburg Times*, 8 Aug. 1936, 1. For context, see Calvin W. Gower, "The Struggle of Blacks for Leadership Positions in the Civilian Conservation Corps, 1933–1942," *Journal of Negro History* 61 (April 1976): 123–35, and Charles W. Johnson, "The Army, the Negro, and the Civilian Conservation Corps, 1933–1942," *Military Affairs* 36 (Oct. 1972): 82–88. The apparent bid for black votes in FDR's reelection campaign appears to have drawn little media attention.

21. VRHC videotaped interview with Samuel Tucker.

22. Ibid.; interview with Elsie Tucker Thomas; "Boys Wanted to Read, but Librarians Had Them Jailed," *NJG*, 2 Sept. 1939, 1; S. J. Ackerman, "The Trials of S. W. Tucker," *WP Magazine*, 11 June 2000, 14ff.; Smith, *Managing White Supremacy*, 261–70. On Tucker's career, see also the Samuel Wilbert Tucker Collection, Virginia Black History Archives, VCU.

23. *Mills v. Anne Arundel County Board of Education*, 30 F.Supp. 245 (1939); Kluger, *Simple Justice*, 214–15; Mark V. Tushnet, *The NAACP's Legal Strategy against Segregated Education, 1925–1950* (Chapel Hill, N.C., 1987), 58–65.

24. The pioneer historians of the events in Norfolk were J. Rupert Picott, in "Desegregation of Higher Education in Virginia," *JNE* 27 (summer 1958): 324–31, and subsequently in *History of the Virginia Teachers Association* (Washington, D.C., 1975), chaps. 12–14; and Doxie A. Wilkerson, in "Some Correlates of Recent Progress toward Equalizing White and Negro Schools in Virginia" (Ph.D. diss., New York Univ., 1958), 246–55, and "The Negro School Movement in Virginia: From 'Equalization' to 'Integration,'" *JNE* 29 (winter 1960): 17–29, rept. in *The Making of Black America*, vol. 2, *The Black Community in Modern America*, ed. August Meier and Elliott Rudwick (New York, 1969), 259–73.

Later treatments include Kluger, *Simple Justice*, 214–17; McNeil, *Groundwork*, 140–55; Ware, *William Hastie*, 62–65; Tushnet, *NAACP's Legal Strategy*, 77–81; Henry Lewis Suggs, *P. B. Young, Newspaperman: Race, Politics, and Journalism in the New South, 1910–1962* (Charlottesville, Va., 1988), 158–63; Earl Lewis, *In Their Own Interests: Race, Class, and Power in Twentieth-Century Norfolk, Virginia* (Berkeley, Calif., 1991), 155–65; and Thomas C. Parramore with Peter C. Stewart and Tommy L. Bogger, *Norfolk: The First Four Centuries* (Charlottesville, Va., 1994), 317–19, 328–30.

25. The story of the litigation is outlined in Kluger, *Simple Justice*, 214–15, and Smith, *Managing White Supremacy*, 256–58. Aline Black's story is sketched in Gil C. Hoffler, "Honor 'Courageous Teachers,'" *NJG*, 18 Dec. 1971, 1, 2.

26. "Plan to Appeal Teachers' Salary Suit Reversal," *NJG*, 10 June 1939, 2.

27. "School Board Breaks Silence," *NJG*, 15 July 1939, 1.

28. Higginbotham interview with Hill, 16; "Again Ask School Board to Equalize Salaries," *NJG*, 7 Oct. 1939, 2.

29. *Alston* v. *School Board of the City of Norfolk*, 112 F.2d 992 (1940); Picott, *Virginia Teachers Association*, 116.

30. "Court Upholds Negroes Plea for Equal Pay," *RTD*, 19 June 1940, 1, 4.

31. *Alston* v. *School Board of the City of Norfolk*, cert. denied 311 U.S. 693 (1940); Picott, *Virginia Teachers Association*, 117; Smith, *Managing White Supremacy*, 271–72. For a full account, see Larissa M. Smith, "Where the South Begins: Black Politics and Civil Rights Activism in Virginia, 1930–1951" (Ph.D. diss., Emory Univ., 2001), 137–68.

32. Tushnet, *NAACP's Legal Strategy*, 70, 80–82, 88–104.

33. PW, "Melvin Ovenus Alston," *ANB* 1:383–84; Hoffler, "Honor 'Courageous Teachers,'" 2; "Pioneer in Teacher Salary Fight Dies," *NJG*, 31 Aug. 1974, 1.

34. "Negroes Here Accept Plan on School Pay," *RTD*, 14 Feb. 1942, 1; Wilkerson, "Recent Progress," 252, 364–65.

35. Kluger's transcript of his interview with Hill, 2 (Kluger's papers at Yale include raw notes and a more formal typed transcript; at some points, here or after, I have silently changed his spelling and punctuation, for the transcript is a working document). Jurisdictions adopting three-year schedules of salary equalization included Loudoun County, Campbell County, and the city of Roanoke (Robert Edward Branson, "From Equalization to Desegregation: Black Virginians' Struggle for Better Education" [history thesis, Univ. of Virginia, 1980], 23).

36. Wilkerson, "Recent Progress," 80, 254–55.

37. "Judge Holds School Board Ignored Order," *RTD*, 27 May 1945, 1, 3; Wilkerson, "Recent Progress," 253–54, 367. Three decades after the struggle in Newport News over teachers' salaries, Dorothy Roles, by that time Dorothy Watkins and having retired as a teacher, was elected a member of the Newport News School Board (Picott, *Virginia Teachers Association*, 117).

38. "To Renew Pleas for Salary Increase, Trades at Huntington," *NJG*, 7 Sept. 1940, 11.

39. Tushnet, *NAACP's Legal Strategy*, 80, mistakenly states that the firing of the three black principals in retaliation for the decision in *Alston* took place in the city of Norfolk, rather than in Norfolk County.

40. "Fight 'Vicious' New Board Edict," *NJG*, 16 Aug. 1941, 2.

41. "Residents of County to Act minus NAACP," *NJG*, 10 Jan. 1942, 10; "Board Answers Complaint of Fired Teachers," *NJG*, 28 Feb. 1942, 10.

42. "Residents of County to Act minus NAACP."

43. "File Action without Aid of NAACP," *NJG*, 10 Jan. 1942, 14; "Board Answers Complaint of Fired Teachers."

44. "File School Bus Suit in Greenville County," *NJG*, 15 March 1941, 1; "Education Chief Raps Inequality," *RAA*, 30 May 1942, 5.

45. "School Bus Discrimination Case Won in High Court," *RAA*, 9 Oct. 1943, 9.

46. Ibid.; VSCOB 44 (1942–45): 265–66. Kluger, *Simple Justice*, 472, errs in dating this development to the late 1940s, after Hill had returned from military service in Europe.

47. "Pupils Sue for Admission to White Va. County Schools," *RAA*, 19 Sept. 1942, 1.

48. Ibid., 1, 23.

49. Ibid., 23.

50. "Refused to Take Jim Crow Seat, Woman Fined," *RAA*, 6 June 1942, 1.

51. Ware, *Hastie*, 185–86; Catherine A. Barnes, *Journey from Jim Crow: The Desegregation of Southern Transit* (New York, 1983), 44–48.

52. Ware, *Hastie*, 186; *Morgan* v. *Commonwealth*, 184 Va. 24 (1945).

53. Irene Morgan's lawyers shared a keen interest in attacking "separate but equal" head on, under the equal protection clause, but they were convinced that this was not the case for doing so, not the time. Had they done so, they were pretty sure the court would have reaffirmed the ancient doctrine of *Plessy* v. *Ferguson*. Thus they persisted in arguing on the basis of the commerce clause, and when Justice Wiley E. Rutledge kept raising the question of whether the Fourteenth Amendment had a bearing, they did what they could to run away from that line of argument. At that time, as Spottswood Robinson put it later, "we did not want to make bad law." Rather, they made the best law possible when in June 1946, by a 6-to-3 margin, the Supreme Court adopted their argument and overturned the statute and the conviction on commerce clause grounds (interview with Robinson, quoted in Ware, *Hastie*, 187–90, at 189; *Morgan* v. *Virginia*, 328 U.S. 373 [1946]; Smith, "Where the South Begins," 207–17).

54. Higginbotham interview with Hill (CRLDP), 21.

55. "Negro Attorney Who Refused to Change Seat on Bus Is Convicted and Test Is in Prospect," *RTD*, 20 Nov. 1946, 1, 2.

56. Ibid., 2; "Hustings Court Reverses Case of Negro Convicted for Disturbance on Bus," *RTD*, 22 Jan. 1947, 2.

57. Ibid.

58. "Virginia Jail Greets Olympic Hero upon Return Home," *RAA*, 25 Sept. 1948, 3; *Lee* v. *Commonwealth*, 189 Va. 890, 891, 894 (1949); "Va. Supreme Court Voids Jim Crow Conviction," *NJG*, 17 Sept. 1949, 2.

59. "Four Citizens Petition Court for Injunction Banning Negroes from Residence in East End," *RTD*, 12 Oct. 1947, B3; "Petition Filed for Ouster of Family," *RTD*, 15 Oct. 1947, 5.

60. "Injunction to Restrict Tenants Denied," *RTD*, 25 Oct. 1947, 5; Clement E. Vose, *Caucasians Only: The Supreme Court, the NAACP, and the Restrictive Covenant Cases* (Berkeley, Calif., 1959), 157.

61. *Shelley* v. *Kraemer*, 334 U.S. 1 (1948); Vose, *Caucasians Only*, 177–210.

62. "Negro Leaders Plan Campaign to End Segregation in State," *RTD*, 17 Dec. 1947, 3; Donald R. McCoy and Richard T. Ruetten, *Quest and Response: Minority Rights and the Truman Administration* (Lawrence, Kans., 1973), chap. 5.

63. "Negro Leaders Plan Campaign to End Segregation."

64. Ibid.; Charles H. Thompson, "Why Negroes Are Opposed to Segregated Regional Schools," *JNE* 18 (winter 1949): 1–8. The organization went on record as "unequivocally" opposed to multistate "regional" public institutions of advanced education for black southerners.

65. "Segregation Hearing Gets Record Crowd," *RTD*, 21 Feb. 1950, 1.

66. Ibid., 1, 4.

67. Ibid., 4; Smith, "Where the South Begins," 273–77. Dr. W. L. Ransome's list might have included the white Democratic primary, except that in Virginia that battle had been won much earlier (see note 72 below).

68. Kluger, *Simple Justice*, 147–49.

69. Ibid.; McNeil, *Groundwork*, 89–95.

70. Eric W. Rise, *The Martinsville Seven: Race, Rape, and Criminal Punishment* (Charlottesville, Va., 1995), 1–52.

71. Ibid., 3, 70–132. For a comparable treatment of the changing contours of criminal justice in the post–World War II South (based on a case in Tennessee), see Gail Williams O'Brien, *The Color of the Law: Race, Violence, and Justice in the Post-World War II South* (Chapel Hill, N.C., 1999). A notorious trial in Virginia in the early 1940s, when a black sharecropper was convicted, by an all-white jury, of first-degree murder in the death of his white landlord, is recounted in Richard B. Sherman, *The Case of Odell Waller and Virginia Justice, 1940–1942* (Knoxville, Tenn., 1992).

72. VRHC videotaped interview with Samuel Tucker. The U.S. Supreme Court declared in 1944, in a case from Texas, *Smith* v. *Allwright*, against black exclusion from Democratic primaries, a point that Virginia had reached more than a decade earlier (see chapter 7 below).

73. Buni, *Negro in Virginia Politics*, chap. 9; Suggs, *Young*, 143–46 (quotation at 145); Smith, "Where the South Begins," 243–54.

74. "Eight of Citizens Slate, Hill Elected to Council," *RTD*, 9 June 1948, 1, 5; "A Long Step Forward for Richmond" (editorial), ibid., 14; Smith, "Where the South Begins," 277–81; Michael B. Chesson, "Richmond's Black Councilmen, 1871–96," in *Southern Black Leaders of the Reconstruction Era*, ed. Howard N. Rabinowitz (Urbana, Ill., 1982), 191–222. Significant as Oliver Hill's accomplishment was, Kluger overstates it when he says Hill "was the first Negro to be elected to that body" (*Simple Justice*, 475).

75. Transcript of Higginbotham's interview with Hill, 37. The first black elected official in Virginia in the twentieth century may have been William A. Lawrence, narrowly elected a member of the Board of Supervisors of Nansemond County the previous November (Buni, *Negro in Virginia Politics*, 156; Suggs, *Young*, 146).

76. "City Hall Reporters Rate Hill 2d Best Councilman," *NJG*, 17 Sept. 1949, 2; "Davenport Is Acclaimed Council's 'Most Valuable,'" *RTD*, 8 Sept. 1949, 1, 3.

77. Elwood interview with Hill, 16.

78. Kluger, *Simple Justice*, 473. Hill has distinguished the two roles: "Politics has got to be the art of what you can accomplish. . . . But as a civil rights advocate, you've got to be more idealistic. You've got to take the higher ground" (Wolf, "Oliver Hill," 40).

79. Kluger, *Simple Justice*, 472–73; Tushnet, *NAACP's Legal Strategy*, 110.

80. Higginbotham's interview with Hill, 18. Kluger, *Simple Justice*, 471, states, "The equalization campaign would be in three stages: first, teachers' salaries, then transportation, and finally school buildings and equipment." Doxey Wilkerson had earlier stated that "in Virginia, there were three successive emphases in this developing interaction between the Negro school movement and the Federal courts—for equal teachers' salaries, for equal school physical facilities, and for integration" ("Negro School Movement," 260; a similar statement is in Wilkerson, "Recent Progress," 248). For that matter, Oliver Hill himself has spoken of a sequence from "unequal pay" to "school facilities" to integration (my transcript of the VRHC interview with Hill, 6). But elsewhere Hill makes clear the broader aim of the late 1940s; for example, "Next thing would be the school facilities and the curricula" (Higginbotham, "Conversations," 14). So, for that matter, does Wilkerson: "During the late 1940s," the "chief issues" were "inequalities in bus transportation, buildings and equipment, and programs of study" ("Negro School Movement," 263). Perhaps Hill himself led Kluger astray (that is, Kluger construed Hill in overly narrow terms) when he stated, "The white school boards were always pleading poverty, but our decision was if we were going to live with separate but equal—the *Gaines* decision was the only relevant Supreme Court decision to help at that time—we were going to make them equal, really equal: teacher

salaries first, then transportation, then the schools themselves" (Kluger's notes from his interview with Hill).

81. *Kelly* v. *School Board of Surry County, Virginia* (E.D. Va., 1948); Wilkerson, "Recent Progress," 256–72; PW, "Charles Sterling Hutcheson," *ANB* 11:584–85.

82. *Freeman* v. *County School Board of Chesterfield County, Smith* v. *School Board of King George County,* and *Ashley* v. *School Board of Gloucester County,* 82 F.Supp. 167 (E.D. Va., 1948), affirmed (per curiam) 177 F.2d 702 (1948); "Court Finds Discrimination in 3 Counties," *RTD,* 9 April 1948, 1; title of editorial, *Virginia Education Bulletin* 25 (May 1948), quoted in Wilkerson, "Recent Progress," 267; Marvin Caplan, "Virginia Schools: A Study in Frustration," *Crisis* 58 (Jan. 1951): 5–11, 61–63.

83. "School Officials of Gloucester, King George Ordered to Court for Possible Contempt Action," *RTD,* 25 Sept. 1948, 2; "Gloucester School Officials Fined for Contempt," *RTD,* 5 May 1949, 1, 3.

84. Wilkerson, "Recent Progress," 256–72; "King George School Drops Four Courses for Whites," *RTD,* 5 Nov. 1948, 1; "Parents Plan Protest Move on Courses," *RTD,* 5 Nov. 1948, 2; "Virginia Negroes Plan School Fight," *RTD,* 9 Jan. 1949, 34; "Court's Order Not Carried Out," *RTD,* 5 May 1949, 1; Nita Morse, "Segregation Rulings Pose New Issues," *RTD,* 25 June 1950, D1.

85. Ann Swain, "Christiansburg Institute: From Freedmen's Bureau Enterprise to Public High School" (M.A. thesis, Radford Univ., 1975); Tracy A. Martin, "Black Education in Montgomery County, Virginia, 1939–1966" (M.A. thesis, Virginia Polytechnic Institute and State Univ., 1996); *Corbin* v. *County School Board of Pulaski County, Virginia,* 84 F.Supp. 253 (W.D. Va., 1949), reversed in part, vacated in part, 177 F.2d 924 (1949); "State Education Officials Feel Pulaski Ruling May Do Harm," *RTD,* 16 Nov. 1949; Morse, "Segregation Rulings Pose New Issues"; transcript of Higginbotham's interview with Hill, 29; Wilkerson, "Recent Progress," 267–69.

86. *Carter* v. *School Board of Arlington County, Virginia,* 87 F.Supp. 745 (E.D. Va, 1949), reversed and remanded, 182 F.2d 531 (1950); Caplan, "Virginia Schools," 8–9; Tushnet, *NAACP's Legal Strategy,* 108–111; Kluger, *Simple Justice,* 473–74.

87. Morse, "Segregation Rulings Pose New Issues."

88. *Sipuel* v. *Oklahoma,* 332 U.S. 631 (1948); *Sweatt* v. *Painter,* 339 U.S. 629 (1950); *McLaurin* v. *Oklahoma,* 339 U.S. 637 (1950); Kluger, *Simple Justice,* 256–84; Tushnet, *NAACP's Legal Strategy,* 120–36; Swanson, statement to Gary Ferguson, *RNL,* in Gregory H. Swanson Papers, Moorland-Spingarn Research Center, Howard Univ., Washington, D.C.

89. "Negro Lawyer Says He Applied for Admission to U. Va. in 1949," *RTD,* 7 July 1950, 6; "Negro Loses Bid to Enter University," *RTD,* 15 July 1950, 1–2.

90. "Negro Sues for Entry into U. Va.," *RTD,* 9 Aug. 1950, 1, 3; "Negro to Air Suit vs. U. Va. in Court Today," *RTD,* 5 Sept. 1950, 6; James Latimer, "Negro Wins Suit to Enter Law School at University," *RTD,* 6 Sept. 1950, 1, 7; "U. Va. Awaits Registration of Swanson," *RTD,* 8 Sept. 1950, 6; "Martinsburg Negro Lawyer Is Admitted to University," *RTD,* 16 Sept. 1950, 4 (photograph). For a fuller analysis of the University of Virginia's partial desegregation beginning in 1950, see Deel, "Virginia's Minimal Resistance," 75–107.

91. "Governor Noncommittal on U. Va. Case," *RTD,* 7 Sept. 1950, 2.

92. Deel, "Virginia's Minimal Resistance," 113–14, 123–33; Godson et al., *College of William and Mary* 2:767. On Virginia Tech and the wider regional context, see PW,

Virginia Tech, chap. 11, and PW, "Black Southerners and Non-Black Universities: Desegregating Higher Education, 1935–1967," *History of Higher Education Annual* 19 (1999): 121–48.

93. Kluger, *Simple Justice*, 466–76. Hill describes the trip to Christiansburg, the stops at Farmville going each way, and the encounter with Barbara Johns (transcript of Higginbotham's interview with him, 25–29, and Higginbotham, "Conversations," 15). The text of the letter from Barbara Johns and Carrie Stokes to Oliver Hill and Spottswood Robinson was published in *RTD*, 2 April 1967, B4, and is quoted in Kluger, *Simple Justice*, 470.

94. Spottswood W. Robinson III, "The Virginia School Fight: A Clarification," *Crisis* 58 (April 1951): 228–29; Tushnet, *NAACP's Legal Strategy*, 106–17, 136–37.

95. Transcript of Kluger's interview with Hill.

96. *Brown v. Board of Education*, 347 U.S. 483 (1954) and 349 U.S. 294 (1955). Kluger, in *Simple Justice*, 476–747, tells the long story through May 1955. Emphasizing the long aftermath are James T. Patterson, *Brown v. Board of Education: A Civil Rights Milestone and Its Troubled Legacy* (New York, 2001), and Peter Irons, *Jim Crow's Children: The Broken Promise of the* Brown *Decision* (New York, 2002), 172–347. See also Austin Sarat, ed., *Race, Law, and Culture: Reflections on Brown v. Board of Education* (New York, 1997), and Michael J. Klarman, "How *Brown* Changed Race Relations: The Backlash Thesis," *Journal of American History* 81 (June 1994): 81–118.

97. Transcript of Higginbotham's interview with Hill, 30, 31; Higginbotham, "Conversations," 15.

98. Tushnet, *Making Civil Rights Law*, chaps. 16–18; Wilkinson, *Harry Byrd*, 113–54; Benjamin Muse, *Virginia's Massive Resistance* (Bloomington, Ind., 1961); James W. Ely Jr., *The Crisis of Conservative Virginia: The Byrd Organization and the Politics of Massive Resistance* (Knoxville, Tenn., 1976); Raymond Wolters, *The Burden of* Brown: *Thirty Years of Desegregation* (Knoxville, Tenn., 1984), 65–127; Robert A. Pratt, *The Color of Their Skin: Education and Race in Richmond, Virginia, 1954–89* (Charlottesville, Va., 1992); and Matthew D. Lassiter and Andrew B. Lewis, eds., *The Moderates' Dilemma: Massive Resistance to School Desegregation in Virginia* (Charlottesville, Va., 1998). For similar developments in the Deep South, see Jeff Roche, *Restructured Resistance: The Sibley Commission and the Politics of Desegregation in Georgia* (Athens, Ga., 1998).

99. Detailing the legal attack on the NAACP is Tushnet, *Making Civil Rights Law*, chaps. 19–20. Case materials from *NAACP v. Button*, 371 U.S. 415 (1963), are in *Landmark Briefs* 56: 1079–1278, with the quoted statements at 1212 (Robert L. Carter's oral argument) and 1092 (petition for writ of certiorari).

100. *Griffin v. County School Board of Prince Edward County*, 377 U.S. 218 (1964). Other court decisions from the series that followed *Brown* were *Griffin v. Board of Supervisors of Prince Edward County*, 203 Va. 321 (1962); *County School Board of Prince Edward County v. Griffin*, 204 Va. 650 (1963); and *Griffin v. Board of Supervisors of Prince Edward County*, 322 F.2d 332 (4th Cir. 1963). Narratives of the saga of the Prince Edward school closings can be found in Bob (Robert Collins) Smith, *They Closed Their Schools: Prince Edward County, Virginia, 1951–1964* (Chapel Hill, N.C., 1965); John Egerton, *Shades of Gray: Dispatches from the Modern South* (Baton Rouge, La., 1991), 105–30; Amy E. Murrell, "The 'Impossible' Prince Edward Case: The Endurance of Resistance in a Southside County, 1959–64," in Lassiter and Lewis, *Moderates' Dilemma*, 134–67; Donald P. Baker, "Closed," *WP Magazine*, 4 March 2001, 8–13, 21–

26; and Kara Miles Turner, "'It Is Not at Present a Very Successful School': Prince Edward County and the Black Educational Struggle, 1865–1995" (Ph.D. diss., Duke Univ., 2001), chaps. 6–7.

101. J. Harvie Wilkinson III, *From Brown to Bakke: The Supreme Court and School Integration, 1954–1978* (New York, 1979), 108–27; Irons, *Jim Crow's Children*, 199–205.

102. *Green v. County School Board of New Kent County*, 391 U.S. 430, 439 (1968). Case materials are in *Landmark Briefs* 66:1–298; Tucker's oral argument is at 209–17.

103. My transcript of the VRHC interview with Oliver Hill, 9.

104. Higginbotham, "Conversations," 12.

105. Transcript of a National Public Radio interview, "Options in Education, Race against Time: School Desegregation," pt. 2 (of 8 parts), 7. Dr. Jerry Thornbery, of The Gilman School in Baltimore, brought this item to my attention.

106. Higginbotham, "Conversations," 16 (first quote); VRHC videotaped interview with Oliver Hill, 12 (second quote).

5. To Sit or Not to Sit

An entry, "*Johnson v. Virginia*," that I published in *Encyclopedia of African-American Civil Rights, from Emancipation to the Present*, ed. Charles D. Lowery and John F. Marszalek (New York, 1992), 286, first led me to Ford Johnson Jr.'s stories. Ford Johnson Sr. and Ford Johnson Jr. themselves told me much of what appears in this chapter: Johnson Sr. responded to my first question about the courtroom case by asking did I know that Johnson Jr. had been in the Thalhimers sit-in case, and I had not, until then, known about such a sit-in or such a case. Early portions of this chapter rely on work done by a former graduate student of mine at Virginia Tech, James R. Clyburn. Together, he and I published "Virginia Sit-Ins, 1960: The Civil Rights Movement in the Urban Upper South," *VSSJ* 38 (2003): 17–32.

1. Pauli Murray, *Song in a Weary Throat: An American Pilgrimage* (New York, 1987), 199–209, 222–31, 322; August Meier and Elliott Rudwick, *CORE: A Study in the Civil Rights Movement, 1942–1968* (1973; rept. Urbana, Ill., 1975), 13–15; Carl L. Graves, "The Right to Be Served: Oklahoma City's Lunch Counter Sit-Ins, 1958–1964," *Chronicles of Oklahoma* 59 (1981): 152–66; Ronald Walters, "The Great Plains Sit-In Movement, 1958–1960," *Great Plains Quarterly* 16 (1996): 85–94; Gretchen Cassell Eick, *Dissent in Wichita: The Civil Rights Movement in the Midwest, 1954–72* (Urbana, Ill., 2001). For an extraordinary overview, see August Meier and Elliott Rudwick, "The Origins of Nonviolent Direct Action in Afro-American Protest: A Note on Historical Discontinuities," in their collection of essays, *Along the Color Line: Explorations in the Black Experience* (Urbana, Ill., 1976), 307–404.

2. William H. Chafe, *Civilities and Civil Rights: Greensboro, North Carolina, and the Black Struggle for Freedom* (New York, 1980); Miles Wolff, *Lunch at the 5 & 10* (1970; rept. Chicago, 1990); Aldon D. Morris, *The Origins of the Civil Rights Movement: Black Communities Organizing for Change* (New York, 1984), chap. 9; David Halberstam, *The Children* (New York, 1998). See also Merrill Proudfoot, *Diary of a Sit-In* (1962; rept. Urbana, Ill., 1990); Martin Oppenheimer, *The Sit-In Movement of 1960* (Brooklyn, N.Y., 1989); James H. Laue, *Direct Action and Desegregation, 1960–1962: Toward a Theory of the Rationalization of Protest* (Brooklyn, N.Y., 1989); Arthur I. Waskow, *From Race Riot to Sit-In, 1919 and the 1960s: A Study in the Connections between Conflict and Violence*

(New York, 1966); David J. Garrow, ed., *Atlanta, Georgia, 1960–1961: Sit-Ins and Student Activism* (Brooklyn, N.Y., 1989).

3. Richard B. Sherman, "'The Last Stand': The Fight for Racial Integrity in Virginia in the 1920s," *JSH* 54 (Feb. 1988): 69–92.

4. James R. Clyburn interview with Dr. Woodrow Benjamin Grant Jr., Baltimore, 10 March 1992. This section draws on Wallenstein and Clyburn, "Virginia Sit-Ins," 18–22, which itself summarizes James R. Clyburn, "Richmond: The Organization of a Movement" (graduate research paper, Department of History, Virginia Tech, April 1992).

5. Tom Howard, "Sit-Downs at Counters Begin Here," *RTD*, 21 Feb. 1960, 1, 5.
6. Ibid.
7. "34 Are Arrested in Sitdowns Here," *RTD*, 23 Feb. 1960, 1.
8. Ibid., 4.
9. Al Coates, "Store Is Picketed; Negroes Ask Boycott," *RTD*, 24 Feb. 1960, 1, 3.
10. "Hill Blasts Va. State Legislature," *RAA*, 5 March 1960, 1–2.
11. Ibid.
12. Al Coates, "Negroes to Spread Boycott," *RTD*, 25 Feb. 1960, 1, 4 (Wyatt Tee Walker's name was rendered "Y. T. Walker"); see also Robert A. Pratt, "William Lester Banks," *DVB* 1:321–23.
13. "Merchants Given Sharp Warning by Trade Newspaper," *RAA*, 5 March 1960, 1, 13. The warning pointed to in the headline—that the arrests were illegal—had been published in *Women's Wear Daily*.
14. "Va. Union Student Tells Nation about Sitdowns," *RAA*, 5 March 1960, 20.
15. "Who Is Defying the Law Now?" *RTD*, 24 Feb. 1960, 14; see PW, "Virginius Dabney," *ANB* 6:381–82.
16. "The Sitdowns," *RNL*, 22 Feb. 1960, 8.
17. James Latimer, "Anti-Trespass Laws Signed to Meet Sit-Down Protests," *RTD*, 26 Feb. 1960, 1 (photo of the governor signing the bills, 2); *Acts* (1963), 113–14 (chs. 97–99).
18. Latimer, "Anti-Trespass Laws Signed," 2.
19. "5 Cincinnati Stores to Be Picketed," *RAA*, 12 March 1960, 17.
20. "Store Is Picketed Again by Negroes," *RTD*, 26 Feb. 1960, 4.
21. Al Coates, "Whites, Negroes Confer on Protest," *RTD*, 27 Feb. 1960, 2.
22. Al Coates, "NAACP Branch Leaders Stand In for Pickets," *RTD*, 28 Feb. 1960, A4.
23. Ibid. For related developments in nearby Petersburg, featuring a March 1960 library sit-in, see Wallenstein and Clyburn, "Virginia Sit-Ins," 24–26.
24. "Judge Says 'This Is No Race Issue,'" *RAA*, 12 March 1960, 1.
25. "Va. U. Students to Appeal Fines," *RAA*, 12 March 1960, 19.
26. "6 VUU Students Fined $20 Each," *RAA*, 19 March 1960, 1, 16; "34 Va. U. Students Now Look to Appeals Hearing," *RAA*, 26 March 1960, 6. Simultaneously with the judicial proceedings, protest activity continued; for a roundup of events in Virginia during spring and summer 1960, see Wallenstein and Clyburn, "Virginia Sit-Ins," 27–29.
27. *Randolph* v. *Commonwealth*, 202 Va. 661, 665 (1961); "Sit-In Case Conviction Is Upheld," *RTD*, 25 April 1961, 1, 3; "Va. Supreme Court Upholds Student Trespass Sentences," *RAA*, 29 April 1961, 1–2.

28. *Randolph* v. *Commonwealth*, 663, 664.

29. Ibid., 666.

30. "Sit-In Case Conviction Is Upheld," 3; "34 Students in Sit-Ins Plan Appeal," *RTD*, 26 April 1961, 8.

31. *Garner* v. *Louisiana*, 368 U.S. 157 (1961). See also Loren Miller, *The Petitioners: The Story of the Supreme Court of the United States and the Negro* (Cleveland, 1966), 392–98; Derrick A. Bell Jr., *Race, Racism, and American Law*, 2d ed. (Boston, 1980), 279–89; Bernard Schwartz, *Super Chief: Earl Warren and His Supreme Court—A Judicial Biography* (New York, 1983), 402–4.

32. *Wells* v. *Gilliam*, 196 F.Supp. 792 (1961).

33. Ibid., 793.

34. Ibid., 794.

35. Ibid., 794, 795.

36. Ibid., 795.

37. Interview with Ford T. Johnson Sr., Richmond, 14 May 1990; interview with Ford T. Johnson Jr., Washington, D.C., 9 Jan. 1992.

38. "Student in Contempt about Court Seats," *RAA*, 5 May 1962, 1–2.

39. Johnson Jr. interview. Similar accounts of the episode can be found in "Student in Contempt," 2, and *Johnson* v. *Virginia*, 373 U.S. 61 (1963).

40. Johnson Jr. interview; Brief for Respondent in Opposition to the Petition for Writ of Certiorari to the Supreme Court of Appeals of Virginia, 2; "To Appeal Court Segregation Case," *RAA*, 23 June 1962, 1.

41. Johnson Jr. interview; "Appeals Case Involving Court Seats," *RAA*, 12 May 1962, 1–2.

42. Johnson Jr. interview.

43. Interview with Roland D. Ealey, Richmond, 22 March 1991; interviews with Johnson Sr. and Johnson Jr.

44. "Student in Contempt," 2; Johnson Sr. interview.

45. "Student in Contempt"; Petition for Writ of Certiorari to the Supreme Court of Appeals of Virginia, 4.

46. "To Appeal Court Segregation Case," 1–2.

47. Ibid.

48. Petition for Writ of Certiorari, 4.

49. VSCOB 50 (1961–63): 464.

50. Petition for Writ of Certiorari, 6, 7, 8.

51. William O. Douglas Papers, box 1282, Library of Congress.

52. Ibid.; *Johnson* v. *Virginia*, 61–62.

53. Anthony Lewis, "High Court Bars Any Segregation in a Courtroom," *NYT*, 30 April 1963, 1, 22; "Courtroom Segregation Held Unconstitutional," *RTD*, 30 April 1963, 1, 3. Lewis wrote about Ford Johnson's case at the time but later left it out of *Portrait of a Decade: The Second American Revolution* (New York, 1964). The deletion helped render the story invisible in subsequent histories of the Civil Rights movement.

54. "The Court Shows Its Impatience," *RAA*, 11 May 1963, 12.

55. *Peterson* v. *City of Greenville*, 373 U.S. 244 (1963). See also Miller, *Petitioners*, 398–403; Bell, *Race, Racism, and American Law*, 289–96; Schwartz, *Super Chief*, 479–86.

56. *Wright* v. *Georgia*, 373 U.S. 284, 285 (1963).

57. Greenberg, *Crusaders in the Courts*, 270–79, 306–11.

58. Dan Day, "Arrests Illegal," *RAA*, 25 May 1963, 1, 5; "High Court Rejects Laws against Peaceful Sit-Ins," *RTD*, 21 May 1963, 1, 3; James Latimer, "Two Implications Are Seen in Supreme Court Action," *RTD*, 21 May 1963; Arthur Krock, "The Court's Segregation Ruling," *NYT*, reprinted in *RTD*, 21 May 1963, 18; "Private Rights Endangered" (editorial), *RTD*, 22 May 1963, 16.

59. *Randolph* v. *Virginia*, 374 U.S. 97 (1963). Within a few weeks of each other in the spring of 1963, the two young lawyers who had spearheaded the case of the Thalhimers Thirty-Four both died, Martin A. Martin, at the age of fifty-two, in April and Clarence A. Newsome, only thirty-six, in May. Neither of them ever knew that the Supreme Court, when it finally handed down its decision in *Randolph* v. *Virginia* on June 10, had ruled in their favor ("Noted Lawyer Dies in Richmond," *RAA*, 4 May 1963, 13; "M. A. Martin, 52, Lawyer, Dies," *RTD*, 28 April 1963, D11; "Sit-In Attorney Dies Unaware of Victory in Supreme Court," *RAA*, 1 June 1963, 1; "Newsome Estate Set at $11,500," *RAA*, 15 June 1963, 1).

60. *Randolph* v. *Virginia*, 97; "State Sit-In Convictions Are Reversed," *RTD*, 11 June 1963, 1, 4; "Sit-In Convictions Reversed; Cases Sent Back to Virginia," *RAA*, 22 June 1963, 9.

61. "Mosque, Parker Field Jim Crow Must Go," *RAA*, 25 May 1963, 1–2.

62. Ibid.; "Parker Field Is Desegregated," *RAA*, 15 June 1963, 1.

63. "Parker Field Is Desegregated"; *Brown* v. *City of Richmond* and *Picott* v. *City of Richmond*, both 204 Va. 471 (1963); Allan Jones, "Few Effects Seen from Court Ruling on Seating Laws," *RTD*, 12 Sept. 1963, 1.

64. "Center City Theatres Now Open to All," *RAA*, June 15, 1963, 1–2; "Fire Hoses Fire Spirit in Danville," ibid.; T. N. Burton, "Restaurants Join Move to Ease Racial Barriers," ibid., 17; Ernest Shaw, "3 Students Appeal Fines Levied in Demonstration," *RAA*, 11 May 1963, 15; "Student Theatre Pickets Ask Adults to Pick up Ball," *RAA*, June 1, 1963, 1; see James W. Ely Jr., "Negro Demonstrations and the Law: Danville as a Test Case," *Vanderbilt Law Review* 27 (1974): 927–68.

65. Cheryl Lynn Greenberg, *"Or Does It Explode?" Black Harlem in the Great Depression* (New York, 1991), chap. 5.

66. Johnson Jr. interview.

67. Robert Mann, *The Walls of Jericho: Lyndon Johnson, Hubert Humphrey, Richard Russell, and the Struggle for Civil Rights* (New York, 1996), 370–73.

68. *Hamm* v. *City of Rock Hill*, 379 U.S. 306, 315 (1964). On one basis or another, the Court had reversed the convictions in every sit-in case that it had agreed to hear. Regarding one of the last in the series of 1960s sit-in cases, *Bell* v. *Maryland*, 378 U.S. 226 (1964), see Peter Irons, *The Courage of Their Convictions: Sixteen Americans Who Fought Their Way to the Supreme Court* (New York, 1988), chap. 6.

69. "Peace Corps in Great Demand," *RTD*, 25 April 1961, 1; "Reports from the Peace Corps" (including one from Ford Johnson), *Panther* (Virginia Union University campus newspaper; commencement edition), 3 June 1963, 3.

70. Johnson Jr. interview. That he would have soon heard anyway—his proud parents promptly shipped off the news and the newspaper—is clear from "Airogram to Africa Notifies Youth of Courtroom Victory," *RAA*, 11 May 1963, 1.

71. Johnson Jr. interview.

72. Johnson Sr. and, later, Johnson Jr. both told me this story.

6. Racial Identity and the Crime of Marriage

Some material in this chapter appeared first in "Race, Marriage, and the Law of Freedom: Alabama and Virginia, 1860s–1960s," *Chicago-Kent Law Review* 70:2 (1994): 371–437. Telephone conversations with Mildred D. Loving contributed substantially to the story, as did a visit with her at the home of one of her children, Donald, and a conversation with Bernard S. Cohen.

1. Robert A. Pratt, "Crossing the Color Line: A Historical Assessment and Personal Narrative of *Loving v. Virginia*," *Howard Law Journal* 41 (winter 1998): 236; see also PW, "Richard Perry Loving," *ANB* 14:22–23.

2. PW, *Tell the Court I Love My Wife: Race, Marriage, and Law—An American History* (New York, 2002), app. 1.

3. Ibid., chaps. 5, 6, 13; *Burns v. State*, 48 Ala. 195 (1872); *Hart v. Hoss and Elder*, 26 La. Ann. 90 (1874); *Honey v. Clark*, 37 Tex. 686 (1872–73).

4. PW, *Tell the Court*; Joshua D. Rothman, *Notorious in the Neighborhood: Sex and Families across the Color Line in Virginia, 1787–1861* (Chapel Hill, N.C., 2003).

5. *Acts* (1877–78), 302 (ch. 7, arts. 3, 8).

6. *Ex parte Kinney*, 14 Fed. Cas. 602, 604 (C.C.E.D. Va., 1879).

7. Ibid., 607.

8. Ibid., 605.

9. Ibid.

10. Virginia, *Annual Report of the Penitentiary* (1879), 24, 28; ibid. (1880), 41; ibid. (1881), 35; ibid. (1882), 29.

11. *Pace v. Alabama*, 106 U.S. 583, 585 (1883); PW, *Tell the Court*, 111–14.

12. *Maynard v. Hill*, 125 U.S. 190, 205 (1888).

13. *Plessy v. Ferguson*, 163 U.S. 537, 540, 545 (1896).

14. "Both Convicted," *Richmond Planet*, 30 Jan. 1909, 8.

15. *Acts* (1910), 581 (ch. 357, art. 49). Regarding litigation in the 1880s, see PW, "Race, Marriage, and the Law of Freedom," 399–405.

16. Regarding twentieth-century definitions of race for purposes of regulating marriage, see Paul Finkelman, "The Color of Law," *Northwestern University Law Review* 87:3 (1993): 955 n. 96, drawn from Pauli Murray, comp., *States' Laws on Race and Color* (1950; rept. Athens, Ga., 1997).

17. Note on the *Moon* case, by James F. Minor and Minor Bronaugh, *Virginia Law Review* 17 (Jan. 1911): 692–99 (quotations at 692 and 698); PW, *Tell the Court*, 138–39.

18. Sherman, "Last Stand"; Paul A. Lombardo, "Miscegenation, Eugenics, and Racism: Historical Footnotes to *Loving v. Virginia*," *U.C. Davis Law Review* 21 (winter 1988): 421–52; Smith, *Managing White Supremacy*, 76–91.

19. *Acts* (1924), 534–35 (ch. 371, secs. 1, 5).

20. Smith, *Managing White Supremacy*, 91, 221–27.

21. Sherman, "Last Stand," 80–81; Lombardo, "Miscegenation, Eugenics, and Racism," 440–46; J. David Smith, *The Eugenic Assault on America: Scenes in Red, White, and Black* (Fairfax, Va., 1993), 71–77; Smith, "Managing White Supremacy," 104–9, and *Managing White Supremacy*, 93–95.

22. Smith, *Managing White Supremacy*, 220–21; *Acts* (1932), 68 (ch. 78). Regarding other cases, see *Keith v. Commonwealth*, 165 Va. 705 (1935), and "Ruled a Negro,

Man Must Quit White Wife," *RTD*, 8 June 1938, 1, discussed in PW, "Race, Marriage, and the Law of Freedom," 411–13.

23. "Miscegenation Case Defendant Fails to Make Bond Request," *RTD*, 30 Dec. 1948, 5; "Salem Court Suspends Term of Negro, 20, on Race Count," *RTD*, 5 March 1949, 3.

24. "Miscegenation Case Defendant Fails"; "Salem Court Suspends Term." Hammond, having reported marrying Hamilton "without doubt that he was white," for that reason escaped being charged for the same crime.

25. *Naim v. Naim*, 350 U.S. 891 (1955); *Naim v. Naim*, 350 U.S. 985 (1956); Chang Moon Sohn, "Principle and Expediency in Judicial Review: Miscegenation Cases in the Supreme Court" (Ph.D. diss., Columbia Univ., 1970), 73–94; "Racial Intermarriage Case Faces High Court," *RTD*, 7 Oct. 1954, 2; "State's High Court Spurns U.S. Order," *RTD*, 19 Jan. 1956, 1. Gregory Michael Dorr provides a full account in "Principled Expediency: Eugenics, *Naim v. Naim*, and the Supreme Court," *American Journal of Legal History* 42 (April 1998): 119–59.

26. "Virginia Ban on Racial Intermarriages Is Upheld," *RTD*, 14 June 1955, 5; Sohn, "Principle and Expediency," 74–75.

27. *Naim v. Naim*, 197 Va. 80, 90 (1955).

28. Ibid., 88.

29. Schwartz, *Super Chief*, 158–62. The clerks are quoted in Dorr, "Principled Expediency," 149 and n. 134.

30. *Jackson v. Alabama*, 348 U.S. 888 (1954); *Naim v. Naim*, 350 U.S. 891 (1955); *Naim v. Naim*, 197 Va. 734 (1956); *Naim v. Naim*, 350 U.S. 985 (1956); Dorr, "Principled Expediency," 155–59; PW, *Tell the Court*, 181–83. Evidence of prosecutions in the late 1950s outside Virginia can be seen in *Ratcliff v. State*, 107 So.2d 728 (Miss., 1958), and *State v. Brown*, 108 So.2d 233 (La., 1959).

31. Gerald Gunther, *Learned Hand: The Man and the Judge* (New York, 1994), 666–70, 782.

32. Ibid., 668; Dorr, "Principled Expediency," 153–55.

33. *Calma v. Calma*, 203 Va. 880 (1962).

34. Ibid., 882.

35. Ibid.

36. *Loving v. Commonwealth* (Record No. 6163), Supreme Court of Appeals of Virginia, 2–4.

37. Phone conversation with Mildred D. Loving, 7 Jan. 1994.

38. Ibid.; Record No. 6163, 2–4.

39. Record No. 6163, 5–6.

40. Phone conversation with Mildred Loving, 7 Jan. 1994; conversation with Mildred Loving, 12 Aug. 1995; *Polk's Washington City Directory* (1962), 226, 950; "The Crime of Being Married," *Life Magazine* 60 (18 March 1966): 85–91.

41. "Transcript of the President's News Conference on Foreign and Domestic Matters," *NYT*, 2 Aug. 1963, 10.

42. Mildred D. Loving to Eleanor Rose, 31 Jan. 1996 (copy in my possession; my thanks to Eleanor Rose); "Anti-Miscegenation Case Move Rejected," *RNL*, 29 Oct. 1964, 21. At the time, no Virginia ACLU affiliate yet existed. The ACLU Archives (Mudd Library, Princeton Univ., Princeton, N.J.) demonstrate the organization's long-term commitment to eradicating the nation's miscegenation laws.

43. Interview with Bernard S. Cohen, Alexandria, Va., 4 Jan. 1994.

44. PW, *Tell the Court*, 218.

45. Interview with Cohen; Motion to Vacate Judgment and Set Aside Sentence, Nov. 6, 1963, *Loving* v. *Commonwealth* (Record No. 6163), 6–7.

46. Interview with Cohen; phone conversation with Philip J. Hirschkop, 18 Aug. 1994; "Pair Files Suit to End State Ban," *RNL*, 28 Oct. 1964, 23; "Anti-Miscegenation Case Move Rejected"; "Couple Begins Legal Attack on Mixed-Marriage Law," *NYT*, 29 Oct. 1964, 26; "Mixed-Marriage Ban Is Fought in Virginia," *NYT*, 29 Dec. 1964, 35.

47. Opinion, *Loving* v. *Commonwealth* (Record No. 6163), 10–12, 15. See also John Edward Lane III, "Leon Maurice Bazile (1890–1967)," in Bryson, *Legal Education in Virginia*, 82–86.

48. "Mixed Couple Case Delayed in Virginia," *NYT*, 28 Jan. 1965, 17; "U.S. Court Defers on Race Question," *NYT*, 13 Feb. 1965, 17; *Perez* v. *Sharp*, 32 Cal. 2d. 711, 734–35 (1948) (J. Carter concurring); *Loving* v. *Commonwealth* (Record No. 6163), 10. For more on *Perez*, see PW, *Tell the Court*, chap. 13.

49. *Loving* v. *Commonwealth*, 206 Va. 924, 929 (1966); "Ban on Interracial Marriages Upheld by Virginia High Court," *NYT*, 8 Mar. 1966, 26.

50. "Virginia Suit Scores Mixed Marriage Ban," *NYT*, 30 July 1966, 9.

51. Exemplifying this approach is Arnold M. Paul, *Conservative Crisis and the Rule of Law: Attitudes of Bar and Bench, 1887–1895* (Ithaca, N.Y., 1960).

52. R. Carter Pittman, "The Fourteenth Amendment: Its Intended Effect on Anti-Miscegenation Laws," *North Carolina Law Review* 43 (1964–65): 92–108 (plus appendix), quoted from 92. Pittman lists (at 107–8 n. 72) the thirty states that had ratified the amendment at the time it went into effect, and he says that "a majority" of those states "retained such laws in 1951." Actually, seven of the thirty had never had such laws, four more had abandoned them by the Civil War, five southern states eliminated them during Reconstruction as inconsistent with the amendment, and five more states (outside the South) repealed them by the 1880s. Therefore, although nineteen of the thirty had such laws at the time they ratified the amendment, only nine had them in 1868 and "retained" them into the second half of the twentieth century.

53. PW, *Tell the Court*.

54. Pittman, "Fourteenth Amendment," 108. Regarding the role of social science in the conceptualization of race, Herbert Hovenkamp concludes that "the significant difference between the Progressive Era and the Warren Court lay not in the use of social science, but rather in the content of the science itself" ("Social Science and Segregation before *Brown*," *Duke Law Journal* [1985]: 624–72 [quotation at 624]; see also Elazar Barkan, *The Retreat of Scientific Racism: Changing Concepts of Race in Britain and the United States between the World Wars* [Cambridge, 1992], and Lee D. Baker, *From Savage to Negro: Anthropology and the Construction of Race, 1896–1954* [Berkeley, Calif., 1998]).

55. Alfred Avins, "Anti-Miscegenation Laws and the Fourteenth Amendment: The Original Intent," *Virginia Law Review* 52 (Nov. 1966): 1224–55 (quotations at 1224–25, 1255). Curiously, in offering evidence that miscegenation statutes had "been upheld as constitutional by every appellate court which has considered the point," Avins failed to list supporting examples from Indiana and Alabama in the 1870s (PW, *Tell the Court*, chaps. 4–5) while ignoring several court decisions any one of which would have invalidated his statement; and despite his claims (1224 n. 4), neither *Grant* v. *Butt*, 198 S.C. 298 (1941), nor *State* v. *Miller*, 224 N.C. 228 (1944), had addressed the question of con-

stitutionality. On such central points, work by Avins, like Pittman, has more value as a primary source from the 1960s than as a reliable historical account of the previous century.

56. William D. Zabel, "Interracial Marriage and the Law," *Atlantic Monthly*, Oct. 1965, 75–79.

57. *State* v. *Brown*, 108 So.2d 233 (La., 1959).

58. "Court in Maryland Avoids a Ruling on Miscegenation," *NYT*, 14 Feb. 1964, 33.

59. *McLaughlin* v. *State*, 153 So.2d 1, 2–3 (Fla., 1963).

60. *Jones* v. *Lorenzen*, 441 P.2d 986, 989–90 (Okla., 1965).

61. *Ratcliff* v. *State*, 234 Miss. 724 (1958); *Rose* v. *State*, 234 Miss. 731 (1958); Charles W. Pickering, "Criminal Law—Miscegenation—Incest," *Mississippi Law Journal* 30 (1958–59): 326–29.

62. Mississippi, *Laws* (1960), 356–57 (ch. 240).

63. *McLaughlin* v. *Florida*, 379 U.S. 184, 188–89, 191–92 (1964).

64. Ibid., 195–96, 198; Tinsley E. Yarbrough, *John Marshall Harlan: Great Dissenter of the Warren Court* (New York, 1992), 267–69; Sohn, "Principle and Expediency," 94–107.

65. "Crime of Being Married," 91.

66. *Landmark Briefs* 64:787–88.

67. Nimetz, 10 Oct. 1966, John Marshall Harlan Papers, box 285, Mudd Library, Princeton Univ.

68. William D. Zabel to Arthur L. Berney, 24 Jan. 1967, ACLU Papers, 1966, vol. 13.

69. *Brown* v. *Board of Education*, 347 U.S. 483 (1954); *Meyer* v. *Nebraska*, 262 U.S. 390, 399 (1923); *Stevens* v. *United States*, 146 F.2d 120 (1944). Regarding *Stevens*, see PW, *Tell the Court*, 174–79.

70. *Landmark Briefs* 64:763, 895, 918; "Supreme Court Agrees to Rule on State Miscegenation Laws," *NYT*, 13 Dec. 1966, 40.

71. *Landmark Briefs* 64:976–1003.

72. Ibid., 960–72, 1003–7. For a full transcript of the oral argument, see ibid., 960–1007. An abbreviated version is in Peter Irons and Stephanie Guitton, eds., *May It Please the Court: The Most Significant Oral Arguments Made before the Supreme Court since 1955* (New York, 1993), 279–85. The same work (277–79, 285–86) includes a brief history of the case, but it is flawed; see PW, *Tell the Court*, 290 n. 26.

73. *Landmark Briefs* 64:971, 1005.

74. Ibid., 971.

75. *Loving* v. *Virginia*, 388 U.S. 1, 7–9 (1967); Schwartz, *Super Chief*, 668–69.

76. *Loving* v. *Virginia*, 8–9.

77. Ibid., 10–12.

78. Ibid., 12.

79. Ibid.; "Justices Upset All Bans on Interracial Marriage," *NYT*, 13 June 1967, 1, 28; "Miscegenation Ban Is Ended by High Court," *RTD*, 13 June 1967, 1, 4. Irons and Guitton, *May It Please the Court*, 277, to the contrary, the *Loving* decision did not rule, as they paraphrase it, that "the freedom to marry is an essential personal right which cannot be infringed by the state." *Loving* removed racial identity as a condition that a state might impose, but it did nothing to diminish states' authority to regulate incest, bigamy, age of consent, or same-sex marriages.

80. "State Couple 'Overjoyed' by Ruling," *RTD*, 13 June 1967, B1; "Mrs. Loving: 'I Feel Free Now,'" *RAA*, 17 June 1967, 1–2; Simeon Booker, "The Couple That Rocked Courts," *Ebony* 22 (Sept. 1967): 78–84.

81. Mildred D. Loving to Eleanor Rose, 31 Jan. 1996.

82. "Caucasian, Negro Wed in Norfolk," *RTD*, 13 Aug. 1967, B2.

83. *McLaughlin* v. *Florida*, 198 (J. Stewart concurring); *Loving* v. *Virginia*, 13 (J. Stewart concurring).

84. From about 1970 on, same-sex couples went to court in various states in efforts to get judges to extend the language in *Loving* about "the freedom to marry" from different-race couples to same-sex couples. Such efforts met with limited success for brief periods in the 1990s in Hawaii and Alaska, and greater and more durable success came in Vermont with a state supreme court decision in late 1999 and subsequent legislation in 2000. For surveys of developments through those three decades, see PW, *Tell the Court*, 240–44, and David L. Chambers, "Couples: Marriage, Civil Unions, and Domestic Partnerships," in *Creating Change: Sexuality, Public Policy, and Civil Rights*, ed. John D'Emilio, William B. Turner, and Urvashi Vaid (New York, 2000), chap. 14.

7. Power and Policy in an American State

Portions of this chapter first appeared as "Federal Courts and Southern Politics in the 1960s: The Reapportionment Revolution in Virginia in Historical Perspective," *VSSJ* 26 (1991): 1–10.

1. For treatments of the judicial politics of reapportionment in the 1960s, see Robert B. McKay, *Reapportionment: The Law and Politics of Equal Representation* (New York, 1965); Robert G. Dixon Jr., *Democratic Representation: Reapportionment in Law and Politics* (New York, 1968); and Schwartz, *Super Chief*, 410–28, 503–8. An early use of the phrase "reapportionment revolution" is in Gordon E. Baker, *The Reapportionment Revolution: Representation, Political Power, and the Supreme Court* (New York, 1966).

2. Glass quotation from Buni, *Negro in Virginia Politics*, 17; Anderson quotation from Holt, *Convention of 1901–2*, 152; see Perman, *Struggle for Mastery*, chap. 10.

3. *Williams* v. *Mississippi*, 170 U.S. 213 (1898); *Debates, 1901–2* 2:2973.

4. *Debates, 1901–2* 1:181; Buni, *Negro in Virginia Politics*, 16–19, 34–49; Holt, *Convention of 1901–2*, 207–12; Moger, *Virginia*, chap. 9.

5. Frank B. Atkinson, *The Dynamic Dominion: Realignment and the Rise of Virginia's Republican Party since 1945* (Fairfax, Va., 1992), 132.

6. Sherman, "Last Stand"; Smith, *Managing White Supremacy*, 57–106.

7. *Nixon* v. *Herndon*, 273 U.S. 536 (1927); Steven F. Lawson, *Black Ballots: Voting Rights in the South, 1944–1969* (New York, 1976), chap. 2; Darlene Clark Hine, *Black Victory: The Rise and Fall of the White Democratic Primary in Texas* (Millwood, N.Y., 1979).

8. *Bliley* v. *West*, 42 F.2d 101 (4th Cir., 1930); "Virginia Primary Law Held Unconstitutional by Federal Judge Here," *RTD*, 6 June 1929, 1.

9. "Richmond White Primary Case Is Set for Hearing," *NJG*, 13 April 1929, 1.

10. Smith, *Managing White Supremacy*, 199–200.

11. Buni, *Negro in Virginia Politics*, 117–23; Smith, *Managing White Supremacy*, 201.

12. Quoted in Smith, *Managing White Supremacy*, 201.

13. *Bliley* v. *West*, 102.

14. *West* v. *Bliley*, 33 F.2d 177, 178 (E.D. Virginia, 1929).

15. Ibid., 178–79.

16. Ibid., 179; *Commonwealth* v. *Wilcox*, 111 Va. 849, 859–60 (1911), quoted ibid.

17. *West* v. *Bliley*, 180.

18. "West Democratic Primary Decision Affirmed by the United States Circuit Court of Appeals," *Richmond Planet*, 21 June 1930, 1 (accompanied by a photo of Cohen).

19. *Bliley* v. *West*, 42 F.2d 101, 103 (1930).

20. Quoted in Smith, *Managing White Supremacy*, 202. Virginia failed to take the case to the nation's highest court, so the trial court decision stood.

21. *Davis* v. *Allen*, 157 Va. 84, 86–87 (1931).

22. Ibid.; Buni, *Negro in Virginia Politics*, 124–31.

23. *Richmond Planet*, 29 March 1930, 1.

24. *Davis* v. *Allen*, 89–91.

25. Ibid., 91, Douglas, *Managing White Supremacy*, 231–33.

26. *Davis* v. *Allen*, 91, 93.

27. Buni, *Negro in Virginia Politics*, 17–32, 131–41.

28. V. O. Key Jr., *Southern Politics in State and Nation* (New York, 1949; rept. Knoxville, Tenn., 1984), 603–9, 644; Frederic D. Ogden, *The Poll Tax in the South* (Tuscaloosa, Ala., 1958), 178–85, 287–90.

29. *Breedlove* v. *Suttles*, 302 U.S. 277, 283 (1937).

30. Ogden, *Poll Tax*, chap. 9; Lawson, *Black Ballots*, chap. 3. Senators from southern states could oppose a congressional repeal measure even if their home states had no poll tax. The Senate, for its part, generated proposals for a constitutional amendment to do away with the tax. Yet, if Congress could not enact a repeal statute, it was hard to see where two-to-one majorities of both houses would come from to send a proposed amendment to the states; and three-fourths of the states had to ratify it before it took effect.

31. *Saunders* v. *Wilkins*, 152 F.2d 235 (4th Cir., 1945); "High Court Asked to Rule on Poll Tax," *RTD*, 17 March 1946, B1.

32. *Saunders* v. *Wilkins*, 236–37.

33. Ibid., 238; "High Court Asked to Rule on Poll Tax."

34. *Saunders* v. *Wilkins*, 237–38; "High Court Asked to Rule on Poll Tax."

35. *Saunders* v. *Wilkins*, 328 U.S. 870 (1946).

36. "Federal Court Dismisses Poll Tax Suit," *RTD*, 11 Sept. 1946, 4.

37. Ibid.

38. Ibid.

39. "Suit to Block State Poll Tax Is Dismissed," *RTD*, 1 Oct. 1946, 1, 4.

40. Ibid.; *Michael* v. *Cockerell*, 161 F.2d 163 (1947).

41. "Suit Is Filed as Challenge to Poll Tax," *RTD*, 8 Jan. 1950, B2; "Arlington Poll Tax Suit Is Dismissed," *RTD*, 25 July 1950, 4; "U.S. Judges Named to Hear Poll Tax Case," *RTD*, 17 Oct. 1950, 3.

42. "Suit Is Filed as Challenge to Poll Tax."

43. Ibid.

44. *Butler* v. *Thompson*, 97 F.Supp. 17, 19 (1951); "Arlington Poll Tax Suit Is Dismissed." State Attorney General J. Lindsay Almond Jr. argued the case for the State Board of Elections.

45. "U.S. Judges Named to Hear Poll Tax Case"; *Butler* v. *Thompson*, 184 F.2d 526, 527 (1950).

46. "State Asks Poll Tax Case Dismissal," *RTD*, 30 Jan. 1951, 6.

47. "Arlington's Poll Tax Suit Is Dismissed," *RTD*, 20 Feb. 1951, 5; James Latimer, "Poll Tax Law Is Sustained on Three New Points," *RTD*, 25 Feb. 1951, B1, B6; *Butler* v. *Thompson*, 24.

48. *Butler* v. *Thompson*, 341 U.S. 937 (1951).

49. "Two Delegates Offer Poll Tax Repeal," *RTD*, 12 Jan. 1950, 4.

50. "Proposal to Retain State Poll Tax Draws Editorial Comments," *RTD*, 14 Sept. 1963, 16.

51. Ibid.

52. *Harman* v. *Forssenius*, 380 U.S. 528, 530–32 (1965).

53. "State Asks Dismissal of Poll Tax Litigation," *RTD*, 24 March 1964, 1, 3; Atkinson, *Dynamic Dominion*, 130–31 (quotation).

54. *Harman* v. *Forssenius*, 537.

55. Ibid., 533–34.

56. Ibid., 541, 544.

57. Ibid., 543.

58. Ibid., 542.

59. "Suit Filed in Norfolk Challenges Poll Tax," *RTD*, 30 Nov. 1963, 1; Parramore et al., *Norfolk*, 388–89, 432. Case materials regarding *Harper* and *Butts* are in *Landmark Briefs* 62:833–1087.

60. *United States* v. *Texas*, 252 F.Supp. 234 (1966), decided 9 Feb.; *United States* v. *Alabama*, 252 F.Supp. 95 (1966), decided 3 March.

61. *Harper* v. *Virginia Board of Elections*, 383 U.S. 663, 665–66, 669–70 (1966).

62. Ibid., 680–81.

63. Ibid., 683–84.

64. Ibid., 683, 686.

65. Ibid., 686.

66. Ibid., 675.

67. Ibid., 670–71, 675, 678.

68. Ibid., 678–79.

69. Brent Tarter, "Evelyn Thomas Butts," *DVB* 2:449–50.

70. *Baker* v. *Carr*, 369 U.S. 186 (1962), and *Reynolds* v. *Sims*, 377 U.S. 533 (1964). Documentation associated with the 1964 cases is in *Landmark Briefs* 58:727–1038. Studies of the major cases on legislative reapportionment focus on Tennessee and Alabama. Richard C. Cortner, *The Apportionment Cases* (1970; rept. New York, 1972), mentions Virginia only in passing, for example, and Gene Graham writes in *One Man, One Vote:* Baker *v.* Carr *and the American Levellers* (Boston, 1972), as though all the world were Tennessee. Even those for whom all the world is Virginia pay little mind. Virginius Dabney, in *Virginia: The New Dominion* (New York, 1971), 552, supplies a single paragraph on reapportionment in the 1960s. Louis D. Rubin Jr., in *Virginia: A History* (New York, 1977), 199, offers one sentence. Wilkinson, in *Harry Byrd*, 248–49, places the case in its context and details its consequences, but he relies on a few newspaper reports for his brief account of the case itself. None of these three writers so much as supplies the name of the decision: the full names were *Harrison Mann et al.* v. *Levin Nock Davis, Secretary, State Board of Elections, et al.*, 213 F.Supp. 577 (1962), and

then *Levin Nock Davis, Secretary, State Board of Elections, et al.* v. *Harrison Mann et al.*, 377 U.S. 678 (1964).

71. At the time of ratification, five states—Alabama, Arkansas, Mississippi, Texas, and Virginia—still employed the poll tax as a condition of voting. None was among the ratifying states. Arkansas changed its constitution to end the poll tax in state and local elections as well; the other four states did not (*Congressional Quarterly Almanac* 20 [1964]: 381–82).

72. White voters split almost evenly in the 1964 presidential election in Virginia. It may be that they gave a thin majority to Goldwater. The poll-tax amendment had no doubt led to a substantial increment of pro-Johnson voters among black Virginians, and it may well be that the amendment also generated more Johnson votes than Goldwater votes among new white voters.

73. Ralph Eisenberg, "Legislative Reapportionment and Congressional Redistricting in Virginia," *Washington and Lee Law Review* 23 (fall 1966): 27–87, and Ralph Eisenberg, "Reapportionment: Journey through a Judicial Thicket," in *Cases in American National Government and Politics*, ed. Rocco J. Tresolini and Richard T. Frost (Englewood Cliffs, N.J., 1966), 183–84.

74. Eisenburg, "Reapportionment," 184–85.

75. Ibid., 185–88.

76. Ibid., 188–91. Cases from nine other states, too—Connecticut, Florida, Idaho, Illinois, Iowa, Michigan, Ohio, Oklahoma, and Washington—came before the Supreme Court at this time (Cortner, *Reapportionment Cases*, 192 n. 1).

77. *Davis* v. *Mann;* see also Robert Austin Jackson, "The Redistricting Process after One Man–One Vote: The Case of Virginia" (Ph.D. diss., Univ. of Virginia, 1976), chap. 4.

78. For an acute portrait of the Virginia political system at midcentury, see Key, *Southern Politics*, chap. 2.

79. PW, "Cartograms," 103, 106.

80. *Selected Speeches of the Honorable Mills E. Godwin, Jr., Governor of Virginia, 1966–1970* (n.p., n.d.), 1–4.

81. Ibid., 361–66, 518–21 (quotation at 518–19); Wilkinson, *Harry Byrd*, 247–351, esp. chap. 11; See also Thomas Learned Wells, "The Legislative Consequences of Urban Growth: The Case of Virginia, 1966" (Ph.D. diss., Univ. of Virginia, 1968), chaps. 3–4, and Anthony Bandeira Cristo, "The Development of the Community College System in Virginia to 1972" (Ph.D. diss., Duke Univ., 1973).

82. *Wesberry* v. *Sanders*, 376 U.S. 1 (1964); Wilkinson, *Harry Byrd*, 314; Dierenfield, *Keeper of the Rules*, 198–200.

83. Dierenfield, *Keeper of the Rules*, 206–34; Atkinson, *Dynamic Dominion*, 163–72.

84. *Reynolds* v. *Sims*, 558 (quoting *Gray* v. *Sanders*, 372 U.S. 368, 381 [1963]), 562.

85. See Introduction, as well as Alexander Keyssar, *The Right to Vote: The Contested History of Democracy in the United States* (New York, 2000), 257–87.

86. PW, "Black Southerners and Non-Black Universities"; PW, *Virginia Tech*, 102–3, 177–93; Laura Fairchild Brodie, *Breaking Out: VMI and the Coming of Women* (New York, 2000); Philippa Strum, *Women in the Barracks: The VMI Case and Equal Rights* (Lawrence, Kans., 2002).

8. From Harry Byrd to Douglas Wilder

1. Donald P. Baker, *Wilder: Hold Fast to Dreams—A Biography of L. Douglas Wilder* (Cabin John, Md., 1989), 3–6, 34–49, 53, 56–62.

2. Ronald L. Heinemann, *Harry Byrd of Virginia* (Charlottesville, Va., 1996), 1–5, 13; see also Alden Hatch, *The Byrds of Virginia* (New York, 1969), 225–37.

3. Heinemann, *Harry Byrd*, 16–47; Hatch, *Byrds*, 415; regarding the laws see above, chap. 6, and Virginia, *Acts* (1924), 14–15 (ch. 15), 46–47 (ch. 43), 57–58 (ch. 62), 90–91 (ch. 88), 533–34 (ch. 370), 568–71 (ch. 394), 668–69 (ch. 446).

4. Heinemann, *Harry Byrd*, 47–105.

5. Ibid., esp. 267 (quotation), 334–35, 410–17.

6. Ibid., 417–20; Wilkinson, *Harry Byrd*, 315 (quotation from *RNL*, 12 May 1966), 333.

7. For good surveys of politics in Virginia from the 1960s on, see Ralph Eisenberg, "Virginia: The Emergence of Two-Party Politics," in *The Changing Politics of the South*, ed. William C. Havard (Baton Rouge, La., 1972), 39–92, and Alexander P. Lamis, *The Two-Party South*, expanded ed. (New York, 1988), chap. 11; see also Dewey W. Grantham, *The Life and Death of the Solid South: A Political History* (Lexington, Ky., 1988), chap. 7.

8. "Justices Upset All Bans on Interracial Marriage," *NYT*, 13 June 1967, 28.

9. See chapter 5, note 59, above.

10. Segal, *Blacks in the Law*, 187–88, 201–4, 228. Sketches of Spottswood W. Robinson III are in "Fighter for Civil Rights," *NYT*, 28 July 1961, 9, and Elliott Cooper, "Judge Robinson Cherishes Old Bank Street Photo," *RTD*, 2 April 1967, B1, B4.

11. For newspaper items regarding Henry Marsh's winning the mayoralty, see Maurice Duke and Daniel P. Jordan, eds., *A Richmond Reader, 1733–1983* (Chapel Hill, N.C., 1983), 408–15. Marsh's recollections are recorded on a videotape (Richmond Community Interviews, 1985) at the VRHC (my transcript, 2–6). See also Margaret Edds, *Free at Last: What Really Happened When Civil Rights Came to Southern Politics* (Bethesda, Md., 1987), 124–47; Thomas R. Morris and Neil Bradley, "Virginia," in *Quiet Revolution in the South: The Impact of the Voting Rights Act, 1965–1990*, ed. Chandler Davidson and Bernard Grofman (Princeton, N.J., 1994), 271–98.

12. "Fourth District," *RTD*, 4 Nov. 1964, A4; "Abbitt Wins 11th Term, Beating Tucker by 3–1 Count," *RTD*, 6 Nov. 1968, A6; *Congressional Quarterly's Guide to U.S. Elections*, 3d ed. (Washington, D.C., 1994), 1253, 1263.

13. Bonnie V. Winston, "Ealey Gets Backing of Crusade [Richmond Crusade for Voters]," *RTD*, 7 Jan. 1983, B1, B3 (quotation); "Democrats Win Three Elections," *RTD*, 12 Jan. 1983, B3; "Ealey Elected as Delegate Here," ibid.; Shelley Rolfe, "By the Way," *RTD*, 15 Jan. 1983, B1, B3; Jeff E. Schapiro, "Del. Ealey Dies of Cancer," *RTD*, 23 March 1992, B1, B3.

14. Baker, *Wilder*, 81. Especially on the race for lieutenant governor, see Dwayne Yancey, *When Hell Froze Over: The Untold Story of Doug Wilder—A Black Politician's Rise to Power in the South* (n.p., 1988).

15. Baker, *Wilder*, 84–86, 107–13.

16. Ibid., 290–94; Margaret Edds, *Claiming the Dream: The Victorious Campaign of Douglas Wilder of Virginia* (Chapel Hill, N.C., 1990).

17. Michael Paul Williams, "Segregation 'Dismantler' Dies at 77," *RTD*, 20 Oct. 1990, 1, 11 (Marsh quotation); "Richmonders Say 'Good-Bye': Mr. Samuel Wilbert Tucker, 1913–1990," *RAA*, 10 Nov. 1990, B1; "Samuel Tucker, 77, Civil Rights Lawyer, Dies," *WP*, 21 Oct. 1990, B7.

18. Hazel Trice Edney, "Friends Say Last Farewell," *RAA*, 3 Nov. 1990, A1, A2.

19. Before the election of Scott, the only African American to serve a Virginia district in Congress had been John Mercer Langston, who was defeated in his bid for reelection in 1890; see Introduction. Scott's district may have reflected efforts to gerrymander according to racial identity, but Scott continued to demonstrate that he could successfully appeal to large numbers of white voters. The 1992 elections also saw the election of Leslie Byrne as the first woman from Virginia in the U.S. House of Representatives; a former member of the state legislature, Byrne lost a bid for reelection to Congress in 1994 but was elected to the Virginia Senate in 1999. In 2001 a black candidate, Donald A. McEachin, won the Democratic nomination to be state attorney general, but he lost in the general election.

20. VRHC videotaped interview with Samuel Tucker.

21. For larger contexts in time and space, see Epstein, *Women in Law*, 237–46; Morello, *Invisible Bar*, 218–47; and Segal, *Blacks in the Law*, 223–34. Regarding the nation's high court, see *Eight Men and a Lady: Profiles of the Justices of the Supreme Court*, by the staff of the National Press (Bethesda, Md., 1990), 113–46, 209–42, and Barbara A. Perry, *A "Representative" Supreme Court? The Impact of Race, Religion, and Gender on Appointments* (New York, 1991), 89–129.

22. For figures on women and the state courts in 1980, see Epstein, *Women in Law*, 243. For comparable figures on race, see Segal, *Blacks in the Law*, 223–34.

23. "The Judgeship," *RTD*, 3 Oct. 1974, A18 (editorial); James Latimer, "Sheffield Is Hinted as Godwin Choice," *RTD*, 4 Oct. 1974, B18; Shelley Rolfe, "Sheffield Is Appointed to Circuit Bench," *RTD*, 5 Oct. 1974, A1, A5; Shelley Rolfe, "By the Way," *RTD*, 9 Oct. 1974, B1 (profile).

24. "Virginia's First Woman Circuit Judge Sworn In," *RTD*, 27 Feb. 1982, B2. On Judge Sheffield, see Megan Rosenfeld, "A Soft-Spoken Judge at the Center of Controversy," *WP*, 20 July 1980, F1-F2.

25. "Thomas Sworn In as Virginia Justice," *RTWN*, 26 April 1983, B1-B2; "Justice Thomas to Quit," *RTWN*, 5 Oct. 1989, B1, B7; transcript of Higginbotham's interview with Hill, 39.

26. Jerry Turner, "One Black on New Court," *RAA*, 8 Dec. 1984, 4; Andy Petkofsky and Tyler Whitley, "Votes Confirm Appeals Judges," *RNL*, 18 Dec. 1984, 15.

27. Margie Fisher, "Robb Picks Woman to Be SCC Judge," *RTWN*, 30 March 1985, A3, A6; Tom Sherwood, "Lacy Breaks Tradition of All-Male SCC in Va.," *WP*, 7 April 1985, C1. A native of South Carolina, Elizabeth B. Lacy grew up in Wisconsin; was graduated with honors in history at St. Mary's, a women's college in Indiana; and earned a law degree from the University of Texas in 1969. As a deputy attorney general in Texas for three years in the 1970s, she had helped draft that state's consumer protection legislation.

28. Frances Schultz, "Mary Sue Grows Up," *Style Weekly* 7 (23 May 1989): 32–37.

29. R. H. Melton and Saundra Torry, "Woman Said Favored for Va. Court," *WP*, 14 Oct. 1988, A17; "Thomas Sworn In as Virginia Justice," *RTWN*, 26 April 1983, B1-B2.

30. "Justice Thomas to Quit," *RTWN*, 5 Oct. 1989, B1, B7; Baker, *Wilder*, 214–15.

31. Christi Harlan and Milo Geyelin, "Virginia Shuffle," *Wall Street Journal*, 12 Dec. 1989, B6.

32. *JHD* (1991), 2, 1021. Two women justices among seven may not constitute parity, but one in seven approximated women's 1980 percentage of all attorneys in Virginia (13%), and two in seven approximated the 1990 figure (25%). A related observation might apply, in a state about 18% black, to one black justice among seven. Judge Keenan's election to the Virginia Supreme Court, however, left the Court of Appeals without a woman judge when a white man took her place. For contrasting photographs of the court—from 1968 and 1993—see PW, "Strange Beings," 221.

33. Marc Davis and Laurence Hammack, "Bench in the Balance," *RT*, 2 Feb. 1997, Horizon 1; "New Justice on Top Court Takes Oath," *RT*, 9 July 1997, B4.

34. "Va.'s First Black Chief Justice Takes Oath," *RT*, 1 Feb. 2003, B1.

35. "New Hampshire Names Woman for Top Court," *NYT*, 27 April 2000, A17.

36. Geraldine R. Segal, *Blacks in the Law: Philadelphia and the Nation* (Philadelphia, 1983) 189, 282–83; Caryle Murphy, "New Robes, Role for Va. Judge," *WP*, 14 Oct. 1986, A1, A4; Tony Germanotta, "Va. Has 1st Woman on U.S. District Bench," Norfolk *Virginian-Pilot*, 4 Nov. 1989, B3; PW, "Strange Beings," 223–24 nn. 67–68.

37. Neil A. Lewis, "Clinton Names a Black Judge; Skirts Congress," *NYT*, 28 Dec. 2000, A1, A18; "Integrating an All-White Court" (editorial); *NYT*, 2 Jan. 2001, A14; Alison Mitchell, "Senators Confirm 3 Judges, Including Once-Stalled Black," *NYT*, 21 July 2001, A16.

Epilogue: Neither Blue Laws nor Black Laws

1. Charles W. Chesnutt, "What Is a White Man?" *Independent* 41 (30 May 1889), reprinted in *Interracialism: Black-White Intermarriage in American History, Literature, and Law*, ed. Werner Sollors (New York, 2000), 37–42 (quotation at 38).

2. Peter Whoriskey, "D.C. Area's First Baby of 2003 Brings Joy to Her 2 Mothers," *WP*, 7 Jan. 2003, B5; Mark Martin letter to editor, "Same Injustice; Different Target," *RT*, 19 Dec. 2002, A18; Linda Kaufman, "About Fairness and My Family," *WP*, 30 March 2003, B7.

3. PW, "Model Universities and Racial Diversity: Undergraduate Enrollment in 24 Public Universities in the South," *Diversity News* 7 (fall 2000): 10–11.

4. "State Felony Disfranchisement Laws," <http:elections.gmu.edu/felony_dis franchisement.htm>; *Los Angeles Times* article, "Executions in the U.S. Increasingly Becoming Southern Phenomenon," rept. in *RT*, 2 Jan. 2003, A7.

5. Tim Kaine, "Legislators Shouldn't Draw Their Own Districts" (op-ed), *RT*, 29 Dec. 2002, Horizon 3.

Index

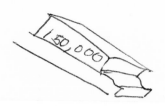

DATE DUE

DEC 0 8 2009		
DEC 1 1 REC'D		
DEC 1 5 2010		
800 800		

GAYLORD

PRINTED IN U.S.A.

BOWLING GREEN STATE UNIVERSITY
DISCARDED
LIBRARY

5+

150,000

KFV 2478 .W35 2004

Wallenstein, Peter.

Blue laws and Black codes